SWORD AND SCALES

Sword and Scales

An Examination of the Relationship between Law and Politics

MARTIN LOUGHLIN

·HART·
PUBLISHING
OXFORD – PORTLAND OREGON
2000

Hart Publishing
Oxford and Portland, Oregon

Published in North America (US and Canada) by
Hart Publishing c/o
International Specialized Book Services
5804 NE Hassalo Street
Portland, Oregon
97213-3644
USA

Distributed in the Netherlands, Belgium and Luxembourg by
Intersentia, Churchillaan 108
B2900 Schoten
Antwerpen
Belgium

Hart Publishing Ltd is a specialist legal publisher based in
Oxford, England.
To order further copies of this book or to request a list of other
publications please write to:

Hart Publishing Ltd, Salter's Boatyard,
Folly Bridge, Abingdon Road, Oxford OX1 4LB
Telephone: +44 (0)1865 245533 or Fax: +44 (0)1865 794882
e-mail: mail@hartpub.co.uk
www.hartpub.co.uk

British Library Cataloguing in Publication Data
Data Available
ISBN 1 901362–51–5 (cloth)
1 901362–52–3 (paperback)

Typeset by Hope Services (Abingdon) Ltd.
Printed in Great Britain on acid-free paper
by Biddles Ltd, Guildford and King's Lynn.

For
Beth and Frances

Contents

Preface

My purpose in writing this book is to provide a concise, accessible introduction to an important though neglected subject: the relationship between law and politics. Although it is an issue on which people often hold strong opinions, their convictions generally manifest themselves either as implicit assumptions or explicit assertions, only rarely as reasoned explanations. The book's objective is to examine these assumptions and assertions, to set them within a framework which facilitates assessment and, in the course of so doing, to expound my own views on the subject.

One immediate obstacle lying in the path of this objective is the fact that the question of law's relationship to politics has itself become politicized. This has resulted in the question generally being presented in a polarized fashion. There is a tendency either to treat law as an exercise in ethical reasoning which is placed categorially above "mere" politics or, alternatively, as the continuation of politics by other means. When deliberation over the relationship between law and politics is reduced to a contest between them, the result is unlikely to be reflective inquiry. Many of the difficulties stem from implicit disagreements about the nature of these activities and the value to be ascribed to them. We are therefore obliged to investigate certain foundational questions. If there is little consensus on whether law is an instrument of politics or provides the normative framework within which politics ought to be conducted, there seems no alternative but to track the inquiry back to its origins. In order to understand the nature of the relationship we must be attentive to its history.

The book is therefore underpinned by a belief that we gain valuable insights into the connection between politics and law by treating the exercise as a study in the history of ideas. Consequently, I explore the nature of the relationship mainly through an examination of the classic texts of political thought. Writers such as Plato and Aristotle, Machiavelli and Hobbes, Locke and Montesquieu, Tocqueville and Burke are likely to be familiar names to students of law. But although each offers an incisive account of the role of law within a political framework, I doubt whether today any of their works is commonly studied for insights into the character of law. One feature of this book will be to search for an understanding of the relationship between politics and law through an examination of the views of these writers on issues such as justice, liberty, sovereignty, democracy, constitutionalism and rights. This is not, it must be emphasized, an essentially theoretical inquiry; my argument is that disputes about the meaning of these ideas colour almost all practical controversies in which the legal and political become bound up with one another. Today's contentious public policy issues cannot sensibly be addressed without giving some consideration to these basic historical and theoretical concerns.

Since one of my main objectives is to introduce students of law to the major works of political thought, throughout the text I have deliberately used direct quotation rather than paraphrase. Such works have survived precisely because these writers were able to present their ideas in a lucid form, and it would be vain to think that my attempts at synthesis could make a better impression. Notwithstanding the strictures of certain historians on the practice, however, I have occasionally modernized spelling or syntax whenever I felt that the original was likely to present an unnecessary distraction.

For assistance on this project, I am pleased to acknowledge the support provided both by the University of Manchester's Research Support Scheme and its Graduate School of Social Science, and also to recognize the help provided by the Audrey Morris Trust. Some early views about the book were presented at the University of Toronto's Legal Theory Workshop and in relation to that visit I should especially like to thank David Beatty, Heather McAllister, Cynthia Langille, Larry Steinberg and, especially, Brian Langille. Although Abi Walker will not recognize much within these covers, through her excellent work as Dean's secretary she has provided the support I needed to permit me to finish the work. I also owe a particular debt of gratitude to the following, who provided valuable comments on early drafts: John Griffith, Dora Kostakopoulou, Tim Murphy, Thomas Poole, David Sugarman, Robert Thomas and Adam Tomkins. Neil Duxbury carried out that task and much more; as my "reader from hell" he has prompted me to keep to the point, to explain myself more clearly, and has done his best to prevent me hiding my ambiguities and confusions behind abstract verbs and portentous phrases. The fact that he has not succeeded is not due to any lack of tenacity. That tribute must be shared with Chris Foley who has lent her refined editorial skills to the task of helping me to make the book more readable. Richard Hart first suggested I might write a general book on law and politics. I am pretty sure he did not expect anything like what follows, but then neither did I when eventually I agreed to take up his suggestion. I would like to thank him for his patience and efficiency in carrying it through to publication.

Martin Loughlin
Dobcross
February 2000

I

Law and Politics in
the Conversation of Mankind

1

Politics and Law

A T THE END of the nineteenth century, the phrase *fin de siècle* was coined to try and identify the distinctive but ambiguous mood of the period. This mood encompassed a certain listlessness or apathy as the old century closed, but also anticipation that a new era was about to dawn; hope and fear wavered in the balance. A century on and we harbour similarly mixed feelings, especially once we turn to the subject of politics.

There is undoubtedly a basis for expressing hope about the future. After all, the century which saw the evolution of ideological politics on a grand scale, but which also witnessed descent into total war, has ended on an optimistic note. The events which took place in eastern Europe and the Soviet Union between 1989 and 1991—exemplified by the destruction of the Berlin Wall and the dissolution of the Soviet Union—mark a transformation of world-historical importance. The great ideological struggle between capitalism and socialism, waged throughout the century, has now apparently been resolved with a victory for economic and political liberalism.[1] In the political sphere, the end of the twentieth century signals the ultimate triumph of liberal democracy.

These epoch-forming developments are of particular significance to the subject of this book. For implicit in the global success of capitalist liberal democracy is the recognition that politics is now seen to be an activity which is subject to a cordon of constraints. To invoke a well-used shorthand, the conduct of politics must be subject to "the rule of law". This aspiration has received universal acknowledgement in the constitutions of the re-formed states of eastern Europe:

"The Czech Republic is a sovereign, unified and democratic law-observing state, based on the respect for the rights and freedoms of the individual and citizen."

Constitution of the Czech Republic, 16 December 1992, Ch. 1, art. 1.

[1] See Francis Fukuyama, *The End of History and the Last Man* (Harmondsworth: Penguin, 1992). Cf. Mark Mazower, *Dark Continent: Europe's Twentieth Century* (Harmondsworth: Penguin, 1998).

"The Republic of Poland shall be a democratic state ruled by law and implementing the principles of social justice."

Constitution of the Republic of Poland, 2 April 1997, art. 2.

Such declarations of the intention to establish "a democratic state ruled by law" suggest that politics and law are being brought into a new and closer relationship.

Important though the developments in eastern Europe are, this trend has had an impact beyond the former communist countries making the transition to democracy. The United Kingdom, for example, is almost unique in lacking a formal written constitution. But many recent developments—including participation in the European project, the devolution of government responsibilities throughout the several parts of the United Kingdom, the passage of the Human Rights Act 1998 and a major expansion in the role of judicial review of governmental action—suggest that we are now taking the steps to transform our "political constitution" into a constitution which rests on a foundation of law.[2] If, as it appears, the end of the century marks a milestone in the universal trend towards inscribing the principles of liberal democracy into the institutional foundations of states, it might also be a timely moment to examine the relationship between law and politics.

Although the onward march of liberal democracy is generally treated as a positive development, it has not been without its detractors. Bringing about a re-alignment of law and politics to ensure that government is responsive to the will of the people, does not abuse its powers, and respects the rights of citizens appears to be a wholly beneficial achievement. For some, however, the contemporary "project" not only forges a new partnership between law and politics to establish a well-ordered and responsive system of government, but marks a triumph of law *over* politics.[3] Such concerns have been voiced by John Gray who argues that the objective of the contemporary liberal project is no less than that "of *abolishing politics*, or of so constraining it by legal and constitutional formulae that it no longer matters what are the

---

[2] Cf. J.A.G. Griffith, "The Political Constitution" (1979) 42 *Modern Law Review* 1; T.R.S. Allan, *Law, Liberty, and Justice: The Legal Foundations of British Constitutionalism* (Oxford: Clarendon Press, 1993). The classic work on the political constitution is Walter Bagehot, *The English Constitution* [1867] R.H.S. Crossman intro. (London: Collins, 1963).

[3] See Chantal Mouffe, *The Return of the Political* (London: Verso, 1993), who refers to the threat that, with the success of liberal democracy, "the political [will be] destroyed by the forces of law and universal reason." (1).

outcomes of political deliberation".[4] Far from working in partnership, Gray believes that law and politics are in a relationship of mutual antagonism, and that for this reason the victory of liberal democracy carries with it certain serious dangers.

The most important threat, it should be emphasized, is not the actual replacement of politics by law, since this utopian ambition can never be realized. Gray's main concern is that the enclosure of politics within the straitjacket of law will have a corrosive effect on social life. Politics is an essential aspect of public activity and if it is unable to perform its vital task of managing basic conflicts effectively, then the virtues of civility on which a stable social order rests are likely to be undermined. The liberal–legalist order, so the argument goes, will be founded on self-interested, rights-bearing, adversarial individuals and this will not be sustainable. This type of social order is likely to aggravate precisely those points of tension in society which any vibrant political process should aim at alleviating. The ultimate danger is that liberal–legalism may, paradoxically, bring about the precise end—despotism—which it is designed to avoid.

A related concern focuses on the impact of the liberal project on the functioning of the State. Throughout the twentieth century, the main political dangers have been located in the threat of an overpowerful State. By contrast, in the twenty-first century, and as the present state of affairs in Russia indicates, it is conceivable that the most basic danger will flow from the debilitating weakness of the State. That is, notwithstanding its evident inefficiencies and mistakes, the State is likely to remain the only institution which is able, with any prospect of success, to deal with the many sizeable social and political problems— e.g., promoting economic success, regulating environmental risks, addressing the challenges of poverty and social exclusion, and guaranteeing security against crime—which remain to be addressed.

The issues which this debate raises are undoubtedly complex. But one thing seems certain: at the heart of the debate lies the relationship between politics and law. An evaluation of the nature of the relationship thus seems timely. Should law and politics be viewed as kindred practices which can form an alliance guaranteeing the maintenance of a responsive, democratic order? Or do they exist in a relationship of mutual antagonism, such that the realization of the principle of government under law might be corrosive of the political order? In this

[4] John Gray, *Enlightenment's Wake: Politics and Culture at the Close of the Modern Age* (London: Routledge, 1995), 76 (emphasis in original).

book, I propose to examine the relationship, starting from the general position that law and politics are vital and related modes of discourse within what Thomas Hobbes termed "the conversation of mankind".[5] I hope to be able to show that, real though these concerns are, politics and law can coexist effectively, although this is most likely to occur only when it is acknowledged that law forms an intrinsic part of the engagement which we call politics.

For the purpose of advancing this inquiry, I propose to examine the influence which certain basic ideas have exerted over the way people think about governance. In undertaking this exercise, we scarcely need move much beyond the articles of the Czech and Polish constitutions which have already been cited. These two brief sentences refer to a number of fundamental concepts—including sovereignty, democracy, social justice, the rule of law, and the rights and freedoms of the citizen—which will form a central part of the review. Once it is recognized that these are basic political ideas incorporated into constitutional documents which will be the subject of interpretation and application by the judiciary, it is evident that we are operating at the interface of politics and law.

THE NATURE OF POLITICS

Politics, it is often suggested, is bound up with questions of power and authority. Understood as a dimension of human experience, politics is the result of contests which occur whenever attempts are made to secure authority over others. In this broad sense, politics is a practice which evolves within all social groupings, which is why people often talk of workplace politics, sexual politics or the politics of the family. Politics is an ubiquitous feature of social life.

But although the pursuit of politics is a basic characteristic of all human associations, the manner in which power is exercised through the agency of government is rather special. Throughout the world, people are organized into states, in the sense that there exists a defined area of territory which is subject to some type of government. The character of this unique association, and particularly its form of government, is to be understood quintessentially in political terms and, whatever form the activity of government takes, the nature of this

[5] Thomas Hobbes, *Leviathan* [1651] Richard Tuck ed. (Cambridge: Cambridge U.P., 1995), 110.

political relationship is distinctive. States, first and foremost, demand the allegiance of their citizens and will brook no rivals. In Max Weber's words, states claim "the monopoly of the legitimate use of physical force within a given territory".[6] Their decrees—the laws of the land— override all other commitments and command our highest loyalty. Infringement of the rules carries with it the threat of a penalty, includ- ing fines, imprisonment and, for certain particularly serious offences against the State, the penalty of death. Also, whenever the State enters into a conflict with another—whether to defend its territory, to vindi- cate a claim, or simply to extend the territorial limits of its power by annexing the land of a weaker neighbour—citizens are expected to respond to the call. When the famous First World War poster pro- claimed, "Your country needs you", millions responded, to fight and die in a war triggered by events of which most had only tenuous know- ledge, for a cause they scarcely understood.[7]

Nevertheless, the fact that the conduct of politics is associated with power, antagonism and conflict, should not obscure the point that pol- itics also constitutes a vital aspect of self-identity and that the evolution of politics is an achievement of considerable human significance. Questions of domination and leadership amongst herds of animals are resolved by force, in accordance with patterns dictated by genetic inheritance. Humans resolve these issues not simply in accordance with the imperatives of instinct but by self-reflection and deliberation on the appropriate pattern of collective life. This is not to deny the fact that such patterns are shaped by biological, geographical and economic forces. But these arrangements of government are also the product of decisions made by people in the light of their understanding of the human condition. It is in this context that we might note Aristotle's observation that "man is by nature a political animal".[8]

It is precisely because these political arrangements have become bound-up with people's sense of identity that the State is able to make such extensive claims on our allegiance. It is not simply the case, for example, that the State has sent thousands of its citizens to their deaths in the cause of conquest; it must also be acknowledged that many have

---

[6] Max Weber, "Politics as a Vocation" [1919] in H.H. Gerth & C. Wright Mills (eds), *From Max Weber: Essays in Sociology* (London: Routledge & Kegan Paul, 1948), 77, 78.

[7] On the psychological aspects of these ties of allegiance see Hans Kelsen, "God and the State" [1922] in his *Essays in Legal and Moral Philosophy* Ota Weinberger intro. (Dordrecht: Reidel, 1973), ch. 3.

[8] Aristotle, *The Politics* [*c*.335–323 BC] T.A. Sinclair trans., Trevor J. Saunders ed. (Harmondsworth: Penguin, 1981), Bk. I, ii.

voluntarily given up their lives in defence of the claims of the State. In Greek and Roman civilizations this was viewed as being the noblest of all actions.[9] And, in the modern era, Wilfred Owen's caustic war poem made such a powerful impact only because *Dulce et decorum est pro patria mori* had never before so openly been called "the old lie".[10] The State, in short, does not merely keep us in order; it also is capable of giving expression to our highest aspirations.

Politics may be a vital aspect of human interaction, but this is not to say that it is always a rational activity. Equipped with intelligence, we nonetheless have only limited knowledge of the world. Possessed of the power of reason, we experience little difficulty in simultaneously maintaining wholly contradictory beliefs. Motivated at times by high ideals, we regularly struggle, often unsuccessfully, with the realities we encounter. For these reasons, political decisions not only have ramifications extending far beyond what was intended, but they may even run directly counter to those objectives. Further, politics is rooted in the distinction between governors and governed, which means that responsibility for making most of these political decisions rests with our representatives.[11] The principle of representation not only complicates the practice, as politicians devise policies which they do not share with the people; it also gives rise to additional misperceptions, such as the belief that the people rule, when it might be more accurate to say that they obey.

Notwithstanding such ironies, confusions and deceptions, the political ideals of citizens are essential to our understanding of politics. Walter Bagehot may not have been wrong when suggesting that the people "yield a deference to . . . the *theatrical show* of society" and to the visible spectacle of an aristocratic order.[12] But this does not mean that their beliefs—including those of equality and democracy—have no impact on political life. Such beliefs—even those which appear to be confused or contradictory—express some of our most basic aspirations, help us to make sense of the world, and provide us with a sense of identity and allegiance. Political decision-making reflects the attempt to give expression to these values, albeit only after having been

---

[9] See C.M. Bowra, *The Greek Experience* (London: Phoenix, 1957), ch. 2; Maurizio Viroli, *For Love of Country* (Oxford: Oxford U.P., 1995).

[10] Wilfred Owen, *Dulce Et Decorum Est* in *The Collected Poems of Wilfred Owen* C. Day Lewis ed. (London: Chatto & Windus, 1963), 55.

[11] See Bernard Manin, *The Principles of Representative Government* (Cambridge: Cambridge U.P., 1997).

[12] Bagehot, above n. 2, 248 (emphasis in original).

refracted through the power structures of the State. Political decision-making may often be subject to scrutiny and revealed as flawed, but these decisions are the product of action in the imperfect world in which we live.

In his influential work, *The Concept of Law*, H.L.A. Hart noted that there have been few questions concerning human society which "have been asked with such persistence, and answered by serious thinkers in so many diverse, strange, and even paradoxical ways as the question 'What is law?'"[13] Hart's own conclusion, that "nothing concise enough to be recognized as a definition could provide a satisfactory answer",[14] warns us of the difficulties. I will not attempt my own definition. My aim is more modest: I propose to outline three conceptions of law which have been particularly influential in the course of political history.

As we have seen, one of the primary means by which the State establishes a system of order is through the promulgation of laws. Law, in this sense, is an instrument of government. This conception, which derives primarily from Hobbes, is most closely identified today with the nineteenth-century jurist, John Austin. Austin contended that law is comprised of the commands of that person or body holding ultimate political authority (what he called the sovereign), commands which are obeyed by citizens because of the threat of sanctions imposed if the rules are infringed.[15] Viewed as the commands of the sovereign authority, law thus presents itself as the output of a political process. Law as command fits particularly well with modern ideas of representative democracy. We the people engage in a form of self-government by establishing a Parliament in which our representatives deliberate and make laws. These laws—Acts of Parliament—are the highest expressions of the will of the people and, in order to sustain a self-governing order, must be obeyed.

This, however, captures only one dimension of the complex phenomenon of law. In other versions, law can be understood as a practice

---

13 H.L.A. Hart, *The Concept of Law* (Oxford: Clarendon Press, 1961), 1.
14 Hart, above n. 13, 16.
15 John Austin, *The Province of Jurisprudence Determined* [1832] Wilfrid E. Rumble ed. (Cambridge: Cambridge U.P., 1995).

which establishes the framework within which political action is taken. That is, far from being a product of politics, law establishes the preconditions for the conduct of politics. This view of law originated with the Greeks,[16] who associated it with the theory of natural law, the origins of which lie in the search for an immutable idea of justice. Having identified the laws of nature that determine the diurnal progress of the sun and the regular cycles of the seasons, the Greeks investigated whether there were similar natural laws governing human conduct. Their answer was that humans, being equipped with the power of reason, have an innate measure of right and wrong. Nature, understood as the dictates of reason and expressed in the form of fundamental laws, is elevated above the purely conventional, which includes the customary political practices of particular societies.

The idea of a natural law operating on a higher level than the conventions of politics seems intelligible only when linked to the existence of a creator: having designed an ordered universe, God placed humans in the unique position of being able to reflect on the rational order of this cosmos. Modern natural rights theories have tried to avoid this dependence of law on theology by devising a conception of law as a construction of reason. The pivotal figure in this movement is the seventeenth-century Dutch jurist, Hugo Grotius. In *De Jure Belli ac Pacis*, Grotius contended that laws would maintain their objective validity "even if we should concede that which cannot be conceded without the utmost wickedness, that there is no God".[17] Grotius believed that given certain natural facts about humans, especially their sociability, the precepts of natural law followed as a matter of logical entailment. This disposition, he maintained, "has been implanted in us partly by reason, partly by unbroken tradition".[18] Although Grotius argued that law embodied principles of just conduct which are revealed through the exercise of our powers of reason, his formulation actually revealed the seeds of two different conceptions of law: reason and tradition.

It is the latter conception—law as tradition or custom—which has been of greater influence within the English system. It is identifiable primarily in the notion of the common law as the law of a people, law which is being both continually adapted and constantly preserved. The

[16] Hannah Arendt, *The Human Condition* (Garden City, NY: Doubleday, 1959), 173–4.

[17] Hugo Grotius, *Prolegomena to the Law of War and Peace* [1625] Edward Dumbald intro. (New York: Liberal Arts Press, 1957) §.11.

[18] Ibid.

paradox is explained by the leading seventeenth century judge and jurist, Sir Matthew Hale, who noted that "the Argonaut's ship was the same when it returned home, as it was when it went out; though in that long voyage it had successive amendments, and scarce came back with any of its former materials."[19] This organic metaphor of law—as a reflection of a latent wisdom distilled from the traditional practices of a cloistered group of lawyers—has given birth to the notion that law is discovered and declared rather than made. Through this appeal to "unbroken tradition", law is thus placed above the merely conventional. It is a tradition which embraces many of the leading figures of the English common law,[20] a tradition in which it might be said that custom takes the form of second nature.

The belief in law as custom has waned in recent times, but the idea of law as a set of principles of just conduct continues to exert a powerful influence over modern thinking. In place of law as custom, a more rationalistic conception has emerged, which Grotius identified as the idea of law as reason, or of right. As Richard Tuck notes, *De Jure Belli ac Pacis* "is in fact the first reconstruction of an actual legal system in terms of rights rather than laws" and thus is "the true ancestor of all the modern codes which have rights of various kinds at their centre".[21] This development sees law elevated above the conventional by assuming the form of a science which is not dependent on experience but on logical deduction. It is primarily through this conception that law, in modern thought, is treated as an activity which is not only distinct from, but also manifestly superior to, politics. This receives its clearest expression in the work of Immanuel Kant, who contended that "politics must bend the knee before right."[22] Kant's views have exerted a powerful influence on contemporary legal thought, often underpinning the conviction that, in carrying out their responsibilities, the judiciary is able to escape from the sort of political conflicts which touch the rest

---

[19] Sir Matthew Hale, *A History of the Common Law of England* [1715] Charles Runnington ed. (London: Butterworth, 6th edn., 1820), 84.

[20] On which see: J.G.A. Pocock, *The Ancient Constitution and the Feudal Law: A Study of English Historical Thought in the Seventeenth Century* (Cambridge: Cambridge U.P., rev. edn. 1987); Pocock, "Burke and the Ancient Constitution—A Problem in the History of Ideas" (1960) 3 *Historical Journal* 125; Gerald Postema, *Bentham and the Common Law Tradition* (Oxford: Clarendon Press, 1986), ch. 1.

[21] Richard Tuck, *Natural Rights and Theories: Their Origin and Development* (Cambridge: Cambridge U.P., 1979), 66.

[22] Immanuel Kant, "Perpetual Peace: A Philosophical Sketch" [1795] in his *Political Writings*, Hans Reiss ed. (Cambridge: Cambridge U.P., 1991), 93, 125.

of society.[23] Consequently, even though it might be accepted that, in the most general sense, law is rooted in the political process, in Ronald Dworkin's words, "some issues from the battleground of power politics [are called] to the forum of principle" and in this rather special arena such "conflicts" are converted into "questions of justice".[24]

The identification of these various conceptions of law has particular importance when we consider the relationship between law and politics. Each conception suggests a different understanding of the nature of that relationship and since each has played an influential role in shaping our system, this means that the inquiry is likely to be complex. Furthermore, the politics surrounding the use of these various conceptions are contentious; focusing on their application, it might even be argued that law is a continuation of politics by other means.[25] At this stage, however, we might simply note that whenever the distinction between law and politics is presented in a highly polarized manner, it is invariably the conception of law as right which is being invoked. In this light, the relationship between law and politics tends to be characterized as one of reason *versus* will, might *versus* right, or justice *versus* power, which not only highlights law's ideal qualities but also presents politics in a negative light.[26] Our inquiry is unlikely to make much headway if we accept such polarities at face value.

MIGHT AND RIGHT

Power, in the sense of might, is often portrayed as the fundamental concept in political science, rather in the manner in which energy is the basic concept in the natural sciences.[27] Although power may take several forms, it is commonly understood as the ability to produce

---

[23] See, e.g., Sir John Laws, "Law and Democracy" 1995 *Public Law* 72.

[24] Ronald Dworkin, *A Matter of Principle* (Cambridge, Mass: Harvard U.P., 1985), 71.

[25] Cf. Carl von Clausewitz, *On War* [1832] Anatol Rapoport ed. (Harmondsworth: Penguin, 1968), 119: "War is a mere continuation of policy by other means."

[26] Cf. Carl Schmitt, *The Concept of the Political* [1932] George Schwab trans. (Chicago: University of Chicago Press, 1996), 20: "One seldom finds a clear definition of the political. The word is most frequently used negatively, in contrast to various other ideas, for example in such antitheses as politics and economy, politics and morality, politics and law."

[27] See, e.g., Bertrand Russell, *Power* (London: Allen & Unwin, 1938), 9; Niklas Luhmann, *The Differentiation of Society* Stephen Holmes and Charles Larmore trans. (New York: Columbia U.P., 1982), ch. 7.

intended effects. We experience power in this sense by observing the behaviour of actors as decisions are made, action is taken and consequences follow.[28] This idea of power as might (symbolized by the sword) may be contrasted with justice or right (the scales). Justice is concerned not with what can be done but with what *ought* to be done. For the purpose of achieving justice, the exercise of power must be tamed and channelled into conduct which produces right consequences. Law understood as right thus seems to exist to control the exercise of politics—understood as an arena of power—and to direct it towards the pursuit of the good. It is in this context that we encounter expressions to the effect that: "Where law ends, there tyranny begins."[29]

Such polarized distinctions seem to have been devised to highlight law's ideal qualities rather than to provide an explanation of law's relationship to politics. Law as right may provide a basis for conceptualizing law as a discrete entity, but it will provide us with a rather skewed perspective if we use it to examine the affinities and distinctions between law and politics as they have emerged historically. Scholars have occasionally treated the evolution of law as the process of working towards a set of principles which express the highest ideals of reason and justice.[30] But even within the highest echelons of the legal profession, there has always been scepticism about such claims. In one celebrated formulation, Justice Holmes contended that "the life of the law has not been logic; it has been experience". Elaborating, Holmes suggested that "the felt necessities of the times"—by which, we can assume, he meant the necessities of the powerful—"and even the prejudices which judges share with their fellow-men, have had a good deal more to do than the syllogism in determining the rules by which men should be governed."[31] Holmes here presents a variant of the

---

[28] See, e.g., Robert A. Dahl, *Who Governs? Democracy and Power in an American City* (New Haven: Yale U.P., 1961). Cf. Steven Lukes, *Power: A Radical View* (London: Macmillan, 1974), labelling Dahl's conception a "one-dimensional view".

[29] This phrase, often attributed to William Pitt the Elder (see speech in the House of Lords, 9 January 1770), derives from Locke. See John Locke, *Second Treatise of Government* in his *Two Treatises of Government* [1680] Peter Laslett ed. (Cambridge: Cambridge U.P., 1988), §.202.

[30] See, e.g., Roscoe Pound, *Interpretations of Legal History* (Cambridge: Cambridge U.P., 1923). Many who adopt this view invoke Lord Mansfield's metaphor that "the common law works itself pure by rules drawn from the fountain of justice": *Omychund v. Barker* (1744) 1 Atk. 21, 33. See, e.g., Ronald Dworkin, *Law's Empire* (London: Fontana, 1986), ch. 11.

[31] Oliver Wendell Holmes, Jr., *The Common Law* (Boston: Little, Brown & Co., 1881), 1.

conception of law as custom, one which seems openly to acknowledge the fact that law is bound up with the conduct of politics. And, of course, once the conception of law as command is brought into the discussion, law and politics are seen to be intimately connected. Indeed, it could be argued that polarization of the issue in terms of right *versus* might illustrates one powerful ideological function of law: the association of law with justice provides a mask which conceals the way in which the powerful govern in accordance with their own interests.

This ideological debate has an ancient lineage. In Book I of *The Republic*, written almost two thousand four hundred years ago, Plato presents a variant of the debate in dialogue form. In a discussion on justice, Thrasymachus argues that justice "is the interest of the stronger party". "Each ruling class makes laws that are in its own interest", he continues, "and in making these laws they define as 'right' for their subjects what is in the interests of themselves, the rulers."[32] In response to this argument, Socrates first disputes Thrasymachus's formulation on the ground that a ruler exercises his authority not in accordance with his own interests but with the objective of promoting the common good. But before Socrates is able to proceed to outline the principles of justice and demonstrate their virtues, Adeimantus poses an interesting question: if justice is nothing more than the interests of the strong, why do the strong go to great lengths to make their actions appear just? Answering his own question, he suggests that, even if we accept the view of Thrasymachus that people are motivated purely by self-interest, the strong will value justice for the social prestige which it brings. "I must put up a façade that has all the outward appearance of virtue", Adeimantus contends, because justice "will bring me no advantage . . . unless I also have a reputation for justice."[33]

Adeimantus might be wrong in assuming that virtue, respect and reputation can be willed by power-holders,[34] but he takes us closer to the intricacies of law and politics. He indicates, on the one hand, that although "might is right" may be a popular slogan, it is flawed. Law cannot adequately be expressed as a purely empirical phenomenon, as the conception of law as command implies. The view that "laws are merely statements of a power relationship"[35] is unable to capture the

---

[32] Plato, *The Republic*, [*c*.380 BC] H.D.P. Lee trans. (Harmondsworth: Penguin, 1955), para. 338.

[33] Ibid. para. 365.

[34] See Jon Elster, *Political Psychology* (Cambridge: Cambridge U.P., 1993), 51–3.

[35] Griffith, above n. 2, 19. Griffith here expresses an Austinian view: see Austin, above n. 15.

complexity of the legal experience. The reason for this is that the ideal aspect of the appeal to justice can never entirely be ignored when trying to understand how people engage with, and respond to, the law. On the other hand, Adeimantus is not saying that law ought to be obeyed because of its moral virtue or because it establishes a political structure which embodies authoritative moral values. Right conduct remains a matter of politics and, notwithstanding the speculations of countless philosophers, it cannot easily be elevated onto a higher plane. Adeimantus expresses the view not only that the normative dimension of law—the appeal to ideals—cannot be eliminated from our experience of law but also that this appeal to legal values remains inextricably bound up with the pursuit of politics.

A variation of this Platonic debate has recently been instigated by E.P. Thompson's study of the Black Act of 1723.[36] That Act had created many new offences against property which carried the sanction of capital punishment, mainly in relation to poaching. Working within a Marxist framework in which law is part of a superstructure determined by economic power relations,[37] Thompson calls the Act "a bad law, drawn by bad legislators, and enlarged by the interpretations of bad judges."[38] But the conclusions he reaches on the relationship between law and politics are surprising. Thompson adopts an orthodox Marxist line (a variant of law as command) in maintaining that "when considered as institution (the courts, with their class theatre and class procedures) or as personnel (the judges, the lawyers, the Justices of the Peace)" the law can be assimilated to the interests of the ruling class.[39] He accepts that law performs an important ideological role in mediating class relations, thereby helping to legitimate them. Nevertheless, he stops short of treating law as the pliant tool of the ruling class. Although class relations are mediated by the law, he recognizes that they are also expressed through the distinctive forms of law. Consequently, although capable of being manipulated by the powerful, these legal forms also have the potential to impose inhibitions on the actions of the powerful. In part, he suggests, this is because of law's ideological function; most people have a strong sense of justice and if the law is evidently partial and unjust "it will mask nothing, legitimise

[36] E.P. Thompson, *Whigs and Hunters: The Origin of the Black Act* (Harmondsworth: Penguin, 1975).

[37] See, e.g., Karl Marx and Frederick Engels, *The German Ideology* [1845–6], C.J. Arthur ed. (London: Lawrence & Wishart, 1977).

[38] Thompson, above n. 36, 267.

[39] Ibid. 260.

nothing, contribute nothing to any class's hegemony".[40] But it is also because law has its own characteristic traditions and methods, drawing on those concepts which make an appeal to universal ideals of equity. Thompson here invokes a conception of law as custom. He contends that in order to be effective, even in its function as ideology, law must "display an independence from gross manipulation and shall seem to be just", and it cannot do so "without upholding its own logic and criteria of equity" and occasionally "by actually *being* just".[41]

Thompson's comments, which provoked intense debate on the left,[42] reflect a sophisticated appreciation of the dimensions of command, custom and right, and they generate a more interesting analysis of the relationship between politics and law than that which the contest between might and right implies. But Thompson's position on this issue does not seem to differ greatly from that of Adeimantus: both agree that, although law can mask the presence of political power, it can also structure and check the way in which that power is exercised. This seems a better position from which to take forward a discussion of the relationship between law and politics.

At the heart of the debate lies the tension between power and justice. But although power is a central concept of politics, the concept of political power has little in common with might or force. Political power, the ability to achieve intended effects, is a highly complex phenomenon: it is a form of decision-making power which can only be exercised through institutions and processes, and therefore, in part at least, through the medium of law.[43] Political power is *relational*; it neither originates with the king (as divine rights theorists claim) nor with the people (the contention of theorists of popular sovereignty) but is a product of the relationship between the State and its citizens.[44] This type of power is maximized when the ties of allegiance are strong—

---

[40] Ibid. 263.

[41] Ibid. (emphasis in original).

[42] See Douglas Hay, "Property, Authority and the Criminal Law" in Hay *et al.* (eds), *Albion's Fatal Tree* (Harmondsworth: Penguin, 1975); M.J. Horwitz, "The Rule of Law: An Unqualified Human Good?" (1977) 86 *Yale Law Journal* 561; Alan Merrett, "The Nature and Function of Law: A Criticism of E.P. Thompson's *Whigs and Hunters*" (1980) 7 *Brit. J. of Law & Society* 195; Perry Anderson, *Arguments within English Marxism* (London: Verso, 1980); Bob Fine, *Democracy and the Rule of Law: Liberal Ideals and Marxist Critiques* (London: Pluto, 1984).

[43] See Helmuth Plessner, "The emancipation of power" (1964) 31 *Social Research* 155.

[44] Cf. F.R. Ankersmit, *Aesthetic Politics: Political Philosophy Beyond Fact and Value* (Stanford, Calif.: Stanford U.P., 1996), 50–1. Ankersmit cites the words of Emmanuel-Joseph Siéyès: "All power originates in representation."

which cannot be a product of will[45]—and when the nature, purpose and limitations of the State are understood. Since law in its various conceptions performs a vital role in sustaining this political relationship, power and justice appear almost as flip sides of the same coin. From this perspective, rather than existing in opposition to one another, politics and law can be understood as each performing important roles in the activity of creating and maintaining a normative universe. It is therefore to this issue of how such normative worlds are established and maintained that we now turn.

[45] See Elster, above n. 34.

2

Ways of World-Making

The sun always moves
The sun never moves

WHICH OF THE above statements is true? Everyday perception tells us that it must be the former, and both the daily and seasonal rhythms of our lives are organized around the apparent truth of that statement. But at least since the time of Copernicus scientists have questioned this geocentric perspective, and the belief that the earth forms the centre of the universe is now generally accepted as false. According to the modern heliocentric view, the sun lies at the centre of our planetary system and the earth, along with eight other planets, is constantly revolving around an essentially static sun. Does this mean that one of these versions is true, and the other confined to the realm of fiction? Or are we to say that, in accordance with their particular frames of reference, both are true?

Some scientists maintain that their world-view provides the truth about the way the world is, and that all other versions are either capable of being transformed into a scientific understanding or are to be rejected as false or meaningless. But this dichotomy is both implausible and unhelpful. There are many scientific frames for making sense of phenomena—those of physics, biology and psychology are, for example, rather different—and there seems to be no accepted method of transmuting one form of scientific explanation into another. If this is true for the natural sciences, then similarly it makes little sense to reduce the visions of Mohammed, Monet, Mozart, or Mussolini to rudimentary units of mind or matter. Surely it is better to acknowledge that there are many different, non-reducible ways of understanding the world.

These various ways of making sense of the world are constructions.[1] Such constructions are conjured into existence through the employment of a standard repertoire of techniques. The methods which are

---

[1] See Peter L. Berger and Thomas Luckmann, *The Social Construction of Reality: A Treatise in the Sociology of Knowledge* (Harmondsworth: Penguin, 1967).

commonly employed include: drawing distinctions or highlighting likenesses; placing emphasis or stress on certain features; adopting a particular mode of ordering of entities; overlooking certain material or adding new material; or reshaping or distorting what we find.[2] Consider some illustrations of the use of these techniques. *Likeness*: "like cases must be decided alike" is a basic maxim of the law, but it actually tells us very little unless we already have a pretty clear idea of what counts as relevant criteria for comparison. *Emphasis*: artists often accentuate certain features in their drawings and consequently are not aiming to sketch a strictly representational likeness, but in the process they often provide us with fresh insights into, and knowledge of, their subjects. *Ordering*: all measurement is based on particular modes of ordering, whether it is the division of the day into hours, minutes and seconds or the identification of the standard eight-tone musical scale, and such patterns greatly influence the way we experience the world. *Overlooking*: when carrying out the routine business of our lives (as psychologists will be quick to point out) we are likely to be blind to those things around us which neither help nor hinder us. *Reshaping*: the scientist who plots experimental data as points on a graph invariably packages the results as a smooth curve which best fits those scattered dots. These are some of the ways in which we seek to understand the world. And the various versions are as much *depictions* of the world as they are *descriptions*; they are not simply *found* in the world but are the result of our attempts to *build* a world.

Given that our attempts to understand the world depend on such depictions, unity cannot be sought in some objective yardstick which exists beyond these versions. Since we know the world only through such constructions, truth can never be tested by determining whether any particular version is in agreement with the world as-it-is. It is disconcerting but unavoidable that the appeal to literal truth is generally unhelpful. Goodman expresses this well: "Some truths are trivial, irrelevant, unintelligible, or redundant; too broad, too narrow, too boring, too bizarre, too complicated; or taken from some other version than the one in question, as when a guard, ordered to shoot any of his captives who moved, immediately shot them all and explained that they were moving rapidly around the earth's axis and around the sun."[3] Though the witness in a trial may be required under oath to tell "the

---

[2] See Nelson Goodman, *Ways of World-Making* (Hassocks: Harvester, 1978), 7–17. I draw extensively on Goodman's work in this section.
[3] Ibid. 120–1.

truth, the whole truth and nothing but the truth", this is an entirely perverse injunction for those seeking to devise a conception of the world. The whole truth is too much, since we would be swamped with trivia, and nothing but the truth would be too little, since some versions that we believe to be right may not be true.[4] There can, in short, be no immaculate conception.

This apparent displacement of truth from its lofty pedestal prompts some difficult questions. If each construction has an intrinsic interest, how are we to evaluate these various worlds? Does it mean simply that "anything goes"? The latter question may easily be answered: "we no more make a world by putting symbols together at random than a carpenter makes a chair by putting pieces of wood together at random."[5] But even if all versions are not equally valid, what does it mean to suggest that a particular version is the right one?

The main tests which we use for evaluating versions of worldmaking are those of credibility, coherence and utility. We accept versions because they confer meaning on the world and give rise to beliefs which—having regard to such notions as probability, inference, confirmation and durability—appear to us to be credible. We also adhere to versions because they seem coherent, by which we mean that they project consistent, non-contradictory pictures of the worlds in which we operate. And we embrace versions because they are useful; they are like maps which enable us to orientate ourselves and to move effectively within these worlds. Rightness, then, is primarily a matter of fit. So whenever we embrace an explanation we should be attentive to the question which it purports to answer. If someone throws herself off a tall building, it may make sense to employ Newtonian physics in order to explain her immediate prospects. But it is also quite obvious that this explanation fails to address other important questions which we may wish to ask about that person's life and fate.

What, it might be asked, is the relevance of this excursus to our examination of law and politics? The basic point should be evident: that the politico-legal world we inhabit is a world that we have made. We create a normative universe which enables us to "maintain a world of right and wrong, of lawful and unlawful, of valid and invalid" and although lawyers generally locate their normative world solely in the rules, practices and institutions of law, these rest on a set of stories or

---

[4] Goodman, *Ways of World-Making*, 19.
[5] Ibid. 94.

traditions which invest them with meaning.[6] Once understood in the context of these narratives, "law becomes not merely a system of rules to be observed, but a [political] world in which we live."[7] It is through this type of process that we develop traditions—meaningful patterns of political behaviour—and a distinctive way of understanding the nature of the political relationship.

MYTH AND SYMBOL

Myths are generally understood as stories which alleviated the anxieties and perplexities confronting primitive peoples. Since their reasoning processes remained underdeveloped, these people tried to come to terms with the unexplained mainly through the pictorial imagery of myth. This mythical world was one of superstition, a world in which gods and spirits were constantly at work. The function of myth was to enable those people who lived in a pre-scientific era to reassure themselves about the conditions of their existence. Through myth we were able to bring the unknown into a more harmonious relationship with the known.

What role has myth to play in the worlds of politics and law? Some might argue that politics and law are arenas in which we shun our most primitive instincts and employ our rational faculties for the purpose of devising systems of order which promote peace and prosperity. By contrast, I think the symbolic aspects of politics and law are critical to any attempt to understand the nature of these discourses. It is through the deployment of myth that we have devised those stories which tell us who we are as a people, how we have come in being as such, and why we are here. Myth remains a medium through which we express our most basic hopes and fears, and which helps us to put things in their proper place. We weave these stories into distinctive patterns and, using such tests as credibility, coherence and utility, stitch together a serviceable view of the world. As the product of our attempts to endow the world with meaning, myth has been one of the most powerful influences in the shaping of human civilization.

Once viewed as a set of intelligible narratives which helps us to overcome our anxieties and conceive an ordered world out of potential chaos, myth can be recognized as shaping the universe in which our

---

[6] Robert M. Cover, "*Nomos* and Narrative" (1983) 97 *Harvard Law Review* 4.
[7] Ibid., 4–5.

practices of politics and law flourish. Politics and law should thus not be viewed simply as the products of rational thought; they are also symbolic expressions of what people need to believe in order to find comfort in the social order. If we are to examine the foundations of politics and law, we must enter the realm of myth.

This is most apparent with respect to those religious myths which gave humans a special place within a God-given order. In what would otherwise be a cold and isolating universe, people sought comfort in the cyclical rhythms of nature and strove to locate themselves within those regularities. Once the basic laws of nature were identified, people came to see themselves as subject to fundamental natural laws. Such religious myths have exerted a powerful influence on political thinking. The Fall of Man and the associated doctrine of Original Sin, for example, is seen by Joseph de Maistre as an idea which "explains everything, and without which nothing can be explained".[8] Further, the Babel story, in which God confounds the language of Nimrod's followers "that they might not understand one another's speech"[9] is often treated as a symbol not only of the difficulties humans face in coming together in any great co-operative venture but also of the consequences of human impiety and of the absolute nature of the barrier which divides humanity from the divine.[10] And how are we to understand the idea of monarchy, expressed in such doctrines as the divine right of kings, except by way of religious borrowings?[11]

Even if the wellsprings of political and legal thought are to be found in myth, it might still be contended that in the modern era such primitive devices have been abandoned in favour of rational concepts. "When I was a child, I spake as a child, I understood as a child", wrote St. Paul in his first letter to the Corinthians, "but when I became a man, I put away childish things. For now we see through a glass, darkly; but then face to face."[12] Is this idea of a gradual evolution in consciousness from mythical to scientific thought convincing? In modern times a

[8] Joseph de Maistre, "The Saint Petersburg Dialogues" [c.1802–17] in Jack Lively (ed.), *The Works of Joseph de Maistre* (London: Allen & Unwin, 1965), 183, 196.

[9] Genesis 11:7.

[10] See Michael Oakeshott, "The Tower of Babel" in his *On History* (Oxford: Blackwell, 1983), 165. See also Oakeshott, "The Tower of Babel" in his *Rationalism in Politics* (London: Methuen, 1962), 59.

[11] See Ernst H. Kantorowicz, *The King's Two Bodies: A Study in Mediaeval Political Theology* (Princeton: Princeton U.P., 1957), ch. 3; A. London Fell, *Origins of Legislative Sovereignty and the Legislative State*. Vol. 3. *Bodin's Humanistic Legal System and Rejection of "Medieval Political Theology"* (Boston: Oelgeschlager, 1987).

[12] I Corinthians, 13.

more rationalistic mode of discourse has certainly been adopted and we seem much less dependent on symbol and myth. But are the practices of politics and law now to be understood as arising solely from intellectual processes rather than from emotion and feeling? My own view is that politics and myth are, in reality, inextricably bound to one another. As Clifford Geertz puts it: "A world wholly demystified is a world wholly depoliticized."[13] Contemporary images of politics and law may be overtly rationalistic constructions, but they are no less symbolic than many of the images which were adopted in the ancient world.

Plato was the first political thinker who sought a decisive break from the mythical world view. His aim was to empty the world of gods and spirits and to construct a theory of politics and law as a coherent system of thought. We "are not writing stories", he suggests in *The Republic*, "but founding a state".[14] Plato devised a theory of an ideal State by working from first principles. His solution consists of a society which is divided into three classes. One class is composed of the majority who go about the business of everyday life and do not at all participate in government. Government is entrusted to a minority group of Guardians, which divides into two classes: the Rulers, who make all the key policy decisions and run the "ship of State", and the Auxiliaries who perform the roles, similar to the civil service, army and police, of enforcing those decisions. Plato's objective was to construct a State founded on an aristocracy of talent and, as a consequence, he maintained radical views about the role of property, the family and education in society. Although the majority was not to be at all involved in the business of government, Plato nevertheless contended not only that the Philosopher Rulers would govern in the interests of the majority but also with their agreement and consent.

When we ask how this reasoning can be justified, we find that it is to be explained by "some magnificent myth that would in itself carry conviction to our whole community".[15] This foundation myth (sometimes mistranslated as "noble lie") is based on a tale that "when God fashioned you, he added gold in the composition of those of you who are qualified to be Rulers . . . ; he put silver in the Auxiliaries, and iron and

---

[13] Clifford Geertz, *Local Knowledge: Further Essays in Interpretive Anthropology* (New York: Basic Books, 1983), 143.

[14] Plato, *The Republic*, [*c*.380 BC] H.D.P. Lee trans. (Harmondsworth: Penguin, 1955), para. 379.

[15] Ibid. 414.

bronze in the farmers and the rest." It is a basic duty of the Guardians to exercise care to ensure that children are allocated to rank in accordance with their character "since there is a prophecy that the State will be ruined when it has Guardians of silver or bronze."[16] Far from eliminating myth from the realm of politics, then, Plato simply sought to abolish "the stories in Homer and Hesiod and the poets" and replace them with some new tales which better fitted the conditions of the time; "our first business", he notes, "is to supervise the production of stories, and choose only those we think suitable."[17]

Similar processes also seem have been at work in the modern era. At precisely the moment at which Copernicus effected a scientific revolution which shifted humanity from its central position in the universe, Enlightenment thinkers such as Descartes and Kant effected an intellectual revolution which sought to establish the human mind as the pivotal point in the universe. Since the Enlightenment we have seen both the emergence of the "individual" and the growth of political theories based on the rational, liberal, and law-observing individual. This modern individual, however, seems to be just as artificial as Plato's Guardian. It is a symbolic creature, devised for the purpose of making a modern political world. The individual in question in politico-legal thought is certainly not the same individual who appears in modern biology, psychology or psychiatry. We look upon the modern individual through a variety of frames, many of which provide contradictory images. The individual appears simultaneously as equal and unequal, rational and irrational, responsible and irresponsible. Though rarely conscious of the shifts we make, as though "through a glass, darkly", we switch frames with great regularity in our discussions, and the assessment we make of an individual accords with the mode of construction adopted.

Our conception of the individual is not therefore essentially a matter of truth. *Ignorantia juris non excusat* (ignorance of the law does not excuse) has been a basic maxim of law for many centuries, and we maintain that principle today notwithstanding the fact that, not only is the body of contemporary law so complex and voluminous that no one actually possesses a full knowledge of it, but also that it would be irrational for any one individual to try to commit it to memory. The responsible legal subject, just as much as the equal political citizen, is a symbolic creation which exists to give expression to a mode of

---

[16] Ibid. 415.
[17] Ibid. 377.

ordering. In this sense, the politico-legal order constitutes an array of abstract symbols—equality, democracy, sovereignty, the rule of law—each of which are designed to evoke an attitude. The order which is established is ultimately founded on belief and trust. It is sustained by a set of symbols which are not merely products of our intellectual processes, but also stem from our instincts and emotions as expressions of what people need to believe so that they might find comfort in that order. Similarly, the languages of politics and law, although often presenting themselves to us in a strictly logical form, are essentially rhetorical. This does not mean that they are mere ornament or trickery; they are persuasive discourses which employ language not simply to describe a state of affairs but also to express and reinforce certain values. The challenge for politicians (and also for judges) is, as Bagehot put it, "to know the highest truth which the people will bear, and to inculcate and preach that."[18] Consequently, although in the modern era we have jettisoned many of the religious myths which sustained order, we have tended to replace them with new discourses which can be viewed as forms of secular prayer.

ORDER AND DISORDER

Of all the symbols which permeate the languages of politics and law, those of order and disorder are especially potent. There is a strong temptation to characterize these as positive and negative symbols respectively; in our desire to escape the chaos and turmoil of disorder, we strive to achieve the beneficial conditions of an ordered existence. But it is not that simple. Order as well as disorder can be viewed a danger which constantly poses a threat to the world. From this perspective, order and disorder, rather than symbolizing good and evil, are the basic polarities between which politics must negotiate.

The menace of disorder is well enough understood. We need reflect only on the suffering which has resulted from the disintegration of the former Yugoslavian state or, more locally, on the urban riots in Brixton and Toxteth in the 1980s. Such scenes remind us of the problems which can arise when the aspirations of aggrieved, vulnerable or covetous people clash in circumstances where the prevailing structure of authority has all but collapsed. The threat of disorder serves as a constant

[18] Walter Bagehot, *The English Constitution* [1867] R.H.S. Crossman intro. (London: Collins, 1963), 178.

reminder of the achievement of a workable legal order. The security afforded individuals by the State provides the bedrock on which human civilization is able to flourish. In the relatively stable political regimes of western industrial countries, this issue has rarely been at the forefront of public attention, though with the rising crime-levels of the 1990s the question of "law and order" has recently occupied a more prominent place on the political agenda. For the early-modern thinkers who sought to explain and justify the foundations of political order, however, we find that the issue of security often lay at the heart of their concerns.

In *Leviathan*, for example, Thomas Hobbes argues that, in order to escape the threat of disorder, human beings need peace, that for peace they needed stable government, and that for stable government individuals are obliged to bind themselves to obey a sovereign authority.[19] Hobbes explains that, since nature has endowed all humans with a similar degree of strength and intelligence, they are forced ceaselessly to strive for power or security. Life in a state of nature is a condition of perpetual struggle. So, for Hobbes, notions of right and wrong, justice and injustice, here have no meaning; there is a veritable Babel of incomprehension and a condition of "war of every man against every man" in which force and fraud emerge as the cardinal virtues. In this state of nature, there is no industry since its fruits are uncertain, no culture or society and no technological development. Humans live in "continual fear and danger of violent death" and in this state of nature "the life of man [is] solitary, poor, nasty, brutish and short."[20]

Hobbes's portrayal of the state of nature is intended to demonstrate that "where there is no common Power, there is no Law: where there is no Law, no Injustice . . . there be no Propriety, no Dominion, no *Mine* and *Thine* distinct; but only that to be every man's that he can get; and for so long as he can keep it."[21] For Hobbes, the only way to secure peace, security and order is for everyone by covenant to relinquish their natural rights and submit to the authority of a coercive power which, through the threat of punishment, will ensure that promises are kept and rules obeyed. "Covenants without the Sword", Hobbes contends, "are but Words, and of no strength to secure a man at all."[22]

[19] Thomas Hobbes, *Leviathan* [1651] Richard Tuck ed. (Cambridge: Cambridge U.P., 1996).
[20] Ibid. 88, 89.
[21] Ibid. 90 (emphasis in original).
[22] Ibid. 117.

In graphic form, Hobbes highlights the dangers of disorder and makes them the centrepiece of his philosophy. But there are also dangers in the imposition of order. The establishment of a coercive power can certainly overcome pathological internal divisions within society. But this "great Leviathan" or "Mortal God"[23]—which, appropriately, Hobbes portrayed as holding both the sword and the crozier,[24] symbolizing a fusion of law and morality—also poses a threat. If law and justice is the product of the sovereign's command and that authority is unlimited, might not, in Tocqueville's words, "the love of order [be] confused with a taste for oppression"?[25]

It was this concern which, in 1680, motivated John Locke to present a rather different version of the state of nature. In his *Second Treatise of Government*, Locke argues that in the state of nature people were free, equal and independent, and rational enough to be able to distinguish right and wrong. He also contends that the idea of property existed in this natural state, and thus that the state of nature was, to all intents and purposes, a form of civil society without the State. Locke, not surprisingly, concludes that the compact which is forged between people is devised for limited purposes: "The great and chief end of men uniting into commonwealths, and putting themselves under government, is the preservation of their property."[26] Locke asserts that no rational person would agree to surrender authority unconditionally: "what security, what fence is there in such a State against the violence and oppression of this Absolute Ruler? The very question can scarce be born."[27] Absolute power leads to a "long train of abuses, prevarications and artifices" and "he that thinks absolute power purifies men's blood and corrects the baseness of human nature need read but the history of this or any other age to be convinced of the contrary."[28] For Locke, it was not sufficient to answer that the Sword will silence all who dare question the sovereign's authority; government must also act in accordance with, and subject to, the Law. Since order carries as many dangers as disorder, the object of government must be the estab-

[23] Thomas Hobbes, *Leviathan* [1651] Richard Tuck ed. (Cambridge: Cambridge U.P., 1996) 120.

[24] Ibid. xciii (reproducing the frontispiece from the first edition of the book).

[25] Alexis de Tocqueville, *Democracy in America* [1835] Henry Reeve trans., Daniel J. Boorstin intro. (New York: Vintage Books, 1990), vol. 1, 13.

[26] John Locke, *Second Treatise of Government* in his *Two Treatises of Government* [1680] Peter Laslett ed. (Cambridge: Cambridge U.P., 1988), §.123.

[27] Ibid. 93.

[28] Ibid. 92.

lishment of a just order. Political power must be exercised justly—the Sword tempered by the Scales—and order reconciled with liberty.

In Locke's day, the manner in which order imposed by government was to be reconciled with freedom was principally through the principle of the rule of law. This culture of limited government was to be bolstered by the emergence of civil society, by which is meant that network of diverse non-governmental institutions capable of counterbalancing the power of the State and preventing it from becoming too dominant. In modern times, however, some have argued that social, economic and technological developments, and especially the rise of democracy and egalitarianism, have combined to present the threat of order in a new form. No one has expressed this threat more eloquently than Alexis de Tocqueville.

Writing in 1840, Tocqueville warned that the evolution of democracy imposed a pressure towards conformity and a dominant mediocrity of taste and that there would, in particular, be a tendency for government to extend the range of its control over individuals. He recognized that, for this threat, "the old words *despotism* and *tyranny* are inappropriate [for] the thing itself is new". Rather, he predicts a society in which "stands an immense and tutelary power" which watches over the fate of its citizens and which exercises a power that is "absolute, minute, regular, provident and mild". This new Leviathan would not be a repressive force; on the contrary, its main objective would be to satisfy people's wants. But ultimately the government would become the sole arbiter of people's happiness. Tocqueville's concern was that within such an egalitarian system, founded on the sovereignty of the people, an individual's sense of free agency would be circumscribed within an ever narrowing range as the supreme power gradually covers "the surface of society with a network of small complicated rules, minute and uniform". "The will of man is not shattered", he continues, "but softened, bent and guided." This governmental power "does not tyrannize, but it compresses, enervates, extinguishes, and stupefies a people, till each nation is reduced to nothing better than a flock of timid and industrious animals, of which the government is the shepherd."[29]

In this remarkable passage, Tocqueville expresses a concern which has become a recurrent theme throughout the twentieth century. He recognized that, since freedom was possible only within a framework

[29] Tocqueville, above n. 25, vol. 2 [1840], 318–19.

of order, order and liberty could be viewed as complementary values. In another sense, however, they are in direct conflict, since it is through the establishment of order that tyranny is realized. The concern being expressed is that with the rise of democracy government enhances its legitimacy, thereby justifying an extension of its powers. But when government grows it may then come to dominate civil society and pose a threat to liberty. The image which Tocqueville projects is that of a society which is increasingly controlled and regimented. This image recurs in much of the political literature of the twentieth century, ranging from George Orwell's *Nineteen Eighty-Four*, in which the entire aim of Newspeak was to narrow the range of thought, to Michel Foucault's analysis of governmentality, in which, through the application of disciplinary technologies, governmental power becomes both all-encompassing and invisible.[30]

Order and disorder thus constitute two powerful symbols around which many issues of politics and law coalesce. For some, order is the fundamental principle of government. "The first duty of every government," Bagehot noted, "is to maintain order—that is, in plain English, to make the law so powerful that nobody thinks he can defy it with impunity." And it is "its first duty, *not* because the malcontents deserve punishment—they may not deserve it at all, as in the case of a rising of slaves or conquered persons—but because it has pledged itself to all the loyal that it will do it."[31] Bagehot here acknowledges that, for government, order is more important than substantive justice. Whilst recognizing the importance of order, other writers also see the potential threat that it poses; many of these concerns seem in effect to be variations on the theme that "a violent order is disorder."[32] Prominent amongst these voices is that of Tocqueville who reminds us that, especially in the modern era, the values of equality and liberty must each be distinguished.

The manner in which the issue of order/disorder is presented has been of critical importance in shaping particular traditions of politics.

[30] George Orwell, *Nineteen Eighty-Four* (London: Secker & Warburg, 1949); Michel Foucault, *Discipline and Punish: The Birth of the Prison* Alan Sheridan trans. (Harmondsworth: Penguin, 1991); Foucault, "Governmentality" in Graham Burchell, Colin Gordon & Peter Miller (eds), *The Foucault Effect* (Hemel Hempstead: Harvester Wheatsheaf, 1991), ch. 4.

[31] Walter Bagehot, "The Irish Policy of the Liberal Government" [1870] in his *Collected Works*, Norman St John-Stevas ed. (London: The Economist, 1965) vol. III, 112 (emphasis in original).

[32] Wallace Stevens, "Connoisseur of Chaos" in *The Collected Poems of Wallace Stevens* (London: Faber & Faber, 1954), 215.

Whether we embrace the account of Hobbes or Locke on the nature of governmental authority depends less on our assessment of the historical accuracy or scientific validity of their treatises and more on which of their stories about the state of nature we find most compelling. "The more I study the cause of the movement of human affairs", Tocqueville noted, "the more I remain convinced that all political events are consequences except the notions and sentiments dominant in a people: these are the real causes of all the rest."[33] Oakeshott makes a similar point in suggesting that civilization is, at bottom, a kind of collective dream and that "the substance of this dream is a myth, an imaginative interpretation of human existence." Consequently, the role of literature in a civilization "is not to break the dream but perpetually to recall it, to recreate it in each generation, and even to make more articulate the dream-powers of a people."[34]

CONCLUSIONS

Politics and law are critical aspects of the normative world which we have assembled for the purpose of living a relatively ordered existence and through which we are able to manage our differences. We engage in these practices primarily through an institution we call the State. Although the State often manifests itself as a coercive presence, the political power it exercises is, as has already been noted,[35] rather different from brute force. It is a form of power which is generated from the relationship between citizens and the State. In this chapter, I have tried to show how this political relationship is sustained mainly by myth and symbol. Even Hobbes, the greatest of the theorists of the authoritarian State, recognized that "the power of the mighty hath no foundation but in the opinion and belief of the people."[36]

In seeking to understand politics and law we are not in the least concerned with the scientific validity of these sets of beliefs. The "truth" or otherwise of these beliefs is rarely an issue of the first importance. "The

[33] Quoted in Jack Lively, *The Social and Political Thought of Alexis de Tocqueville* (Oxford: Clarendon Press, 1962), 53.
[34] Michael Oakeshott, "The Collective Dream of Civilisation", *The Listener*, 19 June 1947, 966.
[35] See Ch. 1 above, 16–17.
[36] Thomas Hobbes, *Behemoth or The Long Parliament* [1682] Ferdinand Tönnies ed. (London: Cass, 1969), 16. See also G.W.F. Hegel, *Philosophy of Right* [1821] T.M. Knox trans. (Oxford: Oxford U.P., 1967), §.190.

nature of a constitution, the action of an assembly, the play of parties, the unseen formation of a guiding opinion", notes Bagehot, "are complex facts, difficult to know and easy to mistake". And for this reason Bagehot contends that although "[i]t is often said that men are ruled by their imaginations . . . it would be truer to say they are governed by the weaknesses of their imaginations".[37] Instead, our concern must be to appreciate the way in which certain ideas and beliefs gain acceptance as the "dominant sentiments" or "collective dreams" of a society and, being thus sanctified by ritual and consecration, are able to bolster a particular type of politico-legal order.

The main way in which certain political and legal ideas come to form a major part of these dominant sentiments is through the roles which they play in narratives, those stories which give meaning to what may be called a way of life or a tradition of behaviour. In this book, I propose to examine a number of these basic ideas, organized around the themes of Justice, the State and Constitutionalism. My objective will be to indicate how these ideas take on a more precise meaning when located within certain traditions of behaviour. Through this exercise we should be able to see not only how law and politics are related activities in a common venture, but also how within certain configurations they take on distinctive roles. In Chapter 1, for example, I referred to the existence of different conceptions of law. If we look back to the contrasting stories which Hobbes and Locke relate about the transition from a state of nature to a political order, the way in which these differing conceptions of law acquire significance within these narratives— law as command for Hobbes and law as right in the case of Locke—should be apparent. Through this type of approach, we might obtain a more refined understanding of the roles of law and politics in "the conversation of mankind".

---

[37] Bagehot, above n. 18, 82.

3

Practical Engagements

THIS CHAPTER HAS two main objectives. The first is directly to address the concerns of those who remain sceptical about my approach to the subject. Such scepticism is likely to take one of two forms. The first is the sort of exasperated resignation which Woody Allen expresses: "Can we actually know the universe? My God, it's hard enough finding your way around in Chinatown."[1] What I hope to show is that we cannot adequately understand the relationship between law and politics without having regard to the importance of general ideas and beliefs. Those who assert that law and politics are practical engagements which can be understood without regard to ideological frameworks are almost certainly ruled unconsciously by the thoughts of others. "Practical men, who believe themselves to be quite exempt from intellectual influences", Keynes famously commented at the end of *The General Theory of Employment*, "are usually the slaves of some defunct economist. Madmen in authority, who hear voices in the air, are distilling their frenzy from some academic scribbler of a few years back".[2] The ideas which underpin legal and political discourse are an essential part of the inquiry.

There is, additionally, another group of sceptics: those who believe that the relationship between law and politics is best examined as part of a scientific study of who gains and who loses when political interests collide. According to this formulation, politics deals with the clash of material interests, and law should be analysed as a continuation of that process. This approach leads to studies which examine the way groups use the forms and institutions of law to realize their political objectives[3] and which analyse the political impact of judicial

[1] Woody Allen, "My Philosophy" in his *Getting Even* (New York: Vintage Books, 1966), 21, 22.

[2] John Maynard Keynes, *The General Theory of Employment, Interest and Money* [1936] (London: Macmillan, 1960), 383.

[3] See, e.g., Carol Harlow and Richard Rawlings, *Pressure Through Law* (London: Routledge, 1992); J. Cooper and R. Dhavan (eds), *Public Interest Law* (Oxford: Blackwell, 1986).

decision-making.[4] Just as political scientists examine the interplay of interests in the policy-making process, so also legislative and, more contentiously,[5] judicial processes can be investigated in terms of these conflicts of interest. Law is brought into the political arena by examining how law operates to promote particular social interests: employers may win out over workers, the haves over the have-nots, business interests over environmental interests, private property interests over the public interest, whites over blacks, men over women, the organized over the non-organized, the strong over the weak.

This type of work is important, especially in highlighting an often neglected aspect of law's political function. These studies challenge a number of legal myths which surround claims to the neutrality and objectivity of law. But this work does not, through demystification, gain access to the "real" world; this scientific world is also socially constructed and is just as likely to be built on premises which are as contestable as those which have been jettisoned. By debunking so many basic legal myths, the application of the scientific approach to politics deprives law of many of the props which it requires to be able to function effectively. Consequently, although it casts an interesting slant on law, it distorts or ignores much of what makes law a distinctive way of engaging in the world.

Whilst the primary objective of this chapter is to defend my general approach, a secondary objective is to illustrate its relevance. I do so by outlining four studies in which the clash of interests should be clear. These situations extend from international to local issues and cover a range of institutional contexts. My basic aim is to demonstrate a simple point: that we are unable to acquire an adequate grasp of the nature of these disputes unless we accept that certain politico-legal ideas and beliefs lie at their core.

THE GULF CONFLICT

On 2 August 1990, Iraq invaded Kuwait. The primary objective, it appeared, was to acquire Kuwait's vast, oil-derived wealth, thereby

---

[4] See, e.g., J.A.G. Griffith, *The Politics of the Judiciary* (London: Fontana, 5th edn., 1997).

[5] See, e.g., the critical reception which greeted the first edition of Griffith, ibid.: Kenneth Minogue, "The biases of the bench" *Times Literary Supplement*, 6 January 1978, 11 and resulting correspondence on 13 Jan. (B. Crick), 20 Jan. (K. Minogue), 27 Jan. (E.P. Thompson, R. Harrison), 3 Feb. (K. Minogue), 10 Feb (E.J. Hobsbawm, C. Harlow), 17 Feb. (K. Minogue), 24 Feb. (E.J. Hobsbawm).

rescuing Iraq from the verge of bankruptcy caused largely by her exhausting, eight-year war with Iran. The invasion was the final stage in a longstanding dispute between the two countries. Iraq maintained that Kuwait in fact formed part of Iraq and had been artificially separated in 1914 as an act of British colonialism. Invasion was therefore justified on the ground that it would both eliminate colonial action and strengthen pan-Arab security. Saddam Hussein, Iraq's leader, had also claimed that by exceeding OPEC quotas on oil sales and thereby having driven down the price of oil, Kuwait had been engaging in what amounted to an act of economic warfare against the Iraqi economy.

Saddam engaged in a swift operation and, by exploiting the spectre of revived Western colonialism, attempted to contain the conflict within the region. These efforts nevertheless failed to prevent internationalization of the crisis. After economic sanctions had been imposed on Iraq by the major powers, on 17 January 1991 military action was taken. An American-led combined force first used air power on military targets in Iraq and then, on 24 February, embarked on a short land war. This culminated in a ceasefire on 3 March, at which stage the Iraqis had been routed and removed from Kuwait. The war had claimed the lives of two hundred and forty combatants from the coalition forces, an estimated twenty thousand Iraqis, and had cost the coalition governments an estimated $54 billion.[6]

Of critical importance in this conflict was the attitude of the United States. By failing to read the signals, Iraq made a vital miscalculation. The US had earlier insisted that it had no position on the particulars of the Iraq–Kuwait dispute, a stance which reflected their normal foreign policy of avoiding entanglements in purely regional controversies. But this position also seemed to convey—wrongly as it turned out—US indifference to the relative claims of the parties and ambivalence over its commitment to the defence of Kuwait. Iraq's action directly affected US interests. The annexation of Kuwait meant that Iraq controlled twenty per cent of the world's oil reserves, and if—as initially seemed possible—Iraq also moved to annex Saudi Arabia, that figure would have been doubled. The prospect of Iraq becoming the key player in the world oil market was a possibility the US, the world's major importer of oil, could not countenance. It was essential to defend Kuwait in order to ensure the security of world oil supplies.

---

[6] L. Freedman and E. Karsh, *The Gulf Conflict 1990–1991: Diplomacy and War in the New World Order* (Princeton: Princeton U.P., 1993), 408–9, 358.

This brief narrative explains the Gulf conflict almost entirely in the language of power politics. But there is another story to be told. In this version, the Gulf conflict is an episode which vindicates the principle of the rule of law. Iraq's invasion of Kuwait had directly infringed a basic precept of international law. Article 2(4) of the United Nations Charter requires that all members "shall refrain in their international relations from the threat or use of force against the territorial integrity or political independence of any State". Iraq's naked aggression against a fellow member State of the United Nations thus presented the international community with a major challenge. As George Bush, then President of the United States, declared in his address on the State of the Union in January 1991: "What is at stake is more than one small country; it is a big idea: a new world order—where nations are drawn together in common cause to achieve the universal aspirations of mankind: peace and security, freedom and the rule of law." The institutions of the United Nations were compelled to respond to this breach of the rules. The Security Council demanded Iraq's immediate withdrawal and it was through UN Resolutions that, first, economic sanctions were employed and, later, that the use of force was authorized. The international coalition which drove the Iraqi army out of Kuwait and restored the Kuwait government to power was drawn from twenty-eight States and worked under the authority of the UN to vindicate a basic norm of international law.

In each of these accounts, the conflict is explained from a particular perspective; the former, that rooted in international power politics, provides an explanation almost entirely in terms of the strategic interests of states, whereas the latter, that based on international law, explains what happened by reference to the requirements of norms of the international legal order. Accounts which adopt each of these contrasting perspectives on the Gulf conflict are to be found in the literature.[7] Any account which fails to incorporate both of these dimensions, however, is unlikely to capture the complexity of the episode. A political perspective which ignores the normative aspects and a legal interpretation which ignores the political dynamics are each likely to provide skewed explanations of what happened. Certainly, we ought not to accept uncritically the claim that the conflict provides an impres-

---

[7] Cf. Christopher Greenwood, "New World Order or Old? The Invasion of Kuwait and the Rule of Law" (1992) 55 *Modern Law Review* 153; Noam Chomsky, "The Use (and Abuse) of the United Nations" in Micah L. Sifry & Christopher Cerf (eds), *The Gulf War Reader: History, Documents, Opinions* (New York: Random House, 1991), 307.

sive illustration of the world community acting to vindicate the principle of the rule of law. If such norms really are authoritative then they ought to be systematically enforced whenever a serious transgression occurs. Nevertheless, we saw no similar action as a consequence of the Israeli occupation of Arab territories after 1967, or with Turkey's partition of Cyprus in 1974, or Indonesia's annexation of East Timor in 1975, or the Soviet Union's invasion of Afghanistan in 1979, or the US invasion of Grenada in 1983.[8] There was not even condemnation when, in 1980, Iraq took aggressive action and attacked Iran. In that case, Iraq's action seems to have been tolerated because revolutionary Iran was generally regarded as the primary threat to stability in the region. This seems to indicate that Iraqi misbehaviour is condemned only when it offends the interests of the western powers. Greenwood suggests the conflict was unique because it was the first time one UN member State "had attempted to annex the entire territory of another and to extinguish it as a separate State".[9] But lawyers are very skilled at drawing fine distinctions and devising new categories, and for Chomsky the unprecedented response to Saddam's aggression occurred only "because he stepped on the wrong toes".[10]

To view the Gulf conflict simply as an application of the principle that the use of force by one State against another must always be opposed is an inadequate justification and an unconvincing explanation. But the fact that the rules are not enforced systematically does not mean that they can be treated as irrelevant, or as a smokescreen which conceals the reality of what is going on. The most important reason why Iraq found itself so isolated within the international community was that it had blatantly transgressed an elementary rule of international law, and this violation provides the foundation for the attempt to build an international consensus over military action. The end of the cold war, which meant that there was no longer any need to judge every regional issue in terms of its potential for causing confrontation between the superpowers, was certainly an important aspect of the overall picture. But the fact that critical aspects of the conflict concerned the international politics of oil and the reconfiguration of superpower politics, should not blind us to the point that the Gulf

---

[8] See Antonio Cassese, *Self-Determination of Peoples: A Legal Reappraisal* (Cambridge: Cambridge U.P., 1995), 90–9.

[9] Greenwood, above n. 7, 153.

[10] Chomsky, above n. 7, 309.

conflict also involved a struggle about the meaning and significance of basic norms of international law.

International relations is an arena which may not easily offer up generalizations about law and politics. We should therefore turn our attention to an issue which seems more directly to touch on the basic interests of the State. One of the most important political challenges which the United Kingdom has faced throughout the latter half of the twentieth century has been that of her position within Europe. When the European Economic Community was established in 1957, the UK decided not to join. The Community's primary objective was to establish a common market amongst the member States and at that time Britain's trade was felt to be too closely tied with members of the Commonwealth. In the 1960s, the UK, recognizing the growing importance of trade links in Europe, applied to join; it was not until January 1973, however, that the UK actually acceded. Whatever the economic benefits, the political implications of Britain's membership have been hotly contested ever since.[11]

At the core of these political issues lies the vexed question of sovereignty, which we may take here to mean simply a country's ability to exert control for itself over those political decisions which are vital to its interests. On accession to the Community, the British people were informed that nothing fundamental had changed. The Government noted that, like any other treaty, the Treaty of Rome commits its signatories to support agreed aims, but that "the commitment represents the voluntary undertaking of a sovereign state to observe policies which it has helped to form". In particular, the Government stressed that there "is no question of any erosion of essential national sovereignty; what is proposed is a sharing and an enlargement of individual national sovereignties in the general interest."[12] Others, nevertheless, considered that something of greater significance had taken place.[13] In

---

[11] See Hugo Young, *This Blessed Plot: Britain and Europe from Churchill to Blair* (London: Macmillan, 1998).

[12] *The United Kingdom and the European Communities* Cmnd 4715 (London: HMSO, 1971), 8.

[13] See, e.g., J.D.B. Mitchell, S.A. Kuipers & B. Gall, "Constitutional Aspects of the Treaty and Legislation Relating to British Membership" (1972) 9 *Common Market Law Review* 134.

order to ground the issue, I shall outline the elements of a rather mundane dispute which arose from the administration of the EC's common fisheries policy.

As part of the complex process of establishing a single market, a common fisheries policy was established and the traditional fishing grounds of member states were opened up to the nationals of other members. However, in pursuit of a policy of conserving fish stocks within Community waters, each member state was then allocated a fishing quota, which was basically the total annual permissible catch of each of the main fish species. But there was a gap in the system: since there was nothing to prohibit vessels from one country re-registering in another member state, the system of quotas for national fishing fleets could, in practice, be circumvented. This threat became more acute after Spain and Portugal joined the EC in 1986, since with their accession the tonnage of the entire Community fishing fleet was increased by fifty per cent and the number of fishermen doubled. In order to prevent this practice of "quota-hopping", the UK Parliament passed the Merchant Shipping Act 1988, which required British-registered boats (the pre-condition to being able to fish against the British quota) to be owned and controlled by British nationals or by corporations registered in the UK.

When, acting in accordance with the 1988 Act, the Minister refused to register Spanish-owned boats in Britain, the boat-owners challenged the legality of that decision. The essence of their argument was that this refusal to permit registration contravened those articles of the Treaty of Rome prohibiting discrimination on grounds of nationality and establishing the principle of free movement of persons in pursuit of their trade. There then followed a tortuous series of actions through the British and European courts in which the courts eventually ruled: that the UK government could not stop the Spanish vessels from operating pending the resolution of the point of law (which in effect suspended the operation of the 1988 Act);[14] that the nationality requirements in the 1988 Act were contrary to Community law (which in effect rendered the 1988 Act unlawful);[15] and that the UK government must pay damages to the Spanish fishermen for failure to respect

[14] Case C–246/89R, *Commission* v. *United Kingdom* [1989] ECR I–3125; Case C–213/89, R v. *Secretary of State for Transport, ex parte Factortame (No. 2)* [1990] ECR I–2433; R v. *Secretary of State for Transport, ex parte Factortame (No. 2)* [1991] 1 AC 603.

[15] Case C–221/89, R v. *Secretary of State for Transport, ex parte Factortame* [1991] ECR I–3905; [1991] 3 All ER 769.

their rights.[16] These rulings caused great controversy, with MPs arguing that they had been duped when passing the European Communities Act 1972, which gave legal effect to the UK's membership of the EC.[17] To many of the protagonists, quota-hopping seemed far removed from the sharing of resources "in the general interest", the court directives smacked of anything but "voluntary undertakings", and, in nullifying the explicit Parliamentary intent expressed in the 1988 Act, the argument that there was "no question of any erosion of essential national sovereignty" rang hollow.

It is not necessary to enter into a detailed discussion of the intricate legal and constitutional questions to which such developments give rise. The fundamental point is that, by the time the UK entered the European Community, the European Court of Justice—the institution vested with authority to determine the meaning and validity of Community instruments—had already articulated the principle that the EC had brought into existence "a new legal order" for the benefit of which States had limited their sovereign rights.[18] This new legal order did not mesh comfortably with the basic legal principle of the British Constitution: that there is no legal limitation on the power of Parliament to pass whatever legislation it desires, and that such Acts of Parliament must be given full effect by the courts. It was predictable that, as the Community evolved, not only would the ambit of Community competence rapidly extend but also that the principles of the Community legal order which the Court of Justice were developing would assume a broader political significance. Many politicians seem to have been only dimly aware of these implications when the debate over Community membership was conducted. Furthermore, although the Government may have been more attentive to the issue, Ministers did not go out of their way to explain the constitutional significance of accession. This is hardly surprising since, once the Government had determined to seek membership, it became a project to be sold to the people and managed through Parliament.

But the most important issue which for our purposes this example highlights is that of the greatly enhanced importance of the interface between law and politics which has arisen as a consequence of mem-

---

[16] R v. *Secretary of State for Transport, ex parte Factortame (No. 4)* [1996] QB 404; R v. *Secretary of State for Transport, ex parte Factortame (No. 5)* [1999] 4 All ER 905.

[17] See, e.g., HC Debs, vol. 174 cols 923–4 (20 June 1990); HC Debs vol. 175, vol. 141–3w.

[18] Case 26/62, *Van Gend en Loos v. Nederlandse Administratie der Belastingen* [1963] ECR 1; Case 6/64, *Costa v. E.N.E.L* [1964] ECR 585.

bership of the European Union. The question of whether one views the European political project as one of incipient federalism or a "Europe of nation states" (i.e., a confederation) is here little more than a sideshow. The most basic point is that the structure of the European Union—constituted by law and driven by legal instruments—has ensured that issues of legal interpretation are now placed at the centre of the political process. When in 1964 the judiciary ruled that the UK government should pay compensation to a major corporation for destroying its property in wartime and the government did not like the result, it simply promoted an Act which nullified the court ruling.[19] The contrast with the quota-hopping saga thirty years later could scarcely be more stark. In the contemporary world, the language of rights and the decisions of the judiciary are now able to penetrate to the core of power politics.

ARMS TO IRAQ

In November 1992 a criminal trial involving three directors of the Matrix Churchill company collapsed. The directors, who had been responsible for exporting machine tools to Iraq, had been charged with serious breaches of export-control restrictions; it was claimed that they had been less than frank about the intended use of these machines when making applications to the Department of Trade & Industry (DTI) for export licences. Their defence was that the Government had known all along that the tools would be used to manufacture munitions, and indeed that they had been working in co-operation with MI6. The Government had tried to prevent the disclosure in court of certain official documents relevant to the trial, but the judge had ruled that they should be disclosed, and when Alan Clark, former Minister of State at the DTI, confirmed under cross-examination that there had been no deception and that the official guidelines had in fact been modified, the prosecution dropped the case and the defendants were acquitted. Since several aspects of this affair had provoked concern, the Government appointed Lord Justice Scott to examine the practices of government departments in dealing with applications to export defence-related goods to Iraq during the 1980s and to report on whether the

---

[19] *Burmah Oil Co* v. *Lord Advocate* [1964] 2 All ER 348; War Damage Act 1965.

Departments and Ministers had "operated in accordance with the policies of Her Majesty's government".[20]

The Scott Inquiry became the focus of intense debate about the conduct of government, its legal powers and administrative practices, and the efficacy of mechanisms for holding government to account. I do not intend to deal with all these issues here,[21] but I do want to focus on one central point. After a thirty-eight-month investigation, involving an examination of over two hundred thousand official documents, Scott delivered a five-volume report in February 1996 which concluded that Ministers had misled Parliament over changes to the export guidelines.[22] The Government rejected that finding, won a Commons debate on the issue by one vote and, having relegated the Report to constitutional history, proceeded with business as usual. What is the significance of this disagreement between Scott and the Government on the guidelines, and what does it reveal about the relationship between law and politics?

When the Iran–Iraq war commenced in 1980, the UK maintained a position of neutrality. The Government then determined its stance with respect to defence sales to the warring parties, and it was in this context that guidelines were drawn up in December 1984. These guidelines stated that the UK would refuse to supply any lethal equipment to either side and would not approve new orders "for any defence equipment which in our view would significantly enhance the capacity of either side to prolong or exacerbate the conflict".[23] In 1989, at the end of the war but before any treaty had been signed, this guidance was reconsidered and a revised version was circulated. This version stated that new orders would not be approved "for any defence equipment which in our view would be of direct and significant assistance to either country in the conduct of offensive operations".[24] The Government contended that this new formulation was similar in all essentials to the

---

[20] *Return to an Address of the Honourable House of Commons dated 15th February 1996 for the Report of the Inquiry into the Export of Defence Equipment and Dual-Use Goods to Iraq and Related Prosecutions* HC 115 (Session 1995–6) [Scott Report], A2.2.

[21] See, e.g., I. Leigh, "Matrix Churchill, Supergun and the Scott Inquiry" 1993 *Public Law* 630; I. Leigh and L. Lustgarten, "Five Volumes in Search of Accountability: the Scott Report" (1996) 59 *Modern Law Review* 695; B. Thompson and F.F. Ridley (eds), *Under the Scott-Light: British Government seen through the Scott Report* (Oxford: Oxford U.P., 1997); 1997 *Public Law* (Autumn: special issue); Adam Tomkins, *The Constitution After Scott: Government Unwrapped* (Oxford: Clarendon Press, 1998).

[22] Scott Report, above n. 20, D8.16.

[23] Ibid. D1.155.

[24] Ibid. D3.30.

original. Scott, however, found that this contention was "so plainly inapposite as to be incapable of being sustained by serious argument".[25] Such critical language highlights the gulf that separated the judge's view from that of the Government. How is it to be explained? Scott believed that the 1984 guidelines established the normative standard governing decision-making on export licences. However, although these guidelines seemed to be designed to express a policy of even-handedness in dealings with Iran and Iraq, Iraq was in fact receiving around twenty times more defence-related equipment than Iran.[26] This apparently meant that the guidelines were just a presentational device masking the reality of what was going on; hence such statements as those of the Cabinet Secretary that civil servants were "misleading themselves" or the observation from a senior Ministry of Defence official that "truth is a very difficult concept"—expressions which were used to hold officials to ridicule.[27] Further, once the guidelines were identified as the source of the policy, it was clear to Scott that the 1989 formulation was plainly different. Since the 1984 guidelines had been reported to Parliament, Scott concluded that the answers which Ministers gave to parliamentary questions not only failed to inform Parliament of the current state of Government policy but also that "this failure was deliberate and the inevitable result of the agreement between the three Junior Ministers that no publicity would be given to the decision to adopt a more liberal, or relaxed, policy or interpretation of the Guidelines".[28] From this perspective, it is difficult to draw any conclusion other than that those Ministers failed in their constitutional responsibilities. And the fact that they held on to office emphasizes the limitations of the arrangements for holding Ministers to account.

But could it be that truth is, in this context, a difficult concept?[29] Scott was obliged to examine a sphere of government decision-making which generally remains secret and his background in commercial law may not have been ideal training for the task. The conduct of foreign relations is an area in which "ambiguity often seems the safest course" since, being "influenced by many diverse and often contradictory

---

[25] Scott Report, above n. 20, D3.123.

[26] Ibid. D1.6.

[27] R. Norton-Taylor, *Truth is a Difficult Concept: Inside the Scott Inquiry* (London: Fourth Estate, 1995), 34, 95. Under the title, *Half the Picture*, Norton-Taylor even dramatized the Inquiry proceedings for the stage.

[28] Scott Report, above n. 20, D4.42.

[29] See Ch. 2 above, 19–21.

pressures, clarity can appear as the enemy of good government."[30] It is a sphere in which "telling Parliament as little as possible in order to preserve maximum freedom of manoeuvre is quite normal" and therefore, although official statements "are rarely inaccurate, . . . they are invariably incomplete".[31]

From this perspective, reminded of the circuitous ways of foreign relations, Scott may indeed have been rather naïve. Working on the assumption that neutrality meant that each side should have access to the same equipment, Scott considered that the disparity in volume sales between the two countries indicated that the Government had not been even-handed in its defence sales policy.[32] But, as one Foreign Office official observed, although even-handedness meant applying the same criteria over defence sales to Iran and Iraq "the end results are not necessarily even handed".[33] This is because, other than maintaining the formal legal status of neutrality with respect to the war, Britain's relations with Iran and Iraq were very different; revolutionary Iran was regarded as implacably hostile to the west, whereas Iraq—traditionally aligned with the Soviet Union—seemed to be opening up to western influence. These foreign policy considerations pre-dated the 1984 guidelines. Further, contrary to the legalistic perspective of Scott, the guidelines were not the source of the policy: the restriction on the supply of lethal equipment, for example, was in place well before the guidelines were drafted, and the guidelines could more accurately be viewed as "a framework through which the real policy issues were discussed".[34] The Foreign Office saw the guidelines "primarily as a set of criteria for use in defending against public and parliamentary criticism and criticism from the Americans and Saudis, whatever decisions we take on grounds of commercial and political interest".[35] Decisions certainly needed to be consistent with the guidelines, but the guidelines were flexible and "our interests are too finely balanced to allow mechanical application of the guidelines to dictate our policy".[36]

The Foreign Office explanation is a classic statement of politics as a symbolic process through which the business of the State must be nego-

---

[30] L. Freedman, "Even-handedness, Guidelines and Defence Sales to Iraq" 1996 *Public Law* 391, 392–3.
[31] Ibid. 393.
[32] Scott Report, above n. 20, D1.35.
[33] Ibid. D2.28.
[34] Freedman, above n. 30, 409.
[35] Scott Report, above n. 20, D3.132.
[36] Ibid.

tiated. Scott's rule-book mentality, by contrast, not only failed to capture the nuances required in the conduct of foreign policy, but also provided an inadequate account of the development of policy-making in
this field and distorted the guidelines' significance. The 1984 guidelines,
after all, were not actually revealed to Parliament until 29 October
1985, and then only in a written answer to a parliamentary question.[37]
It is not necessary to embrace William Waldegrave's warped logic[38] to
see that there was more continuity in policy than Scott seemed prepared to acknowledge. Parliament and the public may have been given
information "that was by design incomplete and in certain respects
misleading",[39] but is not this normal practice in the Government's conduct of sensitive foreign relations? Perhaps the real failure of government was not its highly flexible interpretation of guidance on defence
sales but the fact that during the late 1980s, at precisely the time that
Saddam was planning to annex Kuwait to plunder the resources needed
to finance his regime, the Government's policy was that of expanding
sales of military-related equipment to Iraq.

The Scott Inquiry was a remarkably detailed investigation into the
inner-most workings of the British system of government. But what is
its significance? Some have seen the Report and its reception as an
index of the futility and ineffectiveness of Parliamentary scrutiny in a
system of parliamentary government;[40] others as raising questions
about the personal integrity of Ministers[41] and the nature of contemporary political culture.[42] But the Report also illustrates what is likely
to happen when a judge is permitted to roam through the treacherous
fields of foreign relations. Some have criticized the use of the judiciary
for such inquiries on the grounds that it will inevitably get drawn into
political controversy,[43] and others because the judge did not afford
proper court-like procedural protections to those criticized in the
course of this inquiry.[44] But the Report also exemplifies a belief that the

[37] HC Debs, vol. 84 col.450w.
[38] Waldegrave, the junior Foreign Office Minister during this period, argued before
Scott that the fact that senior Ministers had not approved the change meant that the
guidelines had not been changed: Scott Report, above n. 20, D3.125.
[39] Scott Report, above n. 20, D4.60.
[40] Leigh and Lustgarten, above n. 21, 724.
[41] Rodney Brazier, "It *is* a Constitutional Issue: Fitness for Ministerial Office in the
1990s" 1994 *Public Law* 431.
[42] Leigh and Lustgarten, above n. 21, 725; Tomkins, above n. 21, ch. 1.
[43] Rodney Brazier, *Constitutional Practice* (Oxford: Clarendon Press, 2nd edn., 1994),
226.
[44] Lord Howe of Aberavon, "Procedure at the Scott Inquiry" 1996 *Public Law* 445.

training and world-view of the lawyer may place a judge at a significant disadvantage when trying to accommodate the subtleties and ambiguities of governmental practice. This is an old refrain. In *Growth of the English Constitution*, Edward Freeman complained that "lawyers' interpretations and lawyers' ways of looking at things have done no small mischief, not only to the true understanding of our history, but to the actual course of history itself". The lawyer's chief virtue, Freeman continued, "is that of acute and logical inference from given premisses; the premisses themselves he is commonly satisfied to take without examination from those who have gone before him. It is often wonderful to see the amazing ingenuity with which lawyers have piled together inference upon inference, starting from some purely arbitrary assumption of their own."[45]

CRIME AND POLITICS

In recent years, as politicians have vied for the mantle of "law and order", crime has become a highly politicized issue. The politicization of criminal justice has been most evident in the way crime is now addressed as a party political question. Recently, the pressures felt by politicians have resulted in their taking action which has drawn them into dispute with the judiciary. At the core of the conflict has been the issue of sentencing.

The Criminal Justice Act 1991 established a relatively liberal regime based on the belief that a custodial sentence should be the remedy of last resort. By the mid-1990s, however, with crime rates rising and the Government trailing in the polls, action on the issue of law and order became imperative. Michael Howard, then Home Secretary, gave a speech to the Conservative Party conference in 1995 which signalled his intentions. There was, he suggested, a "strong case for saying that anyone convicted for the second time of a serious violent or sexual crime should receive an automatic sentence of life imprisonment". Howard continued: "If prison, and the threat of prison, are to work effectively, there's a strong case for greater certainty in sentencing—for stiff minimum sentences for burglars and dealers in hard drugs who offend again and again and again."[46] The Home Secretary's speech provoked an

---

[45] E.A. Freeman, *Growth of the English Constitution* (London: Macmillan, 1876), 127–8.

[46] Michael Howard, speech to the Conservative Party conference, Blackpool, 12 October 1995.

immediate response from England's senior judge, the Lord Chief Justice. Whilst conceding that long sentences were sometimes necessary for the protection of the public, Lord Taylor directly contradicted the Home Secretary's view that longer terms of imprisonment would deter habitual criminals. "What deters them", Lord Taylor contended, "is the likelihood of being caught, which at the moment is small". Instead, he proposed that "the police should be provided with the resources they need in order to bring criminals before the courts".[47] Lord Taylor's statement received widespread media attention and provoked political controversy. Surely this was an unjustified intrusion by the judiciary in the political process?

What appears to have provoked this intervention was the perception that the Government was proposing to step on the judiciary's turf. It is for judges to try cases and, having heard all the evidence, to determine appropriate punishment. "Minimum sentences", the Lord Chief Justice argued, "are inconsistent with doing justice according to the circumstances of each case."[48] The judges were concerned that these proposals would significantly limit their discretion; sentences, they felt, should fit the criminal and not simply the crime. They thus felt compelled to enter the arena of political controversy primarily as a form of defensive action to prevent the Executive encroaching too far on judicial territory.

Although the judiciary engaged in a concerted campaign, this made no obvious impact on the Government. The ensuing White Paper, *Protecting the Public*,[49] maintained the policy of fixing mandatory minimum sentences for repeat offenders of a serious violent offence, serious sexual offence, drug trafficking or burglary. Speaking on the White Paper in the legislative chamber of the House of Lords, the Lord Chief Justice delivered a withering rebuke to the Government: "Never in the history of our criminal law have such far-reaching proposals been put forward on the strength of such flimsy and dubious evidence. The shallow and untested figures in the White Paper do not describe fairly the problems the Government seek to address. Still less do they justify the radical solutions it proposes . . . Quite simply, minimum sentences must involve a denial of justice."[50]

---

[47] Lord Taylor C.J., Press Release, 12 October 1995.
[48] Ibid.
[49] Cm 3190 (London: HMSO, 1996).
[50] HL Debs vol. 572 cols 1025–6 (23 May 1996).

Nevertheless, the Crime (Sentences) Bill was presented in the Commons without modification. Furthermore, since the Bill was not opposed by the Labour party, it came to the House of Lords essentially unchanged and with the clear approval of the elected chamber. But this did not in the least inhibit the judges. Lord Bingham, who had just assumed the office of Lord Chief Justice in succession to Lord Taylor, led the attack. He explained that the provisions for minimum sentences were "irremediably flawed", that they infringed "a cardinal principle of just sentencing" and demonstrated that they were indiscriminate in their impact and led to anomalies of a kind which "are not the stuff of sound law-making". Lord Bingham concluded: "If, as the century and the millennium slide to a close, our penal thinking is to be judged by the thinking which animates this Bill, then I, for one, will shrink from the judgment of history".[51] At last this type of pressure began to make an impact. In the Lords, a Labour amendment was introduced with the judiciary's support which provided that mandatory sentences would not apply if factors existed which would make "the prescribed custodial sentence unjust in all the circumstances". This amendment succeeded in the Lords by eight votes.

But could the amendment survive the Bill's return to the Commons? Fortunately for the judiciary, other political factors intervened. The Government decided to go to the polls in May 1997, and this meant that all legislation had to be cleared through Parliament before the dissolution. And in order to ensure the speedy passage of the Bill, the Government felt obliged to accept the amendment.

Does this episode amount to an unacceptable intrusion by the judiciary into matters of party politics, or is it a case of a wholly proper judicial intervention in a public controversy affecting the administration of justice? Was it an example of unelected oligarchic groups flouting the democratic mandate of the people, or was the action justified by the need to maintain a balance between the functions of Parliament and the judiciary within the constitution? Were judges improperly being drawn into politics, or were politicians improperly interfering with matters of law and justice?

The judges contended that they had a constitutional responsibility to ensure the maintenance of the equilibrium established by the principle of the separation of powers. They also maintained that the Executive's policy on minimum sentences impaired the judicial function; that the

[51] HL Debs vol. 577 cols 983–90 (27 January 1997).

weighing of the scales is needed not only to determine guilt or innocence but also the nature of a just sentence.[52] Behind such arguments lies the belief that one of the important political functions of the judiciary is, in Tocqueville's words, "to neutralize the vices inherent in popular government". The judiciary "secretly oppose their aristocratic propensities to the nation's democratic instincts, their superstitious attachment to what is old to its love of novelty, their narrow views to its immense designs, and their habitual procrastination to its ardent impatience".[53] The unspoken premiss here is that a judiciary insulated from populist pressures may keep a check on the dysfunctions of the political process. But not everyone would agree with this. For John Griffith, this imagery of balance is simply "a pleasing conceit". Judicial activism may be "part of the political context in which government works" but "fine-tuning or delicate balancing it is not".[54] The fact of the matter, says Griffith, is that "political power, the power of government, is exercised by a . . . small number of people, consisting of ministers, senior civil servants, a few heads of industry, banking and commerce and some influential advisers . . . Until recently, the most senior judges . . . have been part of this oligarchy . . . [T]hey have today lost that high status . . . and part of the reason for their present robustness is to be found in their attempt to regain what status they have lost."[55] Judges cannot act as a brake on oligarchical government, Griffith asserts, precisely because they form part of that oligarchy; the battle over sentencing discretion must be seen as a turf war for status within the oligarchical structure of government.

A TANGLED RELATIONSHIP

These short studies are offered to provoke thinking on the relationship between law and politics. They span from the high politics of international diplomacy to the more rudimentary issue of the sentencing of

---

[52] Cf. the position in the United States in which the Supreme Court has held that a mandatory death sentence was unconstitutional because of "its failure to allow the particularized consideration of relevant aspects of the character and record of each convicted defendant before the imposition upon him of the sentence of death": *Woodson v. North Carolina* 428 US 80 (1976).

[53] Alexis de Tocqueville, *Democracy in America* [1835] Henry Reeve trans., Daniel J. Boorstin intro. (New York: Vintage Books, 1990) vol. 1, 278.

[54] Griffith, above n. 4, 331, 332.

[55] Ibid. 335.

offenders and they extend beyond the institutional settings of courts to embrace legislative proceedings, scrutiny mechanisms and international negotiations. Most importantly, surrounding the basic conflict of interest at the heart of each of these disputes, there invariably exists a set of politico-legal concepts, including notions of sovereignty, accountability, the separation of powers, and the rule of law. I have tried to use the studies to bring out a range of interpretations which might be advanced to explain what is happening. A number of points about these studies might be highlighted.

Perhaps the most basic point is that the exercise of trying to make sense of what is going on by viewing the issues from contrasting legal and political perspectives is often illuminating. The logic of legal discourse yields a particular interpretation of events, but that interpretation is invariably susceptible to challenge from what may be called a political perspective. Was action initiated against Iraq because Iraq infringed a basic principle of international law or in order to protect the oil interests of the western powers? Did the judiciary enter the political debate over sentencing policy to promote justice or to protect their own status within government? Presenting these issues in an either/or form obviously is rather crude. But at least it highlights the basic point that there are often a number of competing interpretations of what is taking place, and it suggests that we should be attentive to the limitations of, or assumptions made by, any particular approach.

This point can be extended into the more interesting and more contentious claim that, whenever we are trying to make sense of public affairs, the relationship between law and politics must always be brought into an appropriate perspective. This may, however, not be to say much. It does mean that an approach which maintains that law merely replicates power interests and that politics is to be understood purely in terms of the pursuit of material interests must be rejected. It also implies that those who take legalist claims at face value and believe that we have already entered Schiller's world of the "ethical State" governed by "the sacred empire of law"[56] are simply living out their own fantasies. But few people, I suspect, maintain either of these rather extreme convictions. This leaves us with a broad range of possible interpretations to consider. Between the naïve belief that political events can be understood entirely in terms of legal discourse and the

[56] Friedrich Schiller, *Über die ästhetische Erziehung des Menschen* [1795]; cited in F.R. Ankersmit, *Aesthetic Politics: Political Philosophy Beyond Fact and Value* (Stanford, Calif.: Stanford U.P., 1996), 22.

blind conviction that the normative world of law can be dismissed as empty rhetoric, there remains a multiplicity of perspectives which might be advanced.

It is at this juncture that the claim about narratives comes into play. The basic concepts of politico-legal discourse are all rather protean in character. They take on a more precise form and they acquire a particular meaning only within certain traditions of thought. These traditions of thought are the product of the stories which we relate about our system of government—of how political power is constituted and how the relationship between citizen and State is understood. These stories, Cover notes, "establish a repertoire of moves—a lexicon of normative action—that may be combined into meaningful patterns culled from the meaningful patterns of the past".[57] How we perceive the concepts of "sovereignty" and "the new legal order" shapes the way in which we articulate Britain's position, both politically and legally, within the European Union, just as the way in which we conceptualize "the rule of law" and "the new world order" influences our stance in relation to the Gulf War. Similarly, the recognition which we give to the respective jurisdictions of the executive, parliament and the judiciary will inform our understanding of ideas such as "the separation of powers" and "accountability" and resolve to our own satisfaction the controversies occasioned by the Scott Inquiry and the Sentencing Bill. And by invoking such narratives to resolve these controversies, we will be required to embrace a more culturally-specific conception of law, both as a structure of normative ideas (e.g., sovereignty, the rule of law) and as a set of decision procedures (e.g., with respect to the range of influence of juridical ideas within governance).

It is, in short, through these narratives that we build our political and legal worlds. Our ideas about politics and law are "stories about events cast in imagery about principles."[58] Following Geertz, we may say that politics and law are "crafts of place" which operate by "the light of local knowledge."[59]

---

[57] Robert M. Cover, "*Nomos* and Narrative" (1983) 97 *Harvard Law Review* 4, 9.

[58] Clifford Geertz, *Local Knowledge: Further Essays in Interpretive Anthropology* (New York: Basic Books, 1983), 167, 215.

[59] Ibid.

II
Justice

BLACKWELL RETAIL LTD
53-59 SOUTH BRIDGE
EDINBURGH
M4241436   TID16798305
SWITCH
5641 8201 5239 4107
EXP 07/04
SWIPED   ISSUE 07

SALE

AMOUNT   £12.00
PLEASE DEBIT MY ACCOUNT

_____
THANK YOU
PLEASE KEEP THIS RECEIPT
FOR YOUR RECORDS

15:17 11/10/02
AUTH CODE: 6205
RECEIPT 7009

Please retain this receipt for your records

Barclaycard – the only card worth getting this season

Payment by card –the perfect result

Blackwells Bookshop
53-59 South Bridge
Edinburgh
EH1 1YS

1901362523   1 @   12.00
Sword and Scales   £12.00

TOTAL PURCHASES: £12.00
PAYMENT: SWITCH   £12.00
RECE   6909:111002:1459:06   TECH0

PLEASE KEEP YOUR RECEIPT
VAT NO. GB532585539
www.blackwells.co.uk

4

The Iconography of Justice

THE MOST EVOCATIVE contemporary icon of justice is that of the Roman goddess, Justitia. Though her image has been sketched by many of the great artists in the history of Western painting, she is probably best known to us today in the form of the statue perched on top of the Central Criminal Courts at the Old Bailey in London. This is the image which adorns the covers of countless legal texts, and which unvaryingly provides the decorative backcloth to television news bulletins reporting on current legal controversies. In this representation, Justitia is portrayed as a classical female figure, dressed in Græco-Roman robes. With arms outstretched, she holds an erect sword in her right hand and, in her left, a set of scales.

In fact, this powerful figure has an even longer ancestry than that of the Roman goddess. Its earliest manifestation was in 2,500 BC as the icon of the Egyptian goddess, Ma'at. Daughter of the sun god Ra, Ma'at symbolized justice, peace, order and law and it is from her that we get the imagery of the scales of justice. According to Egyptian mythology, after death forty-two judges known as the Priests of Ma'at interrogate the deceased and then weigh the heart, which symbolizes all the deceased's actions, in the scales. In the other dish rests truth, represented by a feather. The slightest turning of the scales determines the question of salvation or damnation. Those who are acquitted are welcomed into the afterlife by Osiris, King of the Blessed, while the condemned are devoured by Ammit, a horrifying monster with the head of a crocodile, the neck of a lion and the body of a hippopotamus.[1]

In Greek legend, Ma'at reappears as Themis, goddess of justice, who maintains order on Olympus and it is Themis who provides the model for Justitia. In medieval art, Justitia takes her place, alongside Prudence, Fortitude and Temperance, as one of the four cardinal virtues. Only during the Middle Ages does the sword regularly appear alongside the scales in the representation of Justice, and it is also in this

---

[1] David Daube, "The Scales of Justice" (1951) 63 *Juridical Review* 109, 113.

era that Justitia is often shown wearing a blindfold. But the imagery of the scales has assumed an almost universal significance. It is certainly to be found in the Old Testament: "Let me be weighed in an even balance", says the Book of Job, "that God may know mine integrity".[2] The imagery also occurs in Islam; in the Qur'an the balances are used to symbolize Divine Judgment after death.[3]

Although Justitia is one of many icons which emerged within the western tradition as allegorical representations of virtues and vices, most of them have fallen out of fashion. Indeed, Justitia is probably the only one today who is instantly recognizable. What has this particular representation come to signify?

THE SCALES OF JUSTICE

The symbol of the scales of justice seems first to embody the idea that justice is primarily concerned with the maintenance of equilibrium, an idea which was central to Greek political thought. The Greeks believed that the world exhibits a deep, underlying unity which is revealed through *logos, nomos* and *taxis* (reason, legality and order). This unity thus reflects the principles of regularity, proportionality and harmony in the world. According to this depiction, the aim of justice is to maintain the equilibrium which these principles reflect.

The scales affirm that the workings of justice are both objective and impartial. The process of judgment must be independent of the whim of any individual; judgment is concerned with the objective weighing of issues in the balance. Justice demands the evaluation of human behaviour against an objective standard, and it is this objective standard which is reflected through the principles of the law. The scales, used to measure quantities of material things, thus become a metaphor for justice. This metaphor implies that the process is an exact science. Each receives that which is due, neither more nor less, as in *The Merchant of Venice*, when Portia, acting as a learned judge in the Duke's court, entreats Shylock to take his lawful penalty from Antonio in these terms:

---

[2] Job, 31:6. See also Daniel, 5:27: "Thou art weighed in the balances, and art found wanting."

[3] Qur'an, 101.

> Shed thou no blood; nor cut thou less, nor more,
> But just a pound of flesh: if thou tak'st more,
> Or less, than a just pound . . .
>   if the scale do turn
> But in the estimation of a hair,
> Thou diest and all thy goods are confiscate.[4]

Justice here is presented as a precise, detached and absolute process.

The symbolism of the scales also expresses "a deep-rooted tendency to see no shades between black and white, to admit no degrees of right and wrong, to allow no distribution of loss and gain among several litigants, to send a party away either victorious or defeated."[5] When they come to the courts in their quest for justice, litigants certainly expect an answer. This confidence reflects the conviction that a right answer is always to be found to every dispute which arises in law. However novel, complex or ambiguous the issue of contention, the one clear duty of the judge is to provide an answer which will vindicate the apparent rights of one or other of the parties to the litigation. Consider the following mundane dispute. A, a rogue, buys a car from B with a cheque which bounces, immediately sells the car to C for cash, and then disappears with the proceeds. In the subsequent legal action between B and C over title to the car, who succeeds? Is it B, the original owner deprived of the property by fraud, or C, the innocent purchaser? Although various legal systems come up with different answers to this question, what all have in common is the view that in law either B or C is entitled to judgment in their favour. No legal system expects B and C jointly to share the loss. Above all, then, the symbol of the scales is a symbol of order and certainty: the first principle of legal justice is that an answer will be given to all disputes which arise between citizens.

THE ROBES OF JUSTICE

Justitia is generally portrayed as a female figure robed in white. The white robes signify purity; judges, the symbol suggests, must be without any trace of those moral flaws which might impair the exercise of judgment or obstruct the true path of justice. The judicial function can be entrusted only to those of high moral character and possessed of a disposition to act solely in accordance with the requirements of the

---

[4] William Shakespeare, *The Merchant of Venice*, Act IV, sc. 1.
[5] Daube, above n. 1, 109.

law. It has also been inferred that "since judges were rarely if ever women, the use of the female figure suggests a justice removed from actuality".[6] When we petition a judge, we are not appealing to a fellow human being for assistance in remedying our grievance but to a pure medium through which the channel of justice flows.

This sense of the judge being set apart from actuality is reinforced by the mode of dress. The splendour, not to say exuberance, of the judicial regalia emulates the apparel of clerics and kings. The parallel with the priesthood places the judge in the position of mediator between heaven and earth. It is not the judge who rules, but Justice which is ruling through the instrumentality of the judge. The wigs and gowns of the contemporary judiciary are intended to impress upon us the fact that the judges do not exercise personal power but are the medium through which law rules. Nevertheless, judicial robes, together with the pomp and ceremony which attend court functions, also impress upon us the majesty of the law. The spectacle, the display of elaborate ritual ranging from judicial processions of scarlet robes, ermine and full-bottomed wigs to the donning of the black cap to pronounce the sentence of death, can also be viewed as a deliberate process which serves to evoke awe and instil deference amongst the multitude.[7] In the words of a contemporary Scottish High Court judge: "The visible symbols of his office, the way he dresses, the place in which he sits, the manner in which he is addressed, the respect which he is accorded, all are designed to buttress that authority, to intimidate those who might wish to challenge or evade it".[8] The intricate ceremonies surrounding the exercise of the judicial role, oscillating between fear and reverence, signify both the performance of a priestly function and a manifest exercise of the power of the State.

JUSTITIA BLINDFOLDED

The figure of Justitia is often blindfolded, and this image is ambiguous. One interpretation is that it represents freedom from corruption of the senses. This interpretation is rooted in the belief that insight and wis-

---

[6] Dennis E. Curtis and Judith Resnik, "Images of Justice" (1987) 96 *Yale Law Journal* 1727, 1765.

[7] See Douglas Hay, "Property, Authority and the Criminal Law" in Hay *et al.*, *Albion's Fatal Tree: Crime and Society in Eighteenth Century England* (Harmondsworth: Penguin, 1975), 17, esp. 26–31.

[8] Lord McCluskey, *Law, Justice and Democracy* (London: Sweet & Maxwell, 1987), 1.

dom come from within. Any action in the sensual world must be called before the tribunal of pure reason, and here any potentially misleading evidence of the senses will be discounted. In this rendition, the judicial resolution of grievances presents itself as a special procedure which operates at some remove from the world of human experience.

But the idea of justice blindfolded is also open to a less exalted interpretation, one which suggests that the judge may all too easily be led astray. The sightless judge supposedly receives her information only through the filter of the law. Surely, it might be asked, this ideal is flawed? Should we not distrust the magistrate who is not permitted to take into account the rich variety of human experience? How much respect can a judge command whose sentence condemns without having a full understanding of the events surrounding legal action? Thus, the image of the judge who dispenses justice only in strict accordance with the precepts of the law can be counterposed by that of the judge who appears to be thoroughly insensitive to human needs. These competing interpretations assume particular significance when courts struggle to draw lines between relevant information about the dispute obtained during the course of the law suit and impermissible extra-judicial knowledge which the judge is supposed to discount. In such circumstances, judges walk a tightrope between maintaining a focus on the critical issues in the case and displaying an apparent ignorance of current affairs. The mass media regularly expresses its incredulity when in the course of a trial the judge asks a question such as: "who is Gazza?". Before rushing to condemn the judiciary's deep-seated ignorance of contemporary life, it is important to recognize that such questions often proceed from an entirely proper acknowledgement of the special procedures of adjudication; only information which has been subject to the forensic procedures of the court can be treated as being legal knowledge. But even if the judge is genuinely ignorant of such matters of *Zeitgeist*, this degree of seclusion is invariably a function of the formal, elevated position we expect the judiciary to occupy.

The most potent meaning of the symbol of the blindfold, however, is that Justitia represents impartiality. Justitia is blindfolded, not blind. The blindfold represents the self-restraint which ensures that the judge is faithful to the oath of office which requires all judges to "do right to all manner of people after the laws and usages of this realm, without fear or favour, affection or ill-will".[9] The blindfold is a symbol of

---

[9] Promissory Oaths Act, 1868, s. 4.

equality before the law. All who come before the judge come as equals to have their cause tried in accordance with the rules of law. Justitia blindfolded cannot be impressed or intimidated by the power or status of the litigants or witnesses who come to her court; justice, according to the formulation in Magna Carta, must not be sold, denied or delayed.[10] These injunctions are especially important with respect to the judge's relationship with the sovereign. The judiciary are after all Her Majesty's judges and at some level are likely to feel beholden to their employer. The blindfold signifies that the judiciary must maintain critical distance as well as independence from the government. In Britain, this tenet is expressed in the convention that, although Her Majesty is the source of all justice, since the reign of Henry III the monarch has not been able to disturb the fountain or divert the stream from its proper channel, except through the agency of her judges. It was not until after the Stuarts, however, that the tenure of a judge's office was altered from *durante beneplacito* (during the king's good pleasure) to *quamdiu se bene gesserint* (during good behaviour); a judge cannot now be dismissed except because of a conviction for some offence or on an address of both Houses of Parliament.[11]

In these ways, the symbol of the blindfold emphasizes the point that one of Justitia's most important jobs is, in the Quaker maxim, to speak truth to power. This placing of distance between judiciary and Executive not only affords protection for the judge but can also operate to the benefit of the State. That is, it is in the State's interest to maintain that the edicts of the judiciary are authoritative precisely because they are the voice of law, not an expression of politics.

THE SWORD OF JUSTICE

In her right hand, Justitia holds a mighty sword. Justice may indeed be independent of the whim of the government, but the machinery of the State is ready to enforce the orders of the judge. In *De Cive*, Hobbes notes that the sovereign carries two swords, the sword of war and that of justice, and comments that: "Both swords, therefore, as well this of

---

[10] Magna Carta, c. 40: "To no one will we sell, to no one will we deny or delay right or justice."

[11] Act of Settlement 1700, s. 3: ". . . Judges commissions be made *quamdiu se bene gesserint*, and their salaries ascertained and established; but upon an address of both Houses of Parliament it may be lawful to remove them."

war as that of justice, . . . essentially do belong to the chief com-mand."[12] The judges may occupy a unique role, but that function must be recognized as a vital component of the apparatus of the State. Kant draws out the ambivalence of this imagery even more graphically. "The jurist who has taken as his symbol the scales of right and the sword of justice," he comments, "usually uses the latter not merely to keep any extraneous influences away from the former, but will throw the *sword* into one of the *scales* if it refuses to sink".[13] The sword not only symbolizes the role of the State in protecting the judicial process from corruption, but it also suggests that, if only because the function of the judge is to apply the existing laws, the judge will ensure that the inter-ests of the State are properly respected.

Further, although in a general sense, the sword symbolizes the role of justice in protecting the innocent, the sword also more precisely represents the rigour of justice. Justice will not hesitate to punish the guilty, neither does it compromise. When Solomon was faced with the competing claims of two women to be the mother of a child, he pro-posed wielding his sword to cut the child in half, in order that each could claim a share.[14] Though often presented as the judgment of com-promise, the real message of Solomon's provisional judgment is that justice is not only correct but also harsh and unyielding. The image of the sword also reminds us of the potential limitations of formal justice.

THE SYMBOL OF JUSTICE

We live in an age in which the mass media bombards us with a profu-sion of images, most of which are designed to stimulate our desire to consume. In this environment, traditional iconography has generally lost its resonance; few people today, for example, would recognize the allegorical images of the cardinal virtues and vices which adorned the art of the Renaissance. But although much iconography has fallen by the wayside, Justitia remains immediately recognizable as a powerful symbol of law and justice. What accounts for its longevity? Why is that within contemporary society both the State and its citizens remain in

[12] Thomas Hobbes, *On The Citizen* [1642] Richard Tuck & Michael Silverthorne eds (Cambridge: Cambridge U.P., 1998), 79.

[13] Immanuel Kant, "Perpetual Peace: A Philosophical Sketch" [1795] in his *Political Writings* Hans Reiss ed. (Cambridge: Cambridge U.P., 1991), 93, 115 (emphasis in orig-inal).

[14] 1 Kings 3:16–28.

need of this image of justice as a regally-robed, coolly impersonal, blindfolded goddess wielding sword and scales?

One thing seems certain: Justitia has not survived because of richness and complexity of its symbolism. Justitia certainly exhibits ambiguities and tensions which capture much of the power, uncertainties and limitations of the judicial process. While the scales may be taken as a representation of law as right, the sword reminds us of the significance of law as command, and when these are brought together in the icon they are held in a relationship of tension. Nor does Justitia survive as an emblem of human achievement, or tribute to the dignity of the office. No one has a greater claim to our respect, suggested Nietzsche, than one who dispenses justice. If the judge were "a cold demon of knowledge he would spread about him the icy atmosphere of a dreadful suprahuman majesty which we would have to fear." But that the judge "is a human being and yet nonetheless tries to ascend from indulgent doubt to stern certainty, from tolerant mildness to the imperative 'you must', from the rare virtue of magnanimity to the rarest of all virtues, justice . . . and above all that he has every moment to atone for his humanity and is tragically consumed by an impossible virtue—all this sets him on a solitary height as the most *venerable* exemplar of the species man."[15] Eloquent though Nietzsche may be about the magnitude of the judicial task, there is little evidence to suggest that such lofty sentiments have maintained the potency of the image.

The answer which must be given is, I suspect, a rather functional one. The fact of the matter is that the State remains in need of a corps of officials able to enforce order and authorize the imposition of violence over its citizens. Although politics, broadly conceived, involves a process of world-building, the State exists ultimately to maintain a particular form of order, and the special task of the judge lies at the sharp end of this process. As a consequence of the decisions of a judge, citizens lose their liberties, their property and their children. This is indeed an awesome power, and to enable that power to operate effectively, we are obliged to hold on to this image of the judicial process as one which transcends the foibles and flaws which afflict ordinary individuals. We need to believe that the judiciary is capable of rendering legal judgment free from bias and political motivation. Governments might wish for a judiciary which is pliant and which remains attentive to their interests.

[15] Friedrich Nietzsche, "On the uses and disadvantages of history for life" [1874] in his *Untimely Meditations* R.J. Hollingdale trans. (Cambridge: Cambridge U.P., 1983), 59, 88 (emphasis in original).

But they also recognize that, in order to be able to project an image of legitimate political order, their judges must be seen to be independent and to be operating at one remove from politics. It is only through this type of role-bound action within an institutional structure accepted as legitimate that the mass of people are likely to overcome their distaste for violence and accept the need to sanction penalties.[16] Citizens often criticize the judiciary for their aloofness and aristocratic disposition, and might even expect judges to be more evidently representative of contemporary society. But most also seem, deep-down, to acknowledge that both the detachment of the judiciary and the dignity of the office remain integral elements of their unique political role.

[16] See Stanley Milgram, *Obedience to Authority: An Experimental View* (New York: Harper & Row, 1974).

5

The Ancient Idea of the Rule of Law

ONE POWERFUL THEME permeating Greek political thought was the belief in a sense of order and proportion which kept the world in harmony. "Heaven and earth and their respective inhabitants", Plato relates, "are held together by the bonds of society and love, and order and discipline and righteousness, and that is why the universe is called an ordered whole or cosmos and not a state of disorder and licence."[1] Through the apprehension of this order we ascertain the sense of beauty in art, truth in nature and justice in politics. Within the political thought of classical Greece, justice was associated with the notions of order, proportionality and equality and, without justice, it was felt that the State could not properly function.

In this chapter, I propose to examine how these classical ideas on the necessary linkage between justice and the State gave birth to the idea of the rule of law. The rule of law has been a major theme in western political thinking ever since. The meaning of this principle has remained ambiguous and contested. What I hope to show is that this ancient conception of the rule of law carries a distinctive meaning, one which, I shall later suggest,[2] differs from the idea of the rule of law which became influential after the eighteenth century. My primary objective, however, is to indicate that this classical conception of the rule of law has exercised a powerful influence on British constitutional thought.

THE GEOMETRICAL PRINCIPLES OF JUSTICE

Since justice was seen to reflect the fundamental principles of universal order, Plato believed that this order could be revealed through the

---

[1] Plato, *Gorgias* [*c*.399 BC] Walter Hamilton trans. (Harmondsworth: Penguin, 1971), 117–18.
[2] See Ch. 12 below, 183–5.

canons of mathematics. Plato thus sought to transpose the axioms of geometry to the conduct of politics. He believed, as a consequence, that justice could be expressed as the principle of "geometric equality" or right proportion.[3] This philosophy of justice was developed further by Aristotle, who rested the foundations of his conception of justice on a distinction between numerical and geometrical equality. Numerical equality means that each individual counts for one, while geometrical, or proportional, equality accords entitlement to each person in accordance with their ability, achievement or desert. From this distinction, Aristotle differentiates between two conceptions of justice: distributive justice and corrective justice.

Distributive justice, Aristotle notes, "is concerned with the distribution of honour or money or such other assets as are divisible among the members of the community".[4] The claims of justice in distribution are directed to the allocation of wealth and goods in the State in accordance with the merit of citizens. He concedes that political views differ on the question of such merits: "the democratic view is that the criterion is free birth; the oligarchic that it is wealth or good family; the aristocratic that it is excellence."[5] Notwithstanding these differences, Aristotle contends that the common theme is that distributive justice is geometrical: justice is "a sort of proportion" and that proportion "is an equality of ratios".[6] What is just is what is proportional and what is unjust is what violates the proportion: "the man who acts unjustly gets too much and the victim of injustice too little of what is good".[7]

Corrective justice, by contrast, is concerned with the righting of wrongs. If a crime has been committed, a contract broken or some other harm inflicted, then the equilibrium has been disturbed and justice demands that it be restored. Corrective justice is similar in this respect to the *lex talionis*, "an eye for an eye", though the objective is not so much that of requiting evil with evil as of ensuring that any advantage gained by the wrongdoer is eradicated. In considering the issue of corrective justice, the virtue of the respective parties is irrelevant: "it makes no difference whether a good man has defrauded a bad one or vice versa".[8] Corrective justice is thus rooted in the principle of

---

[3] Plato, above n. 1.

[4] Aristotle, *The Nicomachean Ethics* [c.334–323 BC] J.A.K. Thomson trans. (Harmondsworth: Penguin, rev. edn. 1976), 176–7.

[5] Ibid. 178.

[6] Ibid.

[7] Ibid. 179.

[8] Ibid. 180.

isonomia, equality before the law. "All that the law considers", Aristotle insists, "is the difference caused by the injury"; the judge tries only "to equalize the inequality of this injustice".[9] Corrective justice follows an arithmetic proportion: "justice is a mean between a sort of gain and loss".[10] Consequently, when disputes occur, people "look for a judge as an intermediary between them (indeed in some places judges are called 'mediators') in the belief that if they secure a mean they will secure what is just."[11]

Although for Aristotle distributive justice remains essentially a matter of politics, corrective justice is purely a question of law which can be resolved by a judge through the process of adjudication of claims. Aspects of the modern debates on corrective and distributive justice are considered in the two chapters which follow. Here it is enough to note that each conception employs the metaphors of "proportion" and "mean" to reinforce the view that justice is treated as a matter of weighing claims in the scales.

THE GOLDEN CORD OF THE LAW

For Plato and Aristotle, the basic function of the State is to administer justice, and justice here means both the rectification of wrongs (an issue of law) and the allocation of wealth and goods in accordance with the merits of the citizens (a question of politics). But does not law also have a more basic role in helping to ensure that the conditions of justice are realized? In *The Republic*, Plato is concerned to provide an account of the ideal form of government. The conclusion he reaches is that the best form of rule is not the rule of law but the rule of the wise. "The [ideal] society we have described can never grow into a reality or see the light of day, and there will be no end to the troubles of states", Plato suggests, "till philosophers become kings in this world, or till those we call kings and rulers really and truly become philosophers, and political power and philosophy come into the same hands."[12] In this ideal regime of the philosopher-kings, law in the sense of a code of rules will merely constitute an obstacle in the way of justice. Towards the end of

---

[9] Aristotle, above n. 4, 180.
[10] Ibid. 181.
[11] Ibid. 181.
[12] Plato, *The Republic*, [*c*.380 BC] H.D.P. Lee trans. (Harmondsworth: Penguin, 1955), para. 473.

his life, however, Plato seemed to accept that, given the world as we know it, people were unfitted to live under these ideal arrangements. He therefore returned to address the practical issues of government under less than perfect conditions and in *The Laws* he promotes the idea of a State ruled by law, a regime in which the rulers are the servants of the law and that "law is the master of the government and the government is its slave."[13]

In this later study, Plato accepts that law is a civilizing force and acknowledges that without laws people "will be indistinguishable from wild animals of the utmost savagery".[14] In a striking passage, he provides us with a powerful image of law. Let us suppose, he suggests, that all living creatures are puppets of the Gods and that the affections within us, our virtues and vices, are like cords and strings which pull us in different directions. There is one cord, he contends, which we ought always to follow. This leading string, "which is golden and holy, transmits the power of 'calculation', a power which in a state is called the public law".[15] Whereas the other cords are hard and steely, this one is flexible and uniform. And with this leading string of the law we must always co-operate since " 'calculation' is a noble thing, it is gentle, not violent". We must therefore ensure "that the gold in us may prevail over the other substances."[16] Plato here seems to be suggesting both that individuals should live according to reason and that the law of the State is the crystallization of reason. Individuals should therefore maintain a law-abiding disposition towards the State and subordinate themselves to its lawful powers.

Aristotle takes this argument on the supremacy of law one stage further. In *The Politics* he suggests that it is a mistake to view the rule of the wise and the rule of the law as being alternatives, since even the wisest ruler cannot dispense with law. Furthermore, law has an impersonal quality which no ruler, however wise, can attain. "It follows therefore", he contends, "that it is preferable that law should rule rather than any single one of the citizens [and] even if it is better that certain persons rule, these persons should be appointed as guardians of the laws, and as their servants".[17] Anyone who asks "for the rule of a

[13] Plato, *The Laws*, [*c*.340 BC] Trevor J. Saunders trans. (Harmondsworth: Penguin, 1970), 715.

[14] Ibid. 874.

[15] Ibid. 645.

[16] Ibid.

[17] Aristotle, *The Politics* [*c*.335–323 BC] T.A. Sinclair trans., Trevor J. Saunders ed. (Harmondsworth: Penguin, 1981), 226.

human being is importing a wild beast . . . , for desire is like a wild beast, and anger perverts rulers and the very best of men".[18] By contrast, "law is intelligence without appetition";[19] law is reason unaffected by desire.

In *The Nichomachean Ethics*, Aristotle extends this argument by suggesting that "justice is only found among those whose mutual relations are controlled by law".[20] This is why "we do not allow a man to rule, but the principle of law; because a man does so for his own advantage, and becomes a despot, whereas the ruler is the upholder of justice, and if of justice, of equality".[21] Aristotle here provides us with the first clear expression of the principle of the rule of law. Government in accordance with the rule of law—and in contrast with government by personal rule—is consistent with the dignity of the individual. Government under the authority of law vests the ruler with a moral quality which otherwise is missing. The rule of law is the rule of reason and this principle provides the foundation of justice in the State. The rule of law promotes rule by consent, enhances the potential effectiveness of government and forms the bedrock of constitutional government.

THE ARISTOTELIAN IDEA OF RULE OF LAW

Aristotle's account of the rule of law as the rule of reason provides us with an authoritative expression of the ancient conception of the rule of law. In this conception, it must be emphasized, the rule of law has nothing to do with democracy, nor with political equality in the modern sense of that term. Aristotle's account of the rule of law is perfectly compatible with that of a slave society, such as that which existed in ancient Athens, or with those states, such as Nazi Germany and apartheid South Africa, in which a section of the population is declared to be sub-human or is systematically excluded from basic entitlements of citizenship. Aristotle himself believed that only a small group of human beings—the adult male heads of households—were qualified to participate in political affairs. In Aristotle's account, the principle of the rule of law is directed to the governing class, and especially to the

---

18 Ibid.
19 Ibid.
20 Aristotle, above n. 4, 188.
21 Ibid.

judges. On this governing class, he believes, rests the responsibility of maintaining the legal order which best fits the ethical foundations of the State.

The rule of law as the rule of reason in effect requires those holding influential positions within political affairs both to maintain a balanced disposition and also to possess the ability to persuade others to exercise self-restraint. The rule of law is essentially a political ideal; it requires those involved in political deliberation—understood to embrace both law-making and judging—to exhibit the virtue of practical wisdom, what the Greeks called *phronēsis*. Aristotle stresses that practical wisdom, unlike mathematics, is not a form of scientific knowledge; practical wisdom or prudence "also involves knowledge of particular facts, which become known from experience."[22] Practical wisdom is a dispositional habit which is quite different from intelligence. It must be shaped by education and training and, being rooted in experience, is unlikely to be a trait possessed by the young. Practical wisdom is fundamentally a virtue of character.

The Aristotelian account suggests that the single most important condition on which the rule of law rests is that of the worthiness of character of those engaged in legislative and judicial decision-making. Although this worthiness is a precondition for all within the governing class, it impinges most on the judges, since it is through their work that justice is activated into legality. In her commentary on the Aristotelian conception, Judith Shklar emphasizes that the judiciary "must understand exactly just how forensic rhetoric and persuasive reasoning work, while their own ratiocination [must remain] free from irrational imperfections".[23] The judiciary must have a thorough familiarity with the games which lawyers play in representing the interests of their clients, and should be able to move beyond rhetoric so as to reason their way to that decision which is dictated by the requirements of justice. Justice is the constant disposition to act fairly and lawfully and for that "a settled ethical character is as necessary as is intelligence itself".[24]

---

[22] Aristotle, above n. 4, 215.
[23] Judith N. Shklar, "Political Theory and the Rule of Law" in Allan C. Hutchinson and Patrick Monahan (eds), *The Rule of Law: Ideal or Ideology?* (Toronto: Carswell, 1987), 1, 3.
[24] Ibid.

THE ANCIENT CONCEPTION AND THE BRITISH CONSTITUTION

The Aristotelian idea of the rule of law influenced the work of the Roman rhetoricians[25] and, through the study of these classic texts, has permeated the culture of British constitutional understandings. The unwritten British constitution is rooted in a set of traditional practices concerning the business of governing and reflects the deep-seated belief that government is a form of practical knowledge. These characteristics of the British constitution were consolidated during an era of aristocratic government in which political experience was passed down within the governing class from generation to generation, a process which found its clearest institutional expression in the typical progression which young gentlemen made from the Clarendon public schools, through the Oxford and Cambridge colleges, and then on to the Houses of Parliament, the Inns of Court or the administrative class of the civil service. It is a system which Walter Bagehot, in his classic study of *The English Constitution*, identified as one of "club government".[26] The direct influence of the Aristotelian idea of the rule of law is, for example, detectable in the concerns which Bagehot himself expressed about the great "leap in the dark" made by the extension of the franchise in 1867. Together with others who expressed grave concerns about the education of this new political class, Bagehot warned that the reform imposed a great duty on "our statesmen". Since the "common ordinary mind is quite unfit to fix for itself what political question it shall attend to", Bagehot argued that these statesmen, "without saying what they are doing", must guide the new voters and ensure that their attention is settled on questions which, rather than "excit[ing] the lower orders of mankind", will bind "the whole interest of the State".[27] This quite clearly reflects an idea of the rule of law which is rooted in character, the need for a balanced disposition and the maintenance of self-restraint.

---

[25] This work was undertaken mainly by Cicero and Quintilian, who cultivated an image of the *vir civilis*, "the man who knows how to plead in the law courts for justice and to deliberate in the councils and public assemblies of the *res publica* in such a way as to promote policies at once advantageous and honourable": Quentin Skinner, *Reason and Rhetoric in the Philosophy of Hobbes* (Cambridge: Cambridge U.P., 1996), 69.

[26] Walter Bagehot, *The English Constitution* [1867] R.H.S. Crossman ed. (London: Collins, 1963), 156.

[27] Ibid. 274–5.

The Aristotelian conception of the rule of law has also left an indelible impression on our tradition of law. It is deeply embedded in the jurisprudence of Sir Edward Coke, Attorney-General to Elizabeth I, James I's Chief Justice, and one of the great figures in the history of the common law. In one of Coke's most celebrated formulations, he not only sought to distinguish law from policy but also achieved a synthesis of Plato's idea of the "golden cord" and Aristotle's doctrine of the mean: all disputes between citizens, Coke asserted, must "be measured by the golden and straight metwand of the law" rather than being left "to the incertain and crooked cord of discretion".[28] But the Aristotelian influence runs much deeper. Having argued that "reason is the life of the law",[29] Coke received a riposte from Hobbes to the effect that, since all humans are capable of reasoning as well as lawyers, they are "as fit for and as capable of judicature as Sir Edward Coke himself".[30] But Coke would say that Hobbes had misunderstood. Although the common law is reason, it is not a form of scientific reason (intelligence) but practical reason (*phronēsis*): the common law is "an artificial perfection of reason, gotten by long study . . . , and not of every man's natural reason."[31]

This scholarly debate was essentially a replay of a discussion which had already taken place in a more highly charged political arena. During a meeting of the Privy Council in 1607, Coke, having opposed attempts by the ecclesiastical courts to determine temporal issues, became sidetracked on the issue of the powers of the king. James I had expressed the view that, since judges are but delegates of the king, the king was empowered to adjudicate on any matters he pleased. Coke disagreed and averred that the king could not take disputes out of the courts and resolve them himself. According to Coke's report, James (whom Hobbes later echoes) had said that "the law was founded upon reason, and that he and others had reason as well as the judges." But Coke countered by saying that "true it was that God had endowed his Majesty with excellent science and great endowments of nature; but his Majesty was not learned in the laws of his realm of England, and causes

---

[28] Coke, 4 Inst. 41.

[29] Coke, 1 Inst. 1.

[30] Thomas Hobbes, *A Dialogue between a Philosopher and a Student of the Common Laws of England* [1681] Joseph Cropsey ed. (Chicago: University of Chicago Press, 1971), 62.

[31] Coke, above n. 28. For a direct response by the common lawyers see: "Reflections by the Lord Chief Justice Hale on Mr Hobbes in his Dialogue of the Law" [c.1670s] in W.S. Holdsworth, *A History of English Law* (London: Methuen, 1924), vol. 5, 499.

which concern the life, or inheritance, or goods, or fortunes of his subjects are not to be decided by natural reason, but by the artificial reason and judgment of law, which law is an act which requires long study and experience before that a man can attain to the cognizance of it; and that the Law was the golden Metwand and Measure to try Causes of the Subjects, which protected his Majesty in safety and peace."[32]

This statement enshrines one of the most illustrious expressions of the idea of the rule of law: law as the special preserve of the judiciary, not to be usurped by the sovereign. While this means that the sovereign is subject to the law, and therefore the law acts as a constraint on the power of the king, the principle of legality, by establishing an objective structure of rule, also can operate to reinforce and legitimate the sovereign's authority. We might note that Coke's formulation of law is a faithful elaboration of Aristotle's idea of law as practical wisdom. But we should also recognize that this was no academic discourse; Coke had been obliged to remind his sovereign of the limitations on his powers and James I was not amused. The idea that the law protected the king rather than that the king acted as guardian of the law was, James asserted, treason to affirm. Consequently, in the account of one counsellor, "his Majesty fell into that high indignation the like was never known in him" and Coke "fell flat on all fours; humbly beseeching his Majesty to take compassion on him if he thought zeal had gone beyond his duty and allegiance".[33] That Coke's defence of the rule of law had almost landed him in the Tower highlights the tension between power and law and also reminds us that the institutionalization of the idea of the rule of law comes through political struggle.

After Coke, the Aristotelian conception of the rule of law took a firm grip over the construct which might be called "the common law mind". Not for the English a career judiciary, with its connotations of a purely technical function in the service of the State. The English judiciary are appointed not only because of their exalted status as experienced practitioners of the law in the Inns of Court but also because they are respected members of society. Such senior advocates are assumed to appreciate the honour of their commission, and willingly to sacrifice material rewards for the privilege of undertaking one of the highest and most virtuous forms of public service. On the character of this small, closely integrated body of mature practitioners rests the

---

[32] Coke, Twelfth Reports, *Prohibitions del Roy* (1607) 12 Co.Rep. 63.
[33] Sir Rafe Boswell to Dr. Milborne; cited in Roland G. Usher, "James I and Sir Edward Coke" (1903) 18 *English Historical Review* 664, 670.

responsibilities of safeguarding and developing the common law tradition, thereby protecting the basic ethical standards of the State. At the heart of their enterprise lies the idea of the rule of reason. The common law, judges inform us, "is, or ought to be, the common sense of the community crystallized and formulated by our forefathers".[34] But jurists come closer to the essence of the matter when they suggest that reasonableness is "an ideal standard, which is . . . none other than that general consent of right minded and rightly informed men which our ancestors in the profession called reason"; and it is only in this sense that "the duty of the court is to keep the rules of law in harmony with the enlightened common sense of the nation".[35] This, it appears, is what Tocqueville had in mind when he expressed the view that democratic institutions can survive only when combined with "lawyer-like sobriety". It is precisely because "lawyers belong to the people by birth and interest, and to the aristocracy by habit and taste" that lawyers "may be looked upon as the connecting link between the two great classes of society".[36] And at the core of this sentiment lies the idea that a judiciary which maintains the tradition of practical wisdom embodied in the ancient idea of the rule of law is a vital element in a properly functioning democracy.

That the ancient conception of the rule of law lives on in the twentieth century is indicated by a brief but revealing note which Lord Evershed sent to the Lord Chancellor in 1945. The supremacy of the rule of law in England, Evershed contended, "is largely bound up with the immense prestige and personal position accorded to the judges" and this status is bolstered by four main factors: first, because the judiciary are chosen from a "cloistered" and "aristocratic" profession; secondly, because the judge is "the complete master of the trial"; thirdly, because the strict rules of procedure "make the proceedings not only solemn (if not Olympian) but secure a real impartiality"; and, fourthly, because "the rules as to dress (wigs and gowns) plus the rules of common law and precedent have made the law something of a mystery".[37] The rites and rituals of the judiciary—the symbols which are reflected

[34] *Barker v. Herbert* [1911] 2 KB 633, 644–5, *per* Farwell L.J.
[35] Sir Frederick Pollock, "Judicial caution and valour" (1929) 45 *Law Quarterly Review* 293, 294.
[36] Alexis de Tocqueville, *Democracy in America* [1835] Henry Reeve trans., Daniel J. Boorstin intro. (New York: Vintage Books, 1990), vol. 1, 276.
[37] Evershed Memorandum to Viscount Simon L.C., 27 July 1945, LCO 2/3827; cited in Robert Stevens, *The Independence of the Judiciary: The View from the Lord Chancellor's Office* (Oxford: Clarendon Press, 1993), 116.

in the icon of Justitia—are, in this sense, a critical aspect of the ancient idea of the rule of law. The public must have confidence in the virtuous character of the judiciary. The judiciary must be seen to be both independent of government and placed at some remove from the people, and for this to happen they are in need of all the props they can muster.

6

Corrective Justice

CORRECTIVE JUSTICE—THE righting of wrongs—lies at the core of the judicial function. Litigants come to courts to seek compensation for the harms which have been caused by the actions of others, whether through failure to honour a contract or because of negligent behaviour or, especially in the case of public authorities, the abuse of their powers. The courts also exist to punish those found guilty of infringing the basic code of social conduct, the criminal law. In carrying out these responsibilities, judges are required to interpret and apply the laws. The view is often taken that, at least for the most part, this is a relatively straightforward exercise which can confidently be entrusted to those with the appropriate legal training. Nevertheless, there are some who argue that the judicial process is highly indeterminate and, consequently, that judges exercise an extensive personal power. It is on this issue of legal determinacy that the debate about the political function of the judiciary has revolved.

Before examining the parameters of that debate, it should first be noted that the role of the judiciary varies according to the type of government which has been instituted. This point has been highlighted by Montesquieu. Following the categorization of classical political thought, Montesquieu distinguishes three main forms of government: *republicanism*, in which the people have sovereign power; *monarchy*, in which one alone governs, though in accordance with fixed and established laws; and *despotism*, in which one person governs by will and without the constraints of fixed laws. He also recognizes that republicanism takes two main forms: *democracy*, when the people as a body possess sovereign power, and *aristocracy*, when that power is held only by a portion of the people.[1] Having outlined the main forms of government, Montesquieu notes that although under a despotic regime the prince can judge, this cannot be permitted in monarchies since "the

---

[1] Montesquieu, *The Spirit of the Laws* [1748] Anne M. Cohler, Basia Carolyn Miller and Harold Samuel Stone trans and ed. (Cambridge: Cambridge U.P., 1989), Bk.2, chs.1, 2. Cf. Aristotle, *The Politics*, T.A. Sinclair trans., Trevor J. Saunders ed. (Harmondsworth: Penguin, 1981), Bk.IV.

constitution would be destroyed and intermediate dependent powers reduced to nothing".[2] Here he reiterates the basic claim which Coke made in his interview with James I.[3] But Montesquieu also contends that the more that government takes the form of a republic, the more the character of judging becomes "fixed". In monarchies, judges "assume the manner of arbiters; they deliberate together, they share their thoughts, they come to an agreement; one modifies his opinion to make it like another's; opinions with the least support are incorporated into the two most widely held."[4] This, however, is not the style of judging in a republic: although in monarchical States the judges often follow the spirit of the laws, in republican government "it is in the nature of the constitution for judges to follow the letter of the law."[5] Since judges pronounce as agencies of the people, it is expected that issues for judicial resolution will be precisely stated and clearly resolved.

Montesquieu's basic point about the changing style of judgment in republican regimes has subsequently been reinforced as a result of the emergence of democracy as the key legitimating principle of modern government. Law-making is now generally acknowledged to be the primary responsibility of legislatures and, as a more formal distinction is drawn between the making and applying of the law, a clearer institutional differentiation is effected between the roles of the legislature and the courts. Law has come to be viewed as an activity through which human conduct is subjected to the governance of rules. After political deliberation by the people's representatives, laws are enacted by legislatures and applied and enforced through courts. Within this modern framework, judges are presented as strict and impartial rule-appliers.

As a result of these developments, the rule of law has acquired a rather different meaning. Once the emphasis in judging changes from deliberation to rule-application, the ancient idea of the rule of law as the rule of reason is superseded by a modern idea of the rule of law as the rule of rules. We will consider the political significance of this modern version later.[6] For present purposes, it might be noted that since the basic objective of legal rules is to guide conduct, the rules should be clear, stable and prospective, because otherwise citizens will experience difficulties in orientating their behaviour in accordance with the

2 Montesquieu, above n. 1, Bk. 6, ch. 5.
3 Ch. 5 above, 72–3.
4 Montesquieu, above n. 1, Bk. 6, ch. 4.
5 Ibid. Bk. 6, ch. 3.
6 See Ch. 12, below, 183–5.

rules. These criteria of rule-making also promote liberty; if in advance we possess a clear understanding of the rules, it should be possible to identify the sphere within which citizens can carry out their activities free from State interference.[7] It is also claimed that legal rules must be general. Generality in rule-making reflects the aspiration that law should establish a common framework to which all must be bound. Generality thus expresses a belief that justice should be blind, or that the rules should not select particular individuals or groups for specific benefits or burdens. Sir William Blackstone gave expression to such values when in his *Commentaries* he intimated that law "is a rule; not a transient sudden order from a superior to or concerning a particular person; but something permanent, uniform and universal."[8] This modern idea of the rule of law thus reflects the beliefs that citizens are equal in the eyes of the law, that the rule structure should be insulated from gross manipulation and that, as an operative system of rules, legal judgment is quite distinct from political decision-making.

In this chapter, the question of legal determinacy will be examined, primarily with the objective of assessing whether judges, when seeking to fulfil the requirements of corrective justice, are able to avoid engaging in a form of political decision-making. Are judges bound by the structure of legal rules or are they able to exercise choice amongst the competing values at issue?

LEGAL FORMALITY

The ideal type of what might be termed the formalist position on adjudication has been characterized by Max Weber as proceeding from certain basic postulates. First, that the law consists of a gapless system of rules, which means that for every dispute which presents itself for resolution, there is a rule in existence which covers that situation. Secondly, it follows that every judicial decision concerns the application of an existing rule to a given set of facts. And, thirdly, that the process of applying the rules to the facts involves an exercise of logic.[9]

---

[7] See Lon L. Fuller, *The Morality of Law* (New Haven: Yale U.P., rev. edn. 1969), ch. 2; Joseph Raz, "The Rule of Law and its Virtue" in his *The Authority of Law: Essays on Law and Morality* (Oxford: Clarendon Press, 1979), ch. 11.

[8] William Blackstone, *Commentaries on the Laws of England* (Oxford: Clarendon Press, 1765), 44.

[9] Max Weber, *Economy and Society: An Outline of Interpretive Sociology* [1920] Guenther Roth & Claus Wittich eds (New York: Bedminster Press, 1968), vol.2, 657–8.

In this construction, law presents itself as a universal phenomenon and adjudication as a rational and scientific, rather than practical, mode of reasoning. Formalism in adjudication is associated with a declaratory theory of the judicial role. Law is found (in the text) and not made; the role of the judge is to declare what the law is, not to make law in the process of adjudicating disputes. The judiciary might provide a more precise elaboration of the law, as the judge explicates a general rule and applies it to the case at hand, but judicial decision-making does not involve an exercise in policy choice.[10]

In its extreme version, the formalist view of adjudication is one which "enables the legal system to operate like a technically rational machine."[11] Weber argues that, in accordance with this conception, the judge acts as "an automaton into which legal documents and fees are stuffed at the top in order that it may spill forth the verdict at the bottom along with the reasons, read mechanically from codified paragraphs."[12] Weber's formulation was subjected to widespread debate in Germany. Formalism was challenged primarily by the Free Law jurists who characterized the formalist account of adjudication as "slot-machine jurisprudence"[13] and, by highlighting the unavoidability of judicial discretion in applying norms to facts, contested the efficacy of treating law as a closed system of rules.[14] For Carl Schmitt, the controversy was not merely a technical problem in jurisprudence: the attempt to link norms to facts also reflected a basic facet of the political condition. Whilst accepting the necessity of treating law as a normative order, Schmitt stressed the centrality of what he calls "the concrete exception", the autonomous moment of judicial decision.[15] Schmitt argues that every legal concept is "infinitely pliable" and consequently that every judicial decision is a political act; all law is "situational law".[16] Judges, in short, are able to make "sovereign" decisions and, by so doing, to promote particular political values.

The German debates appear to have had a significant influence on American jurisprudence. In particular, the American legal realist

[10] See Duncan Kennedy, "Legal Formality" (1973) 2 *Journal of Legal Studies* 351.

[11] Weber, above n. 9, vol.2, 811.

[12] Ibid. 979.

[13] See Gnaeus Flavius [Hermann Kantorowicz], *Der Kampf um die Rechtswissenschaft* (Heidelberg: Carl Winter, 1906).

[14] See Albert S. Foulkes, "On the German Free Law School (Freirechtschule)" (1969) 55 *Archiv für Rechts- und Sozialphilosophie* 366.

[15] Carl Schmitt, *Political Theology: Four Chapters on the Concept of Sovereignty* [1922] George Schwab trans. (Cambridge, Mass: MIT Press, 1985), 30–5.

[16] Ibid. 17, 13.

movement, which flourished during the 1920s and 1930s and which can be understood as a response to attempts to promote legal formalism in the élite American law schools, has parallels with the German Free Law jurists.[17] Although realism appeared in several guises, criticism of the formalist's view of the judicial decision-making remained a principal refrain. In one of its extreme expressions, Jerome Frank maintained that the belief that legal rules are certain and their application to particular cases is unproblematic is the "basic legal myth". It is widely subscribed to, Frank argued, primarily because law serves as a father substitute—it satisfies the craving which people possess for authority and certainty in an indeterminate world.[18] The search for determinacy in law has been a central theme of twentieth-century American jurisprudence ever since.

THE ENGLISH JURISTIC TRADITION

Although these debates on the question of legal determinacy have figured prominently in both American and continental European jurisprudence, they do not seem—at least until recently—greatly to have excited the interest of English jurists. Part of the explanation undoubtedly relates to the exceptionally powerful role which courts play in the American system. But the main reason, I believe, is that the English, for both cultural and institutional reasons, have managed to avoid many of the rationalizing tendencies of other legal systems. Whilst Americans experienced the phenomenon of overload of decisions as a result of their multiplicity of jurisdictions and therefore faced institutional pressures to rationalize and codify, the English judiciary were able to retain the informality of a club. Such informality was partly the result of the small size of the English higher judiciary, but it also reflected the anti-rationalist traditions of the common law, of working analogically from precedents rather than deductively from norms. For these reasons, we have managed, until very recently, to maintain the deliberative judicial style which Montesquieu associates with monarchical states, and thus have been able to avoid the formalism of republican judges. In deference to the democratic temperament,

[17] See James E. Herget and Stephen Wallace, "The German Free Law Movement as the Source of American Legal Realism" (1987) 73 *Virginia Law Review* 399.
[18] Jerome Frank, *Law and the Modern Mind* [1930] (Gloucester, Mass: Peter Smith, 1970).

lip-service was paid to the formalist account of the judicial process. But in the mouths of the English judiciary this was essentially a rhetorical stance. Although patently not providing an adequate explanation of what it is that the judiciary is actually doing, it became the axiom by which the judiciary sought publicly to explain and justify their role.

This stance was fairly openly acknowledged by the leading Victorian jurists. Sir Henry Maine, for example, noted that we "are well accustomed to the extension, modification, and improvement of law by a machinery which, in theory, is incapable of altering one jot or one line of existing jurisprudence". The process by which judges develop the law, he conceded, was "not so much insensible as unacknowledged". "When a group of facts comes before an English Court for adjudication", Maine elaborated, "it is taken absolutely for granted that there is somewhere a rule of known law which will cover the facts of the dispute now litigated . . . Yet the moment the judgment has been rendered and reported, we slide unconsciously . . . into a new language or train of thought. We now admit that the new decision *has* modified the law."[19] In this account, the rule of law as the rule of artificial—and aristocratic—reason has not so much been abandoned as suppressed.

It could not have been otherwise. "We do not admit that our tribunals legislate", Maine concluded, "and yet we maintain that the rules of the English common law, with some assistance . . . from Parliament, are coextensive with the complicated interests of modern society."[20] Since the latter half of the nineteenth century, however, we have seen the extension of parliamentary democracy in Britain and the assumption by Parliament, acting under the impetus of the Government, of the primary role in law-making. These changes have reinforced the belief that law represents the will of the people as expressed in the sovereign Parliament; the conception of law as command gains ascendancy over the traditional common law view of law as custom.[21] One concern has been that within the British constitutional framework it is difficult to identify any significant restraints on the democratic will. Dicey, for example, believed that the British system was one of "democracy tem-

---

[19] Sir Henry Sumner Maine, *Ancient Law: Its Connection with the Early History of Society and its Relation to Modern Ideas* [1861] (London: John Murray, 10th edn. 1919), 28 (emphasis in original). See also A.V. Dicey, *Introduction to the Study of the Law of the Constitution* [1885] (London: Macmillan, 8th edn. 1915), 18: "the appeal to precedent is in the law courts merely a useful fiction by which judicial decision conceals its transformation into judicial legislation."

[20] Ibid. 30.

[21] See Ch. 1 above, 9–12.

pered by snobbishness."[22] But Tocqueville's comments on the role of lawyers in democracies also seem apposite. In his study of America, Tocqueville had identified lawyers, who "secretly oppose their aristocratic propensities to the nation's democratic instincts", as the most powerful counterpoise to democracy.[23] Although twentieth-century British judges seem generally to have embraced the views of both of these nineteenth century commentators, such beliefs could scarcely be expressly articulated.[24] Rather, when called on to explain their role in modern society, the judges would invariably express their function in essentially mechanical terms. In Lord Birkenhead's memorable phrase, the judiciary presented themselves as "the precision instruments for carrying out the will of Parliament".

For the purpose of giving effect to this instrumental conception of their role, the judiciary embraced the principle of the literal interpretation of statutes. Judges were obliged to give statutes their ordinary meaning; that is, the ordinary dictionary meaning unaffected by considerations of the particular context in which the dispute occurred. Only by so doing, it was felt, could judges maintain the necessary impartiality. "The function of the judiciary", Lord Greene M.R. suggested, "is to interpret and enforce the law", and this meant that it "is not concerned with policy" and that it "is not for the judiciary to decide what is in the public interest."[25] By mid-century, this sentiment was being regularly expressed.[26] "In modern Britain, where no agreement exists on the ends of Society and the means of achieving those ends", Lord Parker C.J. intoned, "it would be disastrous if courts did not eschew the temptation to pass judgment on an issue of policy". Disastrous, that is, because the judiciary would be condemned for

---

[22] A.V. Dicey, *Lectures on the Relationship between Law and Opinion in England during the Nineteenth Century* (London: Macmillan, 1905), 57.

[23] Alexis de Tocqueville, *Democracy in America* [1835] Henry Reeve trans., Daniel J. Boorstin intro. (New York: Vintage Books, 1990), vol.1, 278.

[24] See, e.g., Lord Radcliffe, *The Law and its Compass* (London: Faber & Faber, 1961), 39: "It is to me a matter of surprise that so much pen and ink has been employed by commentators in demonstrating this fairly obvious conclusion [concerning the judge's law-making capacity]. If judges prefer to adopt the formula—for that is what it is—that they merely declare the law and do not make it, they do no more than show themselves wise men in practice."

[25] Lord Greene, "Law and Progress" (1944) 94 *Law Journal* 349.

[26] See, e.g., Robert Stevens, *Law and Politics: The House of Lords as a Judicial Body, 1800–1976* (London: Weidenfeld & Nicolson, 1979), Pt.III ("The Era of Substantive Formalism, 1940–1955").

meddling in politics. Consequently, in the words of the Chief Justice: "Judicial self-preservation may . . . alone dictate restraint."[27]

Whether or not this provided an adequate explanation of what the judges were doing, it became the standard logic of justification of their role. Consequently, to the extent that the judges themselves embraced this rhetoric, it affected judicial self-perception and thereby restrained their action. None the less, adoption of this instrumental explanation carried in its train certain difficulties. First, law is not merely an attempt to subject human conduct to the governance of rules; it is an attempt to guide *the future* through the use of rules. The difficulty here is that legislators have a limited ability to anticipate what the future holds. Consequently, many disputes come to the courts in circumstances where no rule clearly applies, and for the obvious reason that the legislature had never directed its attention to the question of whether the particular facts at issue are governed by the rules. Secondly, law is not simply an attempt to subject human conduct to the governance of rules; it is an attempt *through the use of language* to devise rules. The problem which this presents is that language has an open-textured quality; language, we might say, has a limited grip over reality. There is an inherent vagueness in the ordinary use of language and, because of this, rules—even if we accept that they have a core of settled meaning—are often surrounded by a penumbra of uncertainty.

These limitations were acknowledged by H.L.A. Hart in the early 1960s. In *The Concept of Law*, Hart restated the formalist position on adjudication in a modified form. Accepting implicitly that, open-texturedness notwithstanding, rules generally constrain and that, in the main, the role of the judge is to apply the existing rules, Hart also accepted that, because of a certain legislative indeterminacy of aim and because of a degree of vagueness inherent in the ordinary use of language, judges have an interstitial role in law-making. In these penumbral areas, Hart indicated, the judiciary are effectively legislating. When they do so, however, judges seek to promote justice by legislating in accordance with the general policies of the law.[28] This is presumably intended as a less florid version of what Pollock had in mind

---

[27] Lord Parker, *Recent Developments in the Supervisory Powers of Courts over Inferior Tribunals* (Jerusalem: Magnes Press, 1959), 27–8.

[28] H.L.A. Hart, *The Concept of Law* (Oxford: Clarendon Press, 1961), ch. 7. Cf. *Southern Pacific v. Jensen* 244 US 205, 221 (1917), per Holmes J. (dissenting): "I recognize without hesitation that judges do and must legislate, but they do so only interstitially; they are confined from 'molar to molecular motions'."

when suggesting that the court's duty was "to keep the rules of law in harmony with the enlightened common sense of the nation".[29]

Hart's book has been generally accepted as a major contribution to jurisprudence. But is it a work of normative theory or, as Hart himself conceived it, an exercise in "descriptive sociology"?[30] That is, for our purposes, the question remains: do rules actually constrain judges or is rule-handling merely part of an elaborate game which judges play? This question can best be taken further by considering a specific controversy.

THE CASE OF THE SPELUNCEAN EXPLORERS

Consider Lon Fuller's parable of the Speluncean explorers.[31] Five members of the Speluncean Society, whilst on a pot-holing expedition, become trapped. Once it becomes clear that they are unlikely to survive until the completion of the rescue work, they cast dice to determine who amongst them will be killed in order to provide sustenance for the others. The deed is done, and the remaining four survive and are rescued. They are then indicted to stand trial on the crime of murder. Having been convicted by the jury at the trial, they appeal on the question of whether the facts as established are capable of sustaining a verdict of murder. Fuller's hypothetical Court of Appeal sits in a banc of five judges, and they determine the issue as follows.

Trucpenny C.J. focuses on the provisions of the statute, which states: "Whoever shall wilfully take the life of another shall be punished by death." He notes that the rule permits no exceptions. Since the rule is clear, and given the court's duty faithfully to apply the rule, the Chief Justice upholds the conviction. In conclusion, he states that this seems to be a suitable case in which the principle of executive clemency might be invoked to mitigate the rigours of the law.

Foster J. disagrees with the Chief Justice for two main reasons. First, he contends that laws are predicated on the existence of society and that, in the rather exceptional circumstances of this case in which the defendants had been completely cut off from society, they were placed beyond the law's jurisdiction. In this primeval "state of nature", the

---

[29] See, above, ch. 5, 74.
[30] Hart, above n. 28, vii.
[31] Lon L. Fuller, "The Case of the Speluncean Explorers" (1949) 62 *Harvard Law Review* 616.

explorers had devised their own rules for survival to which all had agreed and "it has from antiquity been recognized that the most basic principle of law or government is to be found in the notion of contract or agreement". By acting on this agreement, the lives of four of the five had been saved. Secondly, Foster argues that, although the letter of the statute may have been infringed, its spirit has not. Every rule of law must be interpreted reasonably, in the light of its evident purpose. It was never the purpose of this rule, he suggests, to embrace those who killed another in self-defence, and he extends that reasoning to the case of the explorers. Foster J. concludes that the conviction must be set aside.

Giving the third opinion, Tatting J. finds each of the previous judgments unconvincing. Foster's argument on the state of nature he considers intriguing since, even if the explorers are found to have been placed beyond civil society, the fact is that the judges of the court are authorized, and have themselves sworn, to administer the laws of the State; on what authority could they be transformed into a court of nature? Further, Tatting believes that the analogies Foster invokes in support of his purposive interpretation do not support his conclusion. When people act in self-defence, they act impulsively and not wilfully, whereas in this case the four defendants had acted both wilfully and with great deliberation. Tatting also invokes a precedent in which a defendant was convicted of theft of a loaf of bread, notwithstanding his defence that he was approaching starvation; if hunger cannot justify the theft of natural food, how can it justify the killing and eating of another man? Although Foster's opinion fails to persuade, Tatting nevertheless finds that of the Chief Justice no more compelling. In particular, he is struck by the absurdity of sentencing four men to death when their lives have been saved only by a heroic rescue attempt during the course of which ten rescuers had been killed. Being unable to disentangle the emotional and intellectual aspects of his reactions, Tatting J. withdraws from the case.

Keen J. also disagrees with Foster's use of a purposive interpretation. This, he suggests, is a device which judges generally use when they wish to circumvent the full rigour of the written rule. How can judges divine the intent of the legislators when this law was drafted? Might the legislators not have expressed a great revulsion of cannibalism and have intended that such a practice, whatever the circumstances, should fall within the ambit of this law? Keen acknowledges that this is a hard case, and that hard decisions are never popular. Nevertheless, he believes that applying the rule would serve an important objective in bringing home to the people and their representatives their own responsibilities in ensuring that the law is carefully and comprehensively drafted.

The final opinion, that of Handy J., expresses considerable impatience at the "obscuring curtain of legalisms" which his colleagues have managed to throw around the issue. Government, Handy asserts, is a human affair: "men are ruled, not by words on paper or by abstract theories, but by other men". Good rulers must ensure that they are in tune with the feelings of the people. Handy notes that public opinion polls had indicated that ninety per cent of the people believed that the defendants should be pardoned or let off with a token punishment. That, for him, is determinative of the issue. He accepts that his judicial colleagues will be horrified. They will maintain that public opinion is emotional, capricious and generally based on half-truths. They will therefore advise that the elaborate safeguards of court procedure are essential in ensuring that every rational consideration is properly brought to bear on the issue. Handy states that, as a novice on the bench, he took a similar view, but gradually has come to realize that the further one becomes entwined in the legal intricacies of a case, the more likely it was that one would end up reaching a state similar to that of Tatting in this case. Common sense, Handy believes, is able to resolve this issue without difficulty, and the conviction should be set aside.

The Court being evenly divided, the conviction and sentence of the trial court stood and, unless the Executive were prepared to respond to the requests for clemency, the defendants would be hanged.

LESSONS OF THE PARABLE

Fuller uses the tale of the Speluncean explorers, and to good effect, for the purpose of "bringing into a common focus certain divergent philosophies of law and government".[32] His article provides a classic illustration of the problems which arise when the court is presented with an issue which seems unlikely to have been within the contemplation of the legislature when it enacted the basic rule. The language is relatively clear, but the simplicity of that rule is confounded by an unanticipated event.

---

[32] Fuller, above n. 31, 645.

The approaches taken by Tatting and Handy should first be addressed. Tatting's position, to be blunt, seems completely untenable. The first principle of legal justice is that judgment must be rendered in all cases argued before the court.[33] The parties come to justice seeking an answer to the dispute, and the idea that a judge can say that the issue is too complex, ambiguous or confusing cuts across our most basic assumptions about the judicial process. As we have seen, the imagery of the scales—indeed, the entire set of myths surrounding the image of Justitia—bolsters the belief that, within the body of the law, an answer is to be found and the judge's basic duty is to give expression to this and render judgment accordingly. Handy's judgment does not fare much better. At first glance, it might be viewed as an expression of Cicero's maxim, *salus populi suprema lex esto* (the welfare of the people is the supreme law).[34] Its application in this context, however, seems inappropriate since Handy fails to acknowledge any differentiation in the functions of the court and the legislature. If Tatting fails in his basic duty to render judgment, Handy's failure is one of failing to maintain fidelity to the rules of law.[35] Handy's judgment in effect rejects legal reasoning altogether and entirely reduces law to a matter of politics; while law may be rhetoric, this does not mean that it is empty rhetoric.

It is in the contrast between the formalism of Truepenny and Keen and its challenge by Foster that an expression of the acute tensions in the nature of the judicial role are to be found. There is much to be said in favour of the formalist position. If it is systematically applied by the courts then it will reinforce the idea of the impersonal nature of the law, bolster the principle of equal treatment before the law, and reduce the likelihood of bias or political influence in the application of the law. Consequently, it may promote predictability, enhance accountability and advance simplicity. We might also acknowledge, within the formalist position, a proper respect being accorded to the different roles of the judiciary and the government; if public opinion is indeed so clearly in favour of leniency, then this is not for the court

---

[33] See, e.g., *Tiverton & North Devon Railway Co.* v. *Loosemore* (1883) 9 App. Cas. 480, 492, *per* Lord Blackburn, L.C.: "I believe it to be of more consequence that this point should be settled than how it is settled."

[34] Cicero, *De Legibus* [*c*.51 BC] Bk III, ch. 6.

[35] Cf. Bill of Rights, 1689, art.2: "That the pretended power of dispensing with laws, or the execution of laws, by regal authority, as it hath been assumed and exercised of late, is illegal."

to take into account but must remain a matter of public policy for the executive.[36]

Foster's opinion, by contrast, highlights a basic tension which afflicts the adjudicative process. This is the tension between formal and substantive justice, or between law and equity. This strain was highlighted by Aristotle, who acknowledging that "all law is universal", recognized that "there are some things about which it is not possible to pronounce rightly in general terms". The error, Aristotle felt, "lies not in the law nor in the legislator, but in the nature of the case"; that is, our actions are often too particular or too complicated to be adequately covered by any general rule. Consequently, Aristotle believed that "when the law states a general rule, and a case arises under this that is exceptional, then it is right . . . to correct the omission by a ruling such as the legislator himself would have given if . . . he had been aware of the circumstances".[37] In making an exception to the literal language of the rule, this is precisely what Foster seems to be doing. Further, his line of reasoning not only illustrates Aristotle's point that "there are some cases that no law can be framed to cover", but also provides a good illustration of what Hart would call interstitial law-making owing to the relative indeterminacy of objective of the basic rule.[38]

The dangers of Foster's purposive approach, however, were articulated by Keen. How are the intentions of the legislature to be identified?

[36] This principle can actually be seen at work in the real case which inspired Fuller's account. See: *R* v. *Dudley & Stephens* (1884) 14 QBD 273, 288 (*per* Lord Coleridge C.J.): "It is not suggested that in this particular case the deeds were 'devilish', but it is quite plain that such a principle once admitted might be made the legal cloak for unbridled passion and atrocious crime. There is no safe path for judges to tread but to ascertain the law to the best of their ability and to declare it according to their judgment; and if in any case the law appears to be too severe on individuals, to leave it to the Sovereign to exercise that prerogative of mercy which the Constitution has intrusted to the hands fittest to dispense it." In this case, the court passed a sentence of death on the defendants, who had killed and eaten their cabin boy while cast away on the high seas. The sentence was subsequently commuted by the Crown to six months' imprisonment. See A.W.B. Simpson, *Cannibalism and the Common Law* (Harmondsworth: Penguin, 1984).

[37] Aristotle, *The Nicomachean Ethics* [*c*.334–323 BC] J.A.K. Thomson trans. (Harmondsworth: Penguin, rev. edn. 1976), 199.

[38] Foster here gives expression to Lord Denning's view, expressed in *Magor & St. Mellons R.D.C.* v. *Newport Corporation* [1950] 2 All ER 1226, 1236 (CA): "It would certainly save the judges trouble if Acts of Parliament were drafted with divine prescience and perfect clarity. In the absence of it, when a defect appears, a judge cannot simply fold his hands and blame the draftsman. He must set to work on the constructive task of finding the intention of Parliament and he must do this not only from the language of the statute, but also from a consideration of the social conditions which gave rise to it, and other mischief which it was passed to remedy, and then he must supplement the written word so as to give 'force and life' to the intention of the legislature."

Is this not just a fiction which judges use when substituting their own sense of the justice of the case? And if, through the adoption of this mode of reasoning, we invite judges to consider the substantive merits, is it not inevitable that their political views will intrude into the adjudicative process?[39] Aristotle's point might have been uncontroversial in an era in which justice was felt to reflect principles of an underlying universal order, but today the idea of justice seems to be inextricably bound up with matters of politics. Foster's approach highlights precisely the way in which judges can play games with the open-textured language of the law and are able either to invoke previous cases as precedents when it suits their argument or, alternatively (and as Tatting's critique of Foster's judgment illustrates), avoid cases or reasoning processes which undermine the line they wish to pursue.[40] The danger of the purposive approach is that it opens up the adjudicative process to a much broader range of considerations and to many more creative modes of reasoning. Once accepted, it implies that the judicial process is likely to exhibit a high degree of indeterminacy. Although judges may be able to construct technically respectable opinions, these opinions have a strong rhetorical aspect and, given that the material with which judges work is highly malleable, it would appear that when adjudicating judges exercise a genuine policy choice.[41]

CONCLUSIONS

During the twentieth century, the English judiciary has embraced a version of legal formalism as an expression of the judicial role in meeting

[39] Keen's concerns on these matters reflect the reply which Lord Simonds gave to Lord Denning's contention (ibid.): "[T]he general proposition that it is the duty of the court to find out the intention of Parliament . . . cannot by any means be supported. The duty of the court is to interpret the words that the legislature has used; those words may be ambiguous, but, even if they are, the power and duty of the court to travel outside them on a voyage of discovery are strictly limited . . . What the legislature has not written, the court must not write. This proposition . . . appears to me to be a naked usurpation of the legislative function under the thin disguise of interpretation." *Magor & St. Mellons R.D.C.* v. *Newport Corporation* [1952] AC 189, 191 (HL).

[40] On this point see Karl N. Llewellyn, *The Bramble Bush: On Our Law and Its Study* [1930] (New York: Oceana Publishing, 1960), 74: "the doctrine of precedent . . . is two-headed . . . [T]here is one doctrine for getting rid of precedents deemed troublesome and one doctrine for making use of precedents that seem helpful."

[41] This argument is most commonly associated with the so-called American legal realist movement, of which Llewellyn's work, ibid., is exemplary. For a contemporary analysis along similar lines, see: Duncan Kennedy, *A Critique of Adjudication {fin de siècle}* (Cambridge, Mass: Harvard U.P., 1997).

the requirements of corrective justice. However, this is often expressed in the language of justification and the evidence that formalism provides an explanation of how judges actually reach decisions is less than compelling. As an expression of how judgments are reached, formalism is faced with two basic difficulties. The first is that the legal order is such that the system is riddled with gaps, uncertainties, and conflicts between rules. Consequently, although rules may be able to guide us in many aspects of ordinary life, in virtually all issues which present themselves for adjudication, the ambiguities are such that judges are, in Hart's terminology, constantly legislating. Though this may appear a controversial statement, it should, on reflection, be fairly self-evident. A former law lord has noted, for example, that "in almost every case, except the very plainest, it would be possible to decide the issue either way with reasonable legal justification", and that this "must be so in view of the large number of decisions which are arrived at by a majority of judicial votes". For Lord Macmillan, it follows "that the judiciary are constantly confronted with the necessity of making a choice among the doctrines of the law alleged to be applicable to the particular case" and that "at this point . . . what may, I think, quite properly be called ethical considerations operate and ought to operate."[42] These uncertainties, inherent in the material, cannot be avoided by embracing a doctrine that simply wishes them out of existence.

The other major problem with formalism is that its seems to embrace a literalist idea of language which fails to convince. Words do not always have simple, literal meanings; they often acquire meaning within particular contexts, a point which is one consequence of the argument made in Chapter 2 about the ways in which we make the worlds we inhabit. But if this is correct, it follows that the formalist attempt to discern the meaning of a rule divorced from the context in which it is designed to operate is likely to fail. Take a simple word like "ball". The word has a variety of meanings, meanings which may be discerned only in context. Consider, for example, two simple rules: "The ball must be made of leather" and "Formal dress must be worn at the ball". Here, the meaning of the word within each rule radically alters. And if that is the case in respect of simple words incorporated into simple rules, imagine the difficulties faced by the use of fancy terminology embedded in highly complex rules.

---

[42] Lord Macmillan, *Law and Other Things* (Cambridge: Cambridge U.P., 1937), 49.

It is for these reasons that formalism fails to provide an adequate explanation of the adjudicative process: fact-finding is a complex and creative process; rules are not self-interpreting; and the rule-structure is riddled with gaps, ambiguities and conflicts. Once confronted with these realities, it seems obvious that, in seeking to right wrongs, judges are inevitably engaged in a creative interpretative task. It is a task in which their own views of the world—the stories which they embrace in order to give meaning to their world—must exert a powerful influence over the judgments they reach. This means not only that judges contribute to the task of law-making, but also that particular moral and political judgments underpin the decisions which they reach.

But does this also mean that law is radically indeterminate and that judges reach decisions in accordance with their partisan political preferences? These consequences do not inevitably follow. Indeterminacy generated as a consequence of the openness of the normative structure of law does not necessarily lead to the conclusion that judges are free to legislate as they wish. There are, for example, various institutional constraints on judicial decision-making which restrict the ambit of their discretion: the principle of *stare decisis*, the requirement of that decisions be reasoned, the exclusion of the judge from the fact-finding process in trials involving juries and the existence of a system of appeals all impose constraints on the discretionary powers of judges. There is, however, a more basic point: the fact that the formal legal materials fail to secure determinate decisions should, I believe, be treated not as an issue of indeterminacy but rather as one of under-determinacy.

This issue of under-determinacy is highlighted in the early work of Schmitt. In *Law and Judgment*, Schmitt argued that a minimum of legal predictability is essential for an effective legal order and this comes less from the binding character of the rules than from the shared values of the judiciary.[43] Consequently, in searching for determinacy, Schmitt suggests that we look not to the connection between the rule and the judge but to the relationship between the judge and his or her peers. He formulated the basic principle in simple terms: "a judicial decision is correct today when it can be assumed that another judge would have decided in the same way."[44] It is not the letter of the law

7

Distributive Justice

ONE BASIC FUNCTION of the State is to formulate and enforce rules of just conduct. The State thus devises rules which prohibit the use of violence, define property rights and regulate its transfer, and otherwise promote voluntary transactions amongst citizens; and the courts are established as those special institutions of the State which exist to ensure the proper enforcement of those rules of just conduct. In rectifying wrongs caused as a result of a breach of the rules, the judiciary gives effect to Aristotle's idea of corrective justice. But corrective justice is only one of two basic Aristotelian conceptions of justice. Aristotle also believed that justice in distribution required that goods and advantages be allocated in proportion to their merits. Aristotle recognized that differences in political views exist over what the merits require, though he himself believed that people were born equipped for particular tasks in life and that society consists of a natural aristocracy. In modern societies, however, the issue of justice in the allocation of social and economic benefits has remained one of the most intractable of political questions.

In today's world—founded in general on the principles of a formal legal and political equality but which operate within societies where the material rewards are unequally allocated—merit remains fundamentally contested. Some argue that justice requires a material equality, which would require the removal of those economic and social privileges rooted in aristocratic status, capitalist wealth, bureaucratic power or racial or sexual supremacy.[1] Some suggest that justice requires simply an equality of opportunity in which careers are open to talent and in respect of which people should be permitted to compete free from the barriers imposed by a hierarchically stratified society.[2] Others again argue that these modern ideas are dangerous, since the attempt to institute any of these conceptions of social justice would

[1] See Michael Walzer, *Spheres of Justice: A Defence of Pluralism & Equality* (Oxford: Blackwell, 1983).

[2] See John E. Roemer, *Equality of Opportunity* (Cambridge, Mass: Harvard U.P., 1998).

destroy all freedom.[3] And lurking in the shadows of this debate lies
Hamlet's question: "use every man after his desert, and who would
'scape whipping?"[4] Given the range of contemporary theories of justice—"to all the same", "to each according to his effort", "to each
according to his need", "to each according to his rank"—it might be
thought that any attempt to place the idea of justice above politics is
highly implausible.

In this chapter, I propose to explain the impact of recent attempts to
devise objective principles of distributive justice and then, having
argued that such efforts have been unsuccessful and that the issue of
justice in distribution remains intensely political, to consider some of
the legal implications of political movements to achieve redistribution
through the agency of the State.

THE GEOMETRIC PRINCIPLE OF JUSTICE REVISITED

The publication in 1971 of John Rawls's *A Theory of Justice* constitutes a landmark in the process of thinking about justice. Until Rawls's
work, most political philosophers had first tried to discern what makes
for a good society and then worked backwards to ask what type of
political institutions were required to reflect those conditions.
However, since the vision of the good is likely always to remain a matter of politics, Rawls suggested that this method was unlikely to resolve
conflicts. Most thinkers adopted a utilitarian idea of justice in which
each person seeks to maximize their own desires and the State, by balancing the competing interests of individuals, promotes the greatest
overall good. But, as Rawls pointed out, requiring individuals to sacrifice their own satisfaction for the overall general welfare is not necessarily just. Consequently, instead of seeking agreement on some
particular conception of the good society, Rawls proposed that we
might try to reach agreement on the ground rules for adjudicating
between different ideas of the good. *A Theory of Justice* seeks to
achieve this objective. It does so by establishing a model of a society in
which citizens may have competing ideas of the good life but can nevertheless agree on the rules of right conduct.

---

[3] See F.A. Hayek, *Law, Legislation and Liberty.* Vol. 2. *The Mirage of Social Justice*
(London: Routledge & Kegan Paul, 1976).
[4] William Shakespeare, *Hamlet*, Act II, sc. ii.

Since there is ineradicable conflict over ends, Rawls focuses on the means by which citizens realize their ends. The basic goods which the State should therefore regulate are those which enable citizens to realize their objectives. These "primary goods", as Rawls calls them, are those rights, opportunities and resources which people need to live the good life. Rawls argues that since there is a conflict over ends and since people count equally the only acceptable way of allocating these rights, opportunities and resources is an equal one. He thus proposes two basic principles of justice. The first is that each person has an equal right to the most extensive liberty compatible with a like liberty for all. The second principle is that any social and economic inequalities in society must operate to everyone's advantage and must attach to positions and offices which are open to all.[5] The first principle takes priority over the second; liberty must be restricted only for the sake of liberty. The second reflects a principle of equal opportunity; since complete material equality would provide no incentive for individuals to undertake training or to apply effort, the principle justifies those inequalities which benefit society overall.

Rawls argues that the type of society which best satisfies these principles is that of a "constitutional democracy" which preserves equal basic liberties, has an economic system based on the market, and is overseen by a government which promotes equality of opportunity and guarantees a social minimum. His, then, is a social democratic theory of justice which addresses the question of how people with different religious and political beliefs might live together in conditions of mutual respect. It might therefore be considered an especially appropriate theory for the contemporary western world. John Dunn thus comments that for a political culture rooted in a respect for individual rights, "Rawls's theory offers an evocative method for specifying a public standard of social justice". But Dunn also notes that it is a standard which clashes fundamentally with ideas of "economic expansion, founded upon private ownership and appropriation minimally impeded by fiscal redistribution", ideas have also played a prominent role in shaping the character of western political culture.[6] But Dunn's most telling point is to note that, if this is social democracy's conception of justice, then it is one which no contemporary, self-styled social democracy comes at all close to meeting.

[5] John Rawls, *A Theory of Justice* (Oxford: Oxford U.P., 1972), 60–2, 302–3.
[6] John Dunn, *The History of Political Theory and other essays* (Cambridge: Cambridge U.P., 1996), 62.

Rawls's theory has also been directly challenged by other recent theories of justice. Perhaps the most notable has been that of Robert Nozick. Starting from certain premisses about the inalienable rights of individuals, Nozick contends that a minimal State—that is, one which is limited to the narrow functions of protection against force, theft and fraud and to the enforcement of contracts—is the only State which can be justified and that any more extensive role for the State will result in a violation of the citizen's right not to be forced to do certain things.[7] Judging from the debates which have arisen between these recent competing theories of justice, it would appear that, notwithstanding the sophistication of the theories, they do not enable us to come much closer to the objective of finding some measure which will enable these basic concerns to be raised above the cut and thrust of politics.

This account, however, has so far ignored what many consider to be the most brilliant feature of Rawls's theory, one which will enable political differences to be transcended and rational agreement on his two basic principles to be reached. This feature is what Rawls calls "the original position". Imagine that we are placed behind a "veil of ignorance", where we have no knowledge of our class or social status in society, or of what abilities and talents we will possess, or even of what our idea of the good life will be. Further, imagine also that we do not know anything about the economic or political organization of the society into which we are about to be plunged, or its level of civilization or type of culture.[8] What Rawls argues is that all people, knowing the general facts about human society but otherwise being situated behind this veil of ignorance, will rationally be obliged to embrace his two principles as being those which are conducive to the achievement of a just society. Through the device of the original position, then, Rawls seeks not simply to provide a theory of justice which social democrats might espouse, but one which all rational human beings should accept. If Rawls is right, then he has indeed been able successfully to postulate the geometric principles of justice.

The device of the original position has, however, been subjected to serious criticism. Some have criticized the original position as an analytical tool, and have argued, for example, that a gambler in that position might rationally choose a hierarchically organized rather than an

[7] Robert Nozick, *Anarchy, State, and Utopia* (Oxford: Blackwell, 1974).
[8] See Rawls, above n. 5, 136–42.

essentially egalitarian society,[9] or have pointed out problems in the argument for giving priority to the principle of equal liberty.[10] Others have identified difficulties in determining why, even if those behind the veil would accept these principles, this should justify our adopting them.[11] Rawls's device has even been criticized on the ground that, since people are social beings, the attempt to abstract from a particular social and historical context becomes, in effect, a theoretical attempt to isolate what cannot be isolated.[12] Ernest Gellner, for example, has noted that in many societies the assumption that "culturally naked men can choose their social order, instead of having it imposed upon them by transcendent authority, would be simply unintelligible". It would, in effect, be to ask such people to perform an "imaginary amputation, . . . to think themselves away, to deny their own existence, to ignore their own deepest moral reactions". Consequently, although intended to overcome local prejudice and vested interest, the device of the veil of ignorance, "is simply an extreme instance and expression of a special set of ethnocentric blinkers, of the way in which our own rather special, mobile and hence egalitarian society feeds its own values back to itself".[13]

Under the barrage of such criticism, Rawls has accepted the difficulty of founding his theory of justice on some notion of disinterested reason, or on what he calls a "comprehensive philosophical doctrine". More recently, he has suggested that the principles of justice can form the subject of an "overlapping consensus" in so far as they might be accepted by every "reasonable comprehensive view" held by members of society.[14] By retreating to this position, Rawls in effect returns the issue of justice to the realm of politics. We can strive to develop a consensus over the issue of justice in society, and Rawls's powerful arguments might help us to build that consensus, but the quest for justice

[9] Benjamin Barber, "Justifying Justice: Problems of Psychology, Politics and Measurement in Rawls" in Norman Daniels (ed.), *Reading Rawls: Critical Studies of "A Theory of Justice"* (Oxford: Blackwell, 1975), ch. 13.
[10] H.L.A. Hart, "Rawls on Liberty and its Priority" (1973) 40 *Univ. of Chicago Law Rev.* 534.
[11] Thomas Nagel, "Rawls on Justice" (1973) 82 *Philosophical Review* 220; cf. Ronald Dworkin, "The Original Position" (1973) 40 *Univ. of Chicago Law Rev.* 500.
[12] Steven Lukes, "No Archimedean Point" in his *Essays in Social Theory* (London: Macmillan, 1977), ch. 10.
[13] Ernest Gellner, *Plough, Sword and Book: The Structure of Human History* (London: Paladin, 1988), 25.
[14] John Rawls, *Political Liberalism* (New York: Columbia U.P., 1993), esp. 58–66, 133–72.

must remain a central issue of political debate. We turn, then, to consider the political tendencies of government in the twentieth century to bring about a greater justice in distribution of material goods.

JUSTICE AND THE ADMINISTRATIVE STATE

Sketching on a rather broad canvas, T.H. Marshall has charted how the concept of citizenship has evolved in modern times. During the eighteenth century, the debate took place mainly over the issues of freedom of speech, thought and religion; that is, over *civil* citizenship. In the nineteenth century, as a struggle occurred over the right of the people to participate in the exercise of political power, the emphasis shifted towards the *political* aspects of citizenship. And during the course of the twentieth century, as may be seen as a result of the emergence of the Welfare State, the debate has moved on to the issue of *social and economic* citizenship.[15] With the evolution of the idea of citizenship, the issue of distributive justice has gradually been placed on the political agenda. Egalitarianism has certainly been a key theme in modern political thinking. Although this idea was originally understood mainly in terms of a formal legal and political equality, during this century the issue has been addressed in relation to the tension between formal equality and material inequality. The extension of the concept of citizenship to the social and economic sphere thus reflects an admission that issues such as education, health and economic well-being are often seen as vital preconditions to the full realization of civil and political citizenship rights.

Although the institutionalization of social and economic citizenship rights has been a central theme of twentieth-century politics, such "rights" have not generally been recognized as enforceable legal rights; to the extent that they have been accepted, they have been acknowledged simply to be political claims. The standard response by government to the claims of social and economic citizenship has been to vest public bodies with a range of discretionary powers to provide services to meet the material needs of citizens. This response has therefore led to the emergence of an administrative State in which public bodies have been given general legal powers to undertake such tasks as that of clear-

---

[15] T.H. Marshall, "Citizenship and Social Class" [1949] in his *Class, Citizenship and Social Development* S.M. Lipset ed. (Westport, Conn.: Greenwood Press, 1976), ch. 4.

ing areas of unfit housing and building new homes, of providing hospitals and operating a national health service, and of undertaking an assessment of welfare needs and then supplying a range of social services. The relationship between citizens and the State in the modern era has, consequently, become bureaucratized. The duties which Parliament may be understood to have imposed on these public bodies are owed essentially to Parliament and they have not generally been recognized as vesting justiciable rights in citizens.[16]

The result has been that, although the pressure to accept the claims of social and economic citizenship rights has effected a change in what may be called the political constitution, these "rights" take the form of political claims which have been filtered through an administrative process and have therefore not explicitly been recognized in the normative structure of positive law. A.V. Dicey recognized this tendency at an early stage when he noted that the political reformers "have inherited a legislative dogma, a legislative instrument and a legislative tendency."[17] What, he implied, has not been devised is a new legal theory which reflects the juridical significance of these political changes. That is, while socio-economic citizenship rights have been the product of an emerging political consensus, because they have been implemented through the use of non-purposive framework legislation, they have not generated new legal principles of justice. Government has used legislation to establish an administrative State but has hoped to be able to insulate these new citizenship challenges from the sphere of the courts.[18] Since, as was contended in the previous chapter, judges engage in a creative interpretative task when adjudicating claims, it seems unlikely that this objective would be entirely successful. How, then, would the judiciary adapt the legal requirements of justice in the light of the political acceptance of socio-economic citizenship rights?

THE ROLE OF THE JUDICIARY IN THE ADMINISTRATIVE STATE

When seeking to give expression of the evolutionary potential of the law, the judiciary has a fondness for invoking a particular organic

---

[16] See, e.g., R.M. Titmuss, "Welfare 'Rights', Law and Discretion" (1971) 42 *Political Quarterly* 113.

[17] A.V. Dicey, *Lectures on the Relation between Law & Public Opinion in England during the Nineteenth Century* (London: Macmillan, 1905), 302.

[18] For a theoretical discussion of the issues raised see Gunther Teubner (ed.), *Dilemmas of Law in the Welfare State* (Berlin: de Gruyter, 1986).

metaphor. Lord Kilmuir, Lord Chancellor between 1954 and 1962, gave eloquent voice to this trope when stating that the law "is not to be compared to a venerable antique, to be taken down, dusted, admired and put back on the shelf". Rather, he continued, "it is like an old but still vigorous tree—rooted firmly in history; but still putting out new shoots, taking new grafts and from time to time dropping dead wood."[19] Would the judiciary be able to put out new shoots in responding to the challenge of meeting the requirements of justice within the administrative State? Some doubted whether the judiciary was up to the task.[20] But, especially since the 1960s, the courts have worked actively to set in place a structure of public law principles which aspire to guide the exercise of public power.[21]

It is this issue—the extension of judicial review, especially in relation to social legislation—which lies at the heart of the many of the most intense British debates about the political role of the judiciary in modern society. The thesis of the critics, exemplified by John Griffith, is essentially (i) that "judges are part of the machinery within the State and as such cannot avoid the making of political decisions", (ii) that judges "have by their education and training . . . acquired a strikingly homogeneous collection of attitudes, beliefs and principles, which to them represent the public interest", (iii) that what is or is not in the public interest is a political question, and (iv) that, given their position as part of the established authority, their conception of the public interest, "is necessarily conservative, not liberal".[22]

Although this perspective on the judicial function is often treated as being dangerously radical,[23] it is in fact one which, in all its essentials, has been consistently articulated by conservative thinkers. We have already seen writers such as Tocqueville and Bagehot giving expression to the necessity for lawyers to promote moderation and maintain

---

[19] Lord Kilmuir, "The State, the Citizen and the Law" (1951) 73 *Law Quarterly Review* 172, 173. See also Hale, Ch. 1 above, 11.

[20] See Sir Patrick Devlin, "The Common Law, Public Policy and the Executive" 1956 *Current Legal Problems* 1.

[21] Note, e.g., *R. v. I.R.C., ex parte National Federation of Self Employed* [1982] AC 617, 641 *per* Lord Diplock: "the progress towards a comprehensive system of administrative law . . . I regard as having been the greatest achievement of the English courts in my judicial lifetime."

[22] J.A.G. Griffith, *The Politics of the Judiciary* (London: Fontana, 5th edn. 1997), 292–3, 295, 296, 336.

[23] See, e.g., Kenneth Minogue, "The biases of the bench", *Times Literary Supplement*, 6 January 1978, 11.

order,[24] and judges such as Lords Evershed and Radcliffe explaining how the higher judiciary, through their "cloistered" and "aristocratic" traditions, are particularly well-suited to perform this function.[25] This is not surprising, since Griffith's thesis is rooted in a representation of the judicial function which accords with the ancient idea of the rule of law. Considered as an expression of the ancient idea, and stripped of its critical tone, it is on all fours with Dicey's views. Dicey openly acknowledged that judges legislate; indeed he contended that "a large part and, as many would add, the best part of the law of England is judge-made law". Further, Dicey accepted that although judges are inevitably influenced by the currents of public opinion, they "are more likely to be biassed by professional habits and feeling than by the popular sentiment of the hour" and are likely to act in such a manner as to maintain "the logic or the symmetry of the law" or to aim "at securing the certainty rather than at amending the deficiencies of the law". For these reasons Dicey believed that "judicial conceptions of . . . the public interest may sometimes rise above the ideas prevalent at a particular era" and that this is not surprising since judges, as the heads of the legal profession, "have acquired the intellectual and moral tone of English lawyers", are "men advanced in life" and "are for the most part persons of a conservative disposition".[26]

The crucial issue is one which remains implicit in Griffith's critique: can the conception of the judicial role implied by the ancient idea of the rule of law survive the emergence of democracy and, in particular, the extension of the legal powers of the administrative State? Montesquieu, we may recall, considered that the ancient "deliberative" role was characteristic of monarchical regimes and would be unlikely to continue once a republican system was instituted.[27] Dicey's response was the somewhat reactionary one of advocating turning back the tides of the administrative State.[28] Since this was unlikely, the question the judiciary faced was: what would be the appropriate response when the Executive used these discretionary statutory powers for the purpose of promoting redistributive objectives?

The *cause célèbre* was the 1920s case of *Roberts* v. *Hopwood*, in which Labour-controlled Poplar Borough Council, acting under a

[24] See Ch. 5, above 71, 74.
[25] See Ch. 5 above, 74; Ch. 6 above, 83.
[26] Dicey, above n. 17, 359, 362, 364, 366, 362.
[27] See Ch. 6 above, 78.
[28] See, e.g., A.V. Dicey, "The development of administrative law in England" (1915) 31 *Law Quarterly Review* 148.

general power to pay its employees "such salaries and wages as [the council] may think fit", fixed a minimum wage which was higher than wage rates in the area and was paid to men and women alike. In declaring this action unlawful, the Law Lords expressed the views that the council had allowed themselves to be guided both by "honest stupidity or unpractical idealism" and "by some eccentric principles of socialist philanthropy" and "a feminist ambition to secure equality of the sexes . . . in the world of labour" and they concluded that the local council's powers do not "authorize them to be guided by their personal opinions on political, economic and social questions in administering the funds which they derive from the rates."[29] This decision highlighted the basic issue in a rather stark form. By striking down a minimum wage of around £200 per annum in this manner, the Law Lords (whose annual salary was £5,000) seemed to be laying themselves open to the criticism that, in the guise of laying down the law, they were acting as "the unconscious servant of a single class in the community".[30] This has been the twentieth-century refrain of the critics: that when dealing with disputes concerning workers' compensation claims, trades union disputes or, more generally, the exercise of governmental powers for progressive social policy purposes, the courts have operated systematically to protect the established power interests in society.[31]

It is for such reasons that many on the left in politics have poured scorn on any embellished notion of the rule of law.[32] For Griffith, when extended beyond the requirement that there exist adequate machinery to ensure that public authorities do not exceed their powers, "it is a fantasy invented by Liberals of the old school in the late nineteenth century and patented by Tories to throw a protective sanctity around certain legal and political institutions and principles which they wish to preserve at any cost."[33] For similar reasons we also find many who wish to limit the scope of judicial review and to restrict the judicial role

---

[29] [1925] AC 578, at 604, 598, 604.

[30] H.J. Laski, "Judicial Review of Social Policy in England" (1926) 39 *Harvard Law Review* 832, 848.

[31] See Griffith, above n. 22; John Griffith, *Judicial Politics since 1920: A Chronicle* (Oxford: Blackwell, 1993); K.W. Wedderburn, *The Worker and the Law* (Harmondsworth: Penguin, 3rd edn. 1986); Robert Stevens, *Law and Politics: The House of Lords as a Judicial Body, 1800–1976* (London: Weidenfeld & Nicolson, 1979); Patrick McAuslan, *The Ideologies of Planning Law* (Oxford: Pergamon, 1980).

[32] See, e.g., W. Ivor Jennings, *The Law and the Constitution* (London: Univ. of London Press, 2nd edn. 1938), 59–61; J.A.G. Griffith & H. Street, *Principles of Administrative Law* (London: Pitman, 5th edn. 1973), ch. 1.

[33] J.A.G. Griffith, "The Political Constitution" (1979) 42 *Modern Law Review* 1, 15.

to that of the literal interpretation of statutes. Lord Devlin echoed their concerns in suggesting that, when judges moved beyond the ordinary meaning of words and "looked for the philosophy behind the Act", they invariably found "a Victorian Bill of Rights, favouring (subject to the observance of the accepted standards of morality) the liberty of the individual, the freedom of contract, and the sacredness of property, and which was highly suspicious of taxation."[34] The problem, as we have seen, is that "literalism", "formalism", "judicial restraint" and such-like are strategies adopted by the judiciary at particular moments. Given that these formulations are indicative of one amongst several possible philosophies of judging, this type of appeal does not avoid the fact that the judiciary must inevitably perform an interpretative role. And since there is a range of interpretative theories that could plausibly be invoked, the critical point, it would appear, is to acknowledge the importance of the politics of legal interpretation.

THE SEARCH FOR COHERENCE

Although some theorists, by highlighting the institutional limitations on the role of courts in the law-making process, have tried to lessen the significance of the politics of legal interpretation,[35] it seems now to be accepted that this issue must be addressed directly. If the meaning of a rule cannot be understood without reference to its purpose, then the judge's role, in undertaking some sort of inquiry in order to ascertain the purpose of the law, must be acknowledged to be both complex and creative.[36] It seems not to be the case, for example, that judges consider policy only when rules run out; once the judicial process is accepted as being interpretative, some understanding of the policy or purpose of the rules becomes a core aspect of the judicial function.

Nevertheless, in exercising this interpretative responsibility, it is generally argued that judges do not apply their personal political views of the underlying policies. They are constrained by what Fuller calls the

---

[34] Lord Devlin, "The Judge as Lawmaker" (1976) 39 *Modern Law Review* 1, 14.

[35] See, e.g., Joseph Raz, "Law and Value in Adjudication" in his *The Authority of Law: Essays on Law and Morality* (Oxford: Clarendon Press, 1979), ch. 10.

[36] In this context, consider, e.g., the implications of the ruling in *Pepper* v. *Hart* [1993] 1 All ER 42. See Kenny Mullan, "The Impact of *Pepper* v. *Hart*" in Paul Carmichael and Brice Dickson (eds) *The House of Lords: Its Parliamentary and Judicial Roles* (Oxford: Hart, 1999), ch. 11.

"structural integrity" of the law;[37] that is, they are obliged by a requirement of interpretative fidelity to the law or by "the consensus of the
interpretative community" within the law to reach a judgment which
best fits the existing normative structure of the law.[38] Consequently,
the role of the judiciary is to treat "the whole existing corpus of rules
(rather than the words of a particular rule) as the product of an implicit
rational plan, and ask [. . .] which of the rules proposed best furthers
that plan."[39] In this sense, the judicial process "is deeply and thoroughly political" since, when engaging in this type of exercise, judges
must seek to discern that political theory, such as that theory of social
justice, which best gives meaning to the existing legal structure.[40]

Can the problem of legal indeterminacy be resolved through this
type of judgment? Some suggest that it can. Most notably, Ronald
Dworkin argues that in all disputes presented for adjudication there is
a right answer, in the sense that there can be identified "a particular
conception of community morality [which is] decisive of legal
issues".[41] Nevertheless, Dworkin's theory remains contentious. The
main difficulty is that, given the open-textured nature of legal materials, a variety of competing theories of interpretation can plausibly be
utilized and the question of which theory might make best sense of the
material must remain controversial. Once again, the issue is revealed as
one of under-determinacy. In this context, however, the Schmittian
solution—that the key to legal determinacy is found in the cultural
homogeneity of the judiciary[42]—is doubly contentious.

The first reason is that the cultural homogeneity of the judiciary is
precisely what lies at the core of the critic's concern. Judges inhabit
social worlds which shape the way in which they think about such
issues as the importance of private property rights, the meaning of sexual or racial equality, and the protection to be given to the rights of the
accused. Once it is accepted that judges must, as part of their decision-
making role, devise implicit theories of the values underpinning the
legal order, then the critics will argue explicitly that the judiciary,

---

[37] Lon L. Fuller, "Positivism and Fidelity to Law—A Reply to Professor Hart" (1958)
71 *Harvard Law Rev.* 630, 670.

[38] Owen Fiss, "Objectivity and Interpretation" (1982) 34 *Stanford Law Rev.* 739.

[39] Duncan Kennedy, *A Critique of Adjudication {fin de siècle}* (Cambridge, Mass:
Harvard U.P., 1997), 33.

[40] Ronald Dworkin, *A Matter of Principle* (Cambridge, Mass: Harvard U.P., 1985),
146.

[41] Ronald Dworkin, *Taking Rights Seriously* (Cambridge, Mass: Harvard U.P., 1977),
126.

[42] See Ch. 6 above, 92–3.

because of their class background and social milieu, are likely to hold theories about the notion of justice embedded in the law which are not only undesirable but also have not been sufficiently responsive to the changes which have been effected in the political constitution. Some critics have responded to this concern by arguing the case for opening up the judicial appointments process and taking positive action to ensure the appointment of under-represented groups.[43] Nevertheless, although such reforms will make the judiciary more broadly representative of society, they are likely to exacerbate the problem of ensuring the predictability of law. If legal determinacy is a function of cultural homogeneity, then recruiting judges from a broader social spectrum is likely to bring greater uncertainty (as the range of theories of justice promoted from the bench increases) and might even undermine the effectiveness of those judicial tasks which require citizens to believe that judges are able to transcend the cut-and-thrust of the political process.

But there is a further reason why the interpretative turn presents particular difficulties in the British system. The British constitution is a political constitution and, as we have seen, the reforms which have been introduced to give effect to social and economic citizenship rights have not generally been expressed in legal form; although using legislative instruments, we have not developed new theories which express the relationship between citizen and State in a modern juridical form. It is therefore not surprising that the judiciary has experienced serious difficulties in adjudicating on those claims which touch on the issue of distributive justice: in addition to being immersed in the culture of the ancient conception of the rule of law, judges are presented with a variety of disputes in which the political values underpinning the reform legislation are almost never expressed in legal form. Political reforms which leave the core of the legal order unreconstructed thus present acute problems for the judiciary. Critics such as Griffith argue that the best solution is strictly to limit the political influence of the judiciary.[44] Reformers such as Dworkin, by contrast, contend that once judges begin to embrace more enlightened theories of justice then the nature of the profession is likely to change quite speedily and it might not necessarily be the case that judicial decisions would be less

---

[43] See, e.g., Carol Harlow, "Refurbishing the Judicial Service" in Harlow (ed.), *Public Law and Politics* (London: Sweet & Maxwell, 1986), ch. 10.

[44] John Griffith, "Constitutional and Administrative Law" in Peter Archer and Andrew Martin (eds), *More Law Reform Now* (Chichester: Barry Rose, 1983), 49.

egalitarian, or even less democratic, than the decisions of majoritarian legislatures under the control of powerful economic interest groups.[45] The politics of the judiciary, in this sense, concerns the deployment by the judiciary of a variety of interpretative theories which are implanted within the legal order. But it is made particularly contentious by the requirement that judges, for the purpose of developing this jurisprudence, must effect a subtle but basic shift in the legal foundations of the political order.[46]

For these reasons, judges are inextricably bound up in the politics of distributive justice. They do not, of course, make distributional decisions in the way a party politician might. Judges are circumscribed not only by a range of institutional constraints on their action, but also by their own ideas about self-preservation and their need to produce a judgment which will comply with the accepted canons of interpretative fidelity. Nevertheless, given the pliability of legal materials and the fact that the range of interpretative theories which judges might legitimately hold seems quite broad, within the strictures of their obligation to forge a serviceable judgment judges are able to exercise some form of policy choice.[47] Consistency, then, has been mainly a product of cultural homogeneity of the judiciary. If the judicial role was confined to the task of meeting the requirements of corrective justice this might have been manageable. Once the State uses law to realize notions of distributive justice, however, the judiciary cannot easily avoid being drawn into matters of political controversy. And although this issue has become a feature of virtually all western democracies, the British challenge—which involves nothing less than transforming the political constitution into a legal constitution—has recently been acutely felt.

[45] Dworkin, above n. 40, ch. 1.

[46] See, e.g., Sir Stephen Sedley, "The Sound of Silence: Constitutional Law without a Constitution" (1994) 110 *Law Quarterly Review* 270; Sir John Laws, "Law and Democracy" [1995] *Public Law* 72.

[47] See N.E. Simmonds, "Bluntness and Bricolage" in Hyman Gross and Ross Harrison (eds), *Jurisprudence. Cambridge Essays* (Oxford: Clarendon Press, 1992), ch. 1.

III
The State

8

Politics as Statecraft

IN THE PRECEDING section on Justice, I examined the techniques which have been deployed for the purpose of distinguishing law, conceived mainly as the conduit of justice, from the pursuit of politics. These range from the elaborate rituals which bolster a belief in the judge as a dispenser of wisdom to those philosophies of adjudication which portray judicial decision-making as an exercise in impartial rule-handling. I suggested that, notwithstanding certain important institutional constraints, judges do exercise important political functions and it is precisely because they cannot avoid performing a role in which they are required to uphold and enforce certain political values that such a degree of pomp and mystique surrounds their activities. But if it is the case that, at some level or other, the judicial function is bound up with politics, then we need to make further inquiries as to the nature of politics. There is, after all, little point in identifying judges with politics unless we have a fairly clear idea of what we mean by politics.

The classical expression of politics is most clearly articulated by Aristotle. In *The Politics*, Aristotle claims that there is a fundamental distinction between the realm of politics and the pre-political realm of the household. Although both the household and the State are forms of human association, Aristotle argues that the roles of the "statesman" and that of the household-manager not only reflect variations in the scale of the task, but also constitute categorial differences. Political action is not simply an exercise in management, nor is it founded on the will of a superior directing the actions of an inferior. The objective of politics is quite distinctive: it is an exercise in self-government through deliberative means by members of a collectivity. Unlike the private sphere of the household, or the economic relationship of master and servant, the public realm of politics is one which is based on the ideals of freedom and self-government.[1]

This Aristotelian idea of politics as an activity within the public realm which is linked to some notion of self-government also recurs in

[1] Aristotle, *The Politics* [c.335–323 BC] T.A. Sinclair trans., Trevor J. Saunders ed. (Harmondsworth: Penguin, 1981), Bk. I, ii.

the Middle Ages. The work of Sir John Fortescue, the most important English political theorist of the fifteenth century, provides an illustration. The basic theme of Fortescue's writing is that the English polity was *dominium politicum et regale*, a dominion both political and royal. By this formulation Fortescue indicates that although the king possessed absolute authority to rule, he could alter the law only with the consent of Parliament.[2] But it goes further than this: he implies also that a regime which is purely *dominium regale*—a form of royal rule in which the king may pass such measures as he pleases—is not *politicum* at all. Fortescue extends this point in *On the Nature of the Law of Nature*,[3] a work in which he suggests that although the idea of royal law—rooted in the maxim "what pleases the prince has the force of law"[4]—appears freer and more powerful than the idea of political law—in which law is enacted through Parliament—this is not in fact the case. The ability to act without constraint, Fortescue contends, is a sign neither of power nor of liberty: "the ability to sin does not belong to power, but is a dangerous impotence and slavery". "If the breath of pride so affects the soul of man that, abandoning humility and modesty, he is raised into ambition and plundering of kingdoms", Fortescue continues, "does not that man's sin then proceed from his impotence?"[5] Fortescue's basic point is that politics is concerned not simply with power (in the sense of might) and its exercise; it should be understood to be an activity intimately linked to the virtues of freedom and civilization. We are familiar with the expression, "Where law ends, there tyranny begins".[6] From this more nuanced perspective on the nature of politics, it might be said that "Where tyranny ends, there politics begins".

This sense of politics as an activity which attempts to achieve the conciliation of differences seems not to be so far removed from that of the judicial role which I portrayed in Part II of the book. Pocock has noted that in Fortescue's work "the king ruling by the law and the king

---

[2] Sir John Fortescue, *The Governance of England* [c.1471] in his *On the Laws and Governance of England* Shelley Lockwood ed. (Cambridge: Cambridge U.P., 1997), 81–123.

[3] Ibid. Appendix A.

[4] This maxim was first formulated by the Roman jurist, Ulpian: see *The Digest of Justinian* [533] Alan Watson ed. (Philadelphia: University of Pennsylvania Press, 1985), I.4.1: "*Quod principi placuit, legis habet vigorem*".

[5] Fortescue, above n. 2, 133, 133–4.

[6] See above Ch. 1, 13.

ruling by counsel are one and the same thing."[7] Could one argue that this observation applies not just to the activity of legislation but also to the exercise of adjudication by those king's counsellors whom we call judges? That is, special though it may be, law—in each of its principal manifestations as legislation and judicial decision—should essentially be understood as a peculiar form of political practice.

Nevertheless, even if this close association between the practices of law and politics can be recognized in classical or medieval thought, the question remains: do these classical and medieval ideas of politics and law survive into the modern era? The answer is, I believe, intimately bound up with the emergence of the modern State. The formation of the modern State effected a shift in both politics and law. Throughout the Middle Ages so much of government was undertaken in the name of law that it could be argued that it is only with the establishment of the modern State that an autonomous practice which we call politics emerges. Also, when considering the issue of justice we focused primarily on the conception of law as a set of customary practices through which judges right wrongs. With the establishment of the modern State, however, we come to see law not solely or even primarily as custom, but mainly as command. Law and politics might indeed be closely related activities, but to understand their relationship we must first examine the developments set in train by the emergence of the State. This is the main objective of Part III of this book.

In this chapter, we will be concerned primarily with the evolution of the modern idea of politics. We begin by trying to understand medieval sensibilities as part of the backcloth against which the modern changes were introduced; this is important because, as I shall argue, the struggle to establish a modern State was an essentially political encounter which took shape primarily as a conflict between Church and State but which effected a shift in world-view. For the purposes of trying to understand the significance of this shift we focus mainly on the work of Niccolò Machiavelli. Machiavelli, it should be emphasized, does not lay the foundations of the modern State; this was achieved later and is considered in chapter 9. Machiavelli's importance is to have provided us with the basic elements of a modern idea of politics as statecraft. And, as we shall see, in devising a modern conception of politics, he casts the relationship between politics and law is an interesting light.

---

[7] J.G.A. Pocock, "A discourse of sovereignty: observations on the work in progress" in N. Phillipson and Q. Skinner (eds), *Political Discourse in Early Modern Britain* (Cambridge: Cambridge U.P., 1993) 377, 395.

THE GREAT CHAIN OF BEING

Aristotle may have articulated the classical conception of politics, but it is important to be conscious of just how far this is removed from a modern view. His entire scheme of thought was bound up with a set of ancient ideas in which human activity was conducted according to a strict hierarchy. This hierarchical principle had been most vividly expressed by Homer who, in *The Iliad*, had revealed that the entire universe is held together by a golden chain which is wrapped about the feet of God, an image which provides a hierarchical scale both of existence and of value, and which ranges in sequence from God to the lowest grade of sentient life.[8] The higher world, the world of celestial bodies, is made of an imperishable substance (ether or the *quinta essentia*), whilst in the everyday earthly world all is impermanent and liable to decay.

This principle of hierarchy, a core idea of classical antiquity, was subsequently adopted by the scholastic philosophers of the medieval era. Scholastic philosophy reflected belief in an order of creation in which everything occupied its particular place on the scale. This mode of ordering was later given poetic expression by Alexander Pope in his *Essay on Man*:

> Vast chain of being, which from God began,
> Natures æthereal, human, angel, man,
> Beast, bird, fish, insect! what no eye can see,
> No glass can reach! from Infinite to thee.[9]

This great chain of being provided the foundation for all distinctions of value. Degree of value depended on degree of being; lower in degree of existence meant, in effect, lower on the ethical scale. Equally, the chain reflected the intrinsic harmony in the order of things. Each link in the chain exists "not merely and not primarily for the benefit of any other link, but for its own sake, or more precisely, for the sake of the completeness of the series of forms, the realization of which was the chief object."[10] In the language of Pope, "order is Heaven's first law".[11] This

---

[8] Homer, *The Iliad* [*c.*750–550 BC] Alexander Pope trans. (Harmondsworth: Penguin, 1996) Bk XV, 19–26.

[9] Alexander Pope, *An Essay on Man* [1734] Maynard Mack ed. (London: Methuen, 1950), Epistle I, 237–40.

[10] Arthur O. Lovejoy, *The Great Chain of Being: A Study of the History of an Idea* (Cambridge, Mass: Harvard U.P., 1936), 186.

[11] Pope, above n. 9, Epistle IV, 49.

image gave rise to the belief that humans were under a duty to maintain their place in this natural order, and certainly should not seek to transcend it. The sin of pride, as the story of Icarus reminds us, is essentially a sin against the laws of order. Further, it was often emphasized that the position of humans, being close to animals but possessing the power of intellect, is not especially high within the chain. As Pope explained:

> Created half to rise, and half to fall;
> Great lord of all things, yet a prey to all;
> Sole judge of Truth, in endless Error hurl'd;
> The glory, jest and riddle of the world.[12]

The chain of being maintained a powerful grip over medieval political thought. Human imperfection was not only indispensable to the fullness of the hierarchy of being; it also meant that creatures so limited were unlikely to be able to attain a high level of political wisdom or to bring about any radical improvement in the organization of society. The hierarchical principles embedded within this chain were also extended to the essentially feudal structures of medieval social organization. Of particular importance was the organization of the Church. The ecclesiastical hierarchy, with the Pope at its summit followed by a descending scale of cardinals, bishops and lower clergy, formed a mirror image of the general hierarchical system and reflected the universal and immutable cosmic order which had been established by God. This theocratic structure was replicated in the political organization of Europe, with the Holy Roman Emperor located at the apex of the system, delegating his authority to inferior princes and dukes.[13]

After the Copernican revolution in the natural sciences, the idea of a higher and lower world was replaced by an astronomical system in which all movement—of the earth as well as other celestial bodies—obeyed the same universal rules. The basic challenge of the Copernican revolution, however, was not so much that of the replacement of a geocentric with a heliocentric view, but rather of a shift from a heliocentric to an acentric one. The former shift might cause us to question whether there is an "above" and a "below". But the latter, in suggesting that there were no privileged points in the universe, and indeed that there might be no discernible order to it, seemed to challenge the entire idea of the chain of being.

---

12 Ibid. Epistle II, 15–18.
13 Ernst H. Kantorowicz, *The King's Two Bodies: A Study in Mediaeval Political Theology* (Princeton: Princeton U.P., 1957), chs.4, 5.

During the fifteenth and sixteenth centuries, the unity of medieval culture came under threat and the hierarchical chain of being which gave everything its right, firm and unquestionable place in the general order of things was strained to breaking point. The schism within the Church endangered the very foundations of Christian dogma; once the catholicity of the Church had been questioned, the idea of goodness could no longer rest simply on the Church's teachings. This, in turn, suggested that if there were to be a universal system of ethics it had to be based on principles that could be accepted by all nations and creeds. This marks the beginnings of a recognizably modern mode of thought, founded on the need to restore the idea of innate human dignity as the basis of an ethical system. And this movement contributed to the emergence of those rationalist theories of natural rights which have exerted great influence over modern ideas of law.[14]

Of greater significance to the conduct of politics, however, was the ensuing struggle for authority between Church and State. In one sense, the Church, being concerned essentially with the question of salvation, had no interest in worldly matters. But since the Church had a duty to oversee human action to ensure that salvation was not endangered, it had been driven to claim the *plenitudo potestatis*, or supreme power.[15] This struggle between Church and State revolved around the attempts of the secular world to resist the Church's earthly claims and to ensure that the Church did indeed render to Caesar the things that were Caesar's. The most vital issue was the struggle of the king to assert ultimate political authority within his kingdom, the fundamental issue of sovereignty. The question of sovereignty is examined in the following chapter. There is, however, a prior issue to consider, and this is the essentially *political* nature of this struggle. This issue is best examined by reference to the attempt to emancipate man's intrinsic political nature from the claims of the Church. It was achieved in part through the revitalization of Aristotle's claim that politics is an autonomous realm of discourse. The struggle took place most prominently in Renaissance Italy and came to fruition in the work of Machiavelli.

---

[14] This is the movement linked to the work of Grotius: see Ch. 1 above, 10. See also Richard Tuck, *Natural Rights Theories: Their Origin and Development* (Cambridge: Cambridge U.P., 1979).

[15] Kenneth Pennington, *The Prince and the Law, 1200–1600: Sovereignty and Rights in the Western Legal Tradition* (Berkeley: University of California Press, 1993), 45–6.

MACHIAVELLI AND THE ART OF THE STATE

The name of Machiavelli retains its currency in contemporary thought primarily as an embodiment of cunning, hypocrisy and cruelty. "Out of his surname", Macaulay observed, "they have coined an epithet for a knave, and out of his Christian name a synonym for the Devil."[16] Elizabethan dramatists had an important role in the shaping of this image. In *Henry VI*, for example, Shakespeare notoriously—if somewhat anachronistically—invokes the spectre of "the murderous Machiavel".[17] For our purposes, Machiavelli's significance rests on the fact that he was the first thinker to break decisively with the scholastic tradition. In particular, he undermined the cornerstone of the medieval order—the hierarchical system—by challenging its divine origins. For Machiavelli, political authority was anything but divine; for political rulers to claim that they derived their power from God was not only absurd but also blasphemous.

Benedetto Croce has concluded that Machiavelli's genius lies in his recognition of "the necessity and autonomy of politics, of politics which is beyond or, rather, below moral good and evil, which has its own laws against which it is useless to rebel, politics that cannot be exorcised and driven from the world with holy water".[18] Although Croce's assessment highlights vital aspects of Machiavelli's work, Isaiah Berlin's suggestion that Machiavelli draws a fundamental distinction between "two incompatible ideals of life"[19] cuts deeper still. In *The Discourses* Machiavelli notes that, rather than extolling the virtues of heroes, Christianity "has glorified humble and contemplative men" and that, by contrast, the ancient religions "did not beatify men unless they were replete with worldly glory".[20] What he is doing, Berlin suggests, is not so much distinguishing morals from politics, but drawing a distinction between what are in effect two forms of morality. The ideals of Christianity—charity, mercy, sacrifice and a belief in the life

---

[16] Thomas Babington Macaulay, "Machiavelli" [1827] in his *Critical and Historical Essays* (London: Dent, 1907), vol. II, 1–2.

[17] William Shakespeare, *Henry VI*, Pt. III, Act III, sc. 2. See Edward Meyer, *Machiavelli and the Elizabethan Drama* [1897] (New York: Burt Franklin, 1964).

[18] Benedetto Croce, *Politics and Morals* (New York: Philosophical Library, 1945), 59.

[19] Isaiah Berlin, "The Originality of Machiavelli", in his *Against the Current: Essays in the History of Ideas* (Oxford: Clarendon Press, 1989), 25, 45.

[20] Niccolò Machiavelli, *The Discourses*, [1531] Bernard Crick ed. (Harmondsworth: Penguin, 1983), Bk. II, ch. 2.

hereafter—may have intrinsic value, but Machiavelli argues that such values are incapable of establishing and sustaining a political society. The Christian faith has "made the world weak" and since "the generality of men, with paradise for their goal, consider how best to bear, rather than how best to avenge, their injuries" has "handed it over as a prey to the wicked".[21] If we are serious about building an effective political society infused with a civic spirit, Machiavelli argues, we must turn to those basic values of the pagan world—strength, courage, fortitude in adversity, and discipline—which were extolled in the ideals of Athens and Rome.

In *The Prince*, Machiavelli provides a guide or crib on how to be a successful ruler. Christian values are not explicitly rejected; his claim is that although mercy, chastity, fair-dealing and the like can be accepted as virtues, it must also be recognized that not all people are good. Since we must take people as we find them, "it is necessary for a prince, if he wants to maintain his position, to develop the ability to be not good, and use or not use this ability as necessity dictates."[22] Those, like Leo Strauss, who regard him as a "teacher of evil"[23] are, I believe, mistaken. Since rulers in building and maintaining their states are obliged to act boldly and even ruthlessly, political conduct is not an activity which can be measured by the values of those who wish to live a virtuous private life. For this task, great ability—what Machiavelli calls *virtù*—is required. It is only by acting with *virtù*—with vigour, vitality and a strength of purpose—that fickle fortune can be tamed and glory secured.

The foundations of the State, Machiavelli suggests, are sound laws and sound arms and although right and might are both important "sound laws cannot exist where there are no sound arms".[24] That is, a powerful agency of force provides the necessary foundation for the establishment of good laws. In this sense, the control of force is even more important than just laws; as he expresses it in one of his celebrated formulations, "all armed prophets are victorious and the unarmed destroyed."[25] Similarly, it is better for a ruler to be feared than be loved "for love is held by a chain of obligation which, since men

[21] Ibid.

[22] Niccolò Machiavelli, *The Prince and Other Political Writings* [1513] (London: Dent, 1995), 89.

[23] Leo Strauss, *Thoughts on Machiavelli* (Chicago: University of Chicago Press, 1958), 9.

[24] Machiavelli, above n. 22, 77.

[25] Ibid. 55.

are bad, is broken at every opportunity for personal gain" whereas fear "is maintained by a dread of punishment which will never desert you".[26] Consequently, although it is praiseworthy to rule with integrity, "experience shows that nowadays those princes who have accomplished great things have had little respect for keeping their word . . . [and] they have overcome those who have preferred honesty".[27]

Machiavelli's basic point is that although we may conceive of two basic ways of ruling—through the use of law and through the use of force—the first, which is rooted in human ideals, is generally not sufficient and rulers must occasionally have recourse to the second, which is based on the animal instinct. The mark of a good ruler, then, is the ability to know how to make good use of both the human and the animal impulse. In making this point, he draws on the legends of ancient Greece and notes that Achilles had been sent to Chiron the Centaur for his education: being half-man and half-beast, the Centaur was well-equipped to teach aspiring rulers how to imitate both natures. A ruler should learn that it is necessary on occasions to act the part of a beast and, in emulating their qualities, Machiavelli suggests that the lion and the fox—symbolizing courage and cunning—provide the appropriate models for political conduct. The ideal ruler must be able to blend the characteristics of each. Since "the lion cannot defend itself from traps and the fox cannot defend itself from wolves", the ruler must be a fox to enable him to find out the snares, and a lion in order to terrify the wolves.[28] Although Machiavelli believes that rulers should govern in accordance with the law,[29] this is essentially a prudential precept and the question of "whether the prince should obey moral law therefore becomes a discussion of when he should obey it."[30]

In *The Discourses*, these insights are developed to consider the form which the State might take if liberty is to be preserved. Following Aristotle,[31] Machiavelli accepts that there are three basic forms of government: *principality* (rule of the one), *aristocracy* (rule of the few) and *democracy* (rule of the many). But he also notes that every state is

---

[26] Machiavelli, above n. 22, 94.

[27] Ibid. 96.

[28] Ibid.

[29] Machiavelli, *The Discourses* above n. 20, Bk III, ch. 5: "princes should learn . . . that they begin to lose their state the moment they begin to break the laws and to disregard the ancient traditions and customs under which men have long lived."

[30] J.G.A. Pocock, *The Machiavellian Moment: Florentine Political Thought and the Atlantic Republican Tradition* (Princeton: Princeton U.P., 1975), 177.

[31] Cf. Aristotle, above n. 1, Bks IV–VI.

divided into an upper and lower class who, being generally placed in opposing factions, will often work against one another to corrupt the established constitutional order. Through such processes, he suggests, *principality* occasionally degenerates into *tyranny*, *aristocracy* is transformed into *oligarchy*, and *democracy* converted into *anarchy*. How, Machiavelli asks, can the pursuit of the common good be prevented from being subordinated to factional interests, thereby preserving liberty? His answer, in the words of Quentin Skinner, is "to frame the laws relating to the constitution in such a way as to engineer a tensely-balanced equilibrium between these opposed social forces, one in which all the parties remain involved in the business of government, and each 'keeps watch over the other' in order to forestall both 'the rich men's arrogance' and 'the people's licence' ".[32] This is an early expression of the principle of "mixed government" as well as a blueprint for the maxim that the price of liberty is eternal vigilance. But, most importantly for present purposes, Machiavelli here articulates the idea that in order to conserve the well-being of the commonwealth, the maintenance and control of political tensions are more fundamental than the precise legal form of the constitution.

MACHIAVELLI'S LEGACY

It is often suggested that Machiavelli's ideas form a gateway to modern thought.[33] In *The Politics*, Aristotle had suggested that a good person is not identical to a good citizen, and Machiavelli's work elaborates on that basic theme. But, in explicating that idea, he presents us with a more realistic notion of politics. In Machiavelli's framework, politics has not only torn itself free of religious and metaphysical ideas, but also attains autonomy quite apart from other aspects of social, ethical and cultural life. Governance is a distinctive type of activity, and politics is the mode through which the business of government is effectively conducted. When engaging in this type of activity, rulers may, for the purpose of promoting the common good, be obliged to exercise guile and cunning and engage in duplicitous practices. We really do not, he suggests, have much choice in the matter. We can choose to lead a wholly private life in which we will be governed by precepts of personal moral-

---

[32] Quentin Skinner, *Machiavelli* (Oxford: Oxford U.P., 1981), 74; see Machiavelli, above n. 20, Bk I, esp. chs 1–10.

[33] See Ernst Cassirer, *The Myth of the State* (New Haven: Yale U.P., 1946), 140.

ity. But if we decide to enter the political arena and participate in the business of governing the State, then we are entering a particular sphere of public life in which special rules of engagement apply. The distinctive nature of these precepts was voiced by Talleyrand who, after hearing that Napoleon had ordered the execution of the Duke of Enghien, is supposed to have commented: "It's more than a crime, it's a mistake!".[34]

In *The Republic*, Plato analysed the ideal principles on which a just State should be founded, and it is precisely this ideal element in Plato which Machiavelli suppresses. Machiavelli "understood political theory as a study of the concrete behaviour of individuals and groups, and of peoples in their specific historical and cultural context, with their passions, their desires, and their memories."[35] Consequently, he does not build any grand ethical principles of justice or law into his account of the State; the art of politics which he articulates has little room for formal principles of justice. In his words, "since the distance between how one lives and how one should live is so great, he who discards what he does for what he should do, usually learns how to ruin rather than maintain himself".[36] Machiavelli's sense of political virtue is certainly linked to the need to adhere to the rule of law. But rulers respect the law not because of normative or ethical considerations but as a matter of prudence. They obey law because it is politically advisable for them to do so.

Drawing on this specific strand of his thought, some commentators have suggested that Machiavelli is one of the principal founders of modern political science. "We are much beholden to Machiavelli", noted Francis Bacon, "who openly and unfeignedly declares and describes what men do, and not what they ought to do."[37] Ernst Cassirer suggests that Machiavelli's political science and Galileo's natural science are based on a common principle, in that both "start from the axiom of the uniformity and homogeneity of nature" and, just as natural events follow the same invariable laws, so also do we find that in politics "all ages are of the same fundamental structure".[38] So Machiavelli studies political actions in the way a scientist studies chemical and physical reactions; just as Galileo had destroyed the medieval

---

[34] Ernst Cassirer, above n. 33, 146.

[35] Maurizio Viroli, *Machiavelli* (Oxford: Oxford U.P., 1998), 9.

[36] Machiavelli, *The Prince*, above n. 22, 89.

[37] Francis Bacon, *De Augmentis Scientarium* [1605] in his *Works* James Spedding ed. (London: Longman, 1858), vol. V, 17.

[38] Ernst Cassirer, above n. 33, 156.

belief structure which was rooted in the distinction between a higher and lower world, so too did Machiavelli destroy the ideal of a Christian commonwealth on earth.

This view of Machiavelli as the founder of political science can, nevertheless, be exaggerated. Maurizio Viroli convincingly argues that Machiavelli practised political theory "not as the work of a philosopher, nor as the work of a scientist, but as the work of an orator"; his objective was "to offer counsel and advice on the most useful way to . . . govern, . . . not to identify political or moral truths, and even less to frame universal laws of politics based upon observation of facts".[39] The rhetorical element cannot be ignored in Machiavelli's work.[40] It is precisely this element which Berlin captures in his suggestion that Machiavelli's genius does not lie in his amoral or scientific treatment of politics, but in his identification of the virtues of Christianity and the pagan world as two opposing value systems. Machiavelli's aim was to promote the values of the pagan world and to advocate a return to those ambitious and bold ideas of ancient Rome, and in this sense he promoted a form of politics founded on the ideals of civic humanism.[41] But he did not argue that one value system is ethically superior to the other and he offered no over-arching normative criterion for determining choice between the two, and this, Berlin argues, is the source of his true originality: "if we choose forms of life because we believe in them, because we take them for granted, or, upon examination, find that we are morally unprepared to live in any other way (although others choose differently) . . . then a picture emerges different from that constructed round the ancient principle that there is only one good for men".[42] And if we admit the possibility of two equally valid modes of being, then we admit the possibility there could be several.

Following Berlin, we might say that Machiavelli, by breaking off the search for one true answer to the question of how we should live, made us aware of "the necessity of having to make agonizing choices between incompatible alternatives in public and in private life (for the two could

---

[39] Viroli, above n. 35, 112.

[40] See Victoria Kahn, *Machiavellian Rhetoric: From Counter-Reformation to Milton* (Princeton: Princeton U.P., 1994).

[41] See Pocock, above n. 30; Quentin Skinner, *The Foundations of Modern Political Thought* (Cambridge: Cambridge U.P., 1978) vol. 1, ch. 6. Others, however, having noted his turn to the values of the ancient world, have emphasized the interpretation of Machiavelli as a reviver of the *arcana imperii*, or ancient mysteries of statecraft. See Peter S. Donaldson, *Machiavelli and Mystery of State* (Cambridge: Cambridge U.P., 1988).

[42] Berlin, above n. 19, 78.

not, it became obvious, be genuinely kept distinct)".[43] Moral and political values are irreducibly plural and conflicts between them are inevitable. Once this is recognized and accepted, the victory of one political ideology over another seems improbable. Consequently, although it was not his intention, Machiavelli's work provides the basis for the toleration of opposing views which has become a defining characteristic of a modern, liberal society.

In a celebrated statement, Friedrich Meinecke argued that "Machiavelli's theory was a sword which was plunged into the flank of the body politic of Western humanity, causing it to shriek and to rear up."[44] The wound that was inflicted was, in part, to the Christian church's earthly claims; it has, for example, been claimed that Machiavelli's teachings were the inspiration behind Henry VIII's decision to break with Rome.[45] More importantly though, Machiavelli's legacy has been to undermine the claims of all political ideologies to have found the scientific key which would unlock the door to utopia. Politics becomes a vital feature of modern life precisely because of the impossibility of establishing a world without antagonism and which is freed from dispute over competing conceptions of the good life. We exist in a world in which we find "a plurality of values not structured hierarchically", a world which "entails the permanent possibility of inescapable conflict between values".[46] Humans are not governed solely by reason, since the life of the mind "always depends on much that has not been subject to critical scrutiny by our intellect".[47] For Machiavelli, *fortuna* was an indispensable element in life. In a modern reformulation, we might say that we lack the scales to be able scientifically to weigh the various competing values in the balance.

This type of approach generates a distinctive view of politics. Politics can be understood to be rooted in what might be termed "agonistic pluralism". This term, derived from the Greek word *agon* denoting contest or competition, means that, since there is an irreducible diversity of basic values, politics must concern itself with the business of making choices between rival, sometimes incommensurable, goods and in circumstances for which there is no overarching rational or objective

[43] Berlin, above n. 19, 79.
[44] Friedrich Meinecke, *Machiavellism: The Doctrine of Raison d'Etat and its place in Modern History* [1924] (London: Routledge & Kegan Paul, 1957), 49.
[45] See Donaldson, above n. 41, 1.
[46] Isaiah Berlin, *The Crooked Timber of Humanity* (London: John Murray, 1990), 80.
[47] John Gray, *Enlightenment's Wake: Politics and Culture at the Close of the Modern Age* (London: Routledge, 1995), 27.

standard or principle for resolving that dispute.[48] Politics is ineluctably located within an arena of antagonism and is the activity through which these antagonisms are managed. Furthermore, although conflict and dissension may seem to threaten cohesion within the State, they are in fact the conditions under which the State is able to thrive.[49] The common theme in the thinking of Aristotle, Fortescue and Machiavelli is that, notwithstanding the vast differences in the societies about which they are writing, politics remains intimately connected to dispute, debate and some notion of self-government, and this tradition is maintained today in a revival of the idea that *deliberation*, rather than simply voting, provides the key aspect of democratic decision-making.[50]

[48] See Chantal Mouffe, *The Return of the Political* (London, Verso, 1993); Gray, ibid. ch. 6.

[49] See F.R. Ankersmit, *Aesthetic Politics: Political Philosophy Beyond Fact and Value* (Stanford, Calif.: Stanford U.P., 1996), 172.

[50] See Jon Elster (ed.), *Deliberative Democracy* (Cambridge: Cambridge U.P., 1998).

9

Sovereignty

SOVEREIGNTY IS THE main organizational principle on which modern political systems are founded. Sovereignty comes about when a group of people within a defined territory are moulded into an orderly cohesion by the establishment of a governing authority which is able to exercise absolute political power within that community. Such a definition links the concept to the emergence of the State. Today, the concept also underpins the international order; it is only since the emergence of sovereign states, for example, that the conduct of international politics can properly be said to have come into existence. Sovereignty thus identifies both the condition of political independence and provides the prop by which many political practices, domestic and international, are sustained. Consequently, the emergence of the State based on the principle of sovereignty is commonly treated in modern political science as "the predominant source of the individual's moral and legal valuations and the ultimate point of reference for his secular loyalties" and the preservation of sovereignty is seen as being the "foremost political concern in international affairs."[1] The State founded on the principle of sovereignty provides the framework through which politics, in the sense explored in the previous chapter, is conducted. In this chapter, I propose to take the inquiry further by focusing on the meaning of this basic principle of sovereignty.

During the sixteenth century, Jean Bodin defined sovereignty as the supreme power which is exercised over citizens and subjects, unrestrained by law. This formulation suggests that sovereignty is closely linked to power and is an essentially empirical phenomenon. This is the approach—sovereignty as the ability to bring about intended effects—which was still being followed by most nineteenth-century jurists. John Austin, for example, defined the sovereign as "a *determinate* human superior, *not* in a habit of obedience to a like superior, receiv[ing] *habitual* obedience from the *bulk* of a given society."[2] During the

---

[1] H.J. Morgenthau, *Politics Among Nations* (New York: Knopf, 6th edn. 1985), 345.
[2] John Austin, *The Province of Jurisprudence Determined* [1832] Wilfrid E. Rumble ed. (Cambridge: Cambridge U.P., 1995), 166 (emphases in original).

course of the nineteenth century, however, legal and political conceptions of sovereignty gradually became differentiated.[3] Sovereignty as a
legal concept was viewed as a more limited idea: it is a normative construct, a concept created by law and concerned only with law. This
normative conception of legal sovereignty received its clearest expression in the work of Hans Kelsen, who defined sovereignty as "the pre-
supposed assumption of a system of norms . . . whose validity is not to
be derived from a superior order".[4] In this formulation, sovereignty is
simply a hypothesis which provides the working principle of a legal
order.

Making sovereignty the basis of the legal order rather begs the question of how it is founded in political practice. Kelsen argued that the
dualism of law and state which underpins the idea of sovereignty "performs an ideological function of extraordinary significance". Legal
theory seems to assume both that "the state, as a collective unity that is
originally the subject of will and action, exists independently of, and
even prior to, the law" and also that the State "is a presupposition of
the law . . . beholden to the law, because obligated and granted rights
by the law".[5] Most British lawyers, not sharing the Germanic taste for
abstract theorization, have come to treat legal sovereignty simply as a
"fact".[6] But, for our purposes, this is an evasion of the issue. Law, like
politics, may indeed be rooted ultimately in questions of power and
authority, but sovereignty expresses a particular way in which power is
wielded by rulers and conceded by the ruled. In examining the relationship between law and politics, we need to analyse how this type of
power relationship came to be expressed through the concept of sovereignty. To do so, we must examine the origins of the concept, consider
how the political and legal aspects have come to be differentiated, and
assess the concept's contemporary relevance. This is a complex

[3] See, e.g., A.V. Dicey, *An Introduction to the Study of the Law of the Constitution*
[1885] (London: Macmillan, 8th edn. 1915), 72; James Bryce, *Studies in History and
Jurisprudence* vol. 2 (Oxford: Clarendon Press, 1901), 51. Bryce contrasts legal sovereignty, which vests in "the person (or body) to whose directions the law attributes legal
force" from the "practical sovereign" or ruler, that "person (or body of persons) who can
make his (or their) will prevail whether with the law or against the law."
[4] Hans Kelsen, "Sovereignty and International Law" in W.J. Stankiewicz (ed.), *In
Defense of Sovereignty* (New York: Oxford U.P., 1969), 115, 119.
[5] Hans Kelsen, *Introduction to the Problems of Legal Theory* (trans. of first edn.
[1934] of *Reine Rechtslehre* by Bonnie L. Paulson and Stanley L. Paulson) (Oxford:
Clarendon Press, 1992), 96–7.
[6] For Dicey sovereignty was "a legal fact": Dicey, above n. 3, 37. In an influential article Sir William Wade treats it as a "political fact": H.W.R Wade, "The basis for legal sovereignty" 1955 *Cambridge Law Journal* 172.

inquiry, but one thing is clear: the concept of sovereignty is inextricably bound up with the emergence of the modern idea of the State.

THE EMERGENCE OF THE MODERN IDEA OF THE STATE

It has been suggested by Clifford Geertz that the idea of the State contains at least three themes: first, status or *estate*, in the sense of station, standing or rank; secondly, *stateliness* with its connotations of display, dignity, presence or pomp; and, thirdly, *statecraft*, by which is meant dominion, regnancy, mastery or governance.[7] Although the modern idea of the State is most closely associated with the third of these meanings, Geertz reminds us not only that this aspect was the latest to emerge through history, but also that it grew out of the former themes. If we are to understand the nature of the modern State we should know something about this process.

During the Middle Ages, the term *status* referred mainly to a condition of stability. The maintenance of the state of the realm (*status regni*) was regarded as being the ultimate right and duty of the king.[8] Furthermore, since the quality of *stateliness* was inherent in the idea of kingship, the presence of majesty itself operated as an ordering force. But medieval society did not recognize this ultimate right as an abstract and absolute power. Within medieval Christian thought, mankind was conceived as an organism, or mystical body, with Christ at its head and the Church, the *Ecclesia*, operating as an indivisible unity which gave expression to a heavenly pattern—the chain of being—and which guided humans from their transitory, earthly existence towards salvation and eternal life.[9] The Church, invoking the authority of the Gospels,[10] claimed the supreme power and, when eventually it occurred, the struggle between Church and State took place primarily over the appropriate spheres of influence between *sacerdotium* and

---

[7] Clifford Geertz, *Negara: The Theatre State in Nineteenth-Century Bali* (Princeton: Princeton U.P., 1980), 121.

[8] See H.C. Dowdall, "The Word 'State'" (1923) 39 *Law Quarterly Review* 98, 101; Gaines Post, *Studies in Medieval Legal Thought* (Princeton: Princeton U.P., 1964), ch. VI.

[9] Otto Gierke, *Political Theories of the Middle Age*, F.W. Maitland trans. (Cambridge: Cambridge U.P., 1900), 9–37.

[10] Matthew, 16: 18–19: "And I say unto thee, that thou art Peter and upon this rock I will build my church . . . And I will give unto thee the keys of the kingdom of heaven: and whatsoever thou shalt bind on earth shall be bound in heaven: and whatsoever thou shalt loose on earth shall be loosed in heaven."

imperium, between ecclesiastical and secular power. Hardly surprisingly, during the course of this struggle monarchs tried to bolster their authority by borrowing all the symbols and metaphors—from the sacramental rites of coronation through to the claims of "the divine right of kings"—which the Church had deployed.[11] As Carl Schmitt expressed it: "All significant concepts of the modern theory of the State are secularized theological concepts".[12]

As the kings and princes of Europe achieved success in resisting both the claims of the Church and the jurisdictional authority of the Holy Roman Empire,[13] the charismatic facets of political leadership were gradually superseded and a more impersonal conception of rulership emerged. In England this manifested itself in a distinction which was drawn between the king and his Crown: while the king referred to the monarch in his personal capacity, the idea of the Crown meant the sovereignty of the entire community of the realm. This distinction gave rise to the legal doctrine of the king's two bodies: that the king "has in him two bodies, viz, a body natural, and a body politic" and that his body politic "is a body that cannot be seen or handled, consisting of policy and government, and constituted for the direction of the people, and the management of the public-weal".[14] This differentiation was not consistently maintained, however, especially since it was generally accepted that, though distinct, the king and the Crown were also inseparable. As Maitland put it, the reign of Henry VIII "was not the time when the king's lands could be severed from the nation's lands, the king's wealth from the common wealth, or even the king's power from the power of the State."[15]

The main impetus for forging a more impersonal conception of rulership came from the growth of new political formations in Europe. Of particular significance was the emergence after the twelfth century of the Italian self-governing republics. Debates were conducted throughout the period of the Renaissance concerning which type of

[11] See E.H. Kantorowicz, *The King's Two Bodies: A Study in Mediaeval Political Theology* (Princeton: Princeton U.P., 1957); Francis Oakley, *Omnipotence, Covenant and Order: An Excursion in the History of Ideas from Abelard to Leibniz* (Ithaca: Cornell U.P., 1984).

[12] Carl Schmitt, *Political Theology: Four Chapters on the Concept of Sovereignty*, G. Schwab trans. (Boston: MIT Press, 1985), 36.

[13] See Walter Ullmann, "The development of the medieval idea of sovereignty" (1949) 64 *English Historical Rev.* 1.

[14] *Case of the Duchy of Lancaster* (1561) 1 Plowden 212, 213.

[15] F.W. Maitland, "The Crown as Corporation" [1901] in his *Collected Papers, vol. III* H.A.L. Fisher ed. (Cambridge: Cambridge U.P., 1911) 244, 248–9.

government—elective or hereditary—was likely to be the best state. During the course of these debates, the term *status* came to refer not only to the condition of princes but also to represent particular systems of government. The term was therefore employed to identify the general framework of government through which order within political communities was maintained. This development came about, Quentin Skinner maintains, not because of the evolution of legal theories about the *status* of kings but rather as a result of the sort of practical political reasoning of which Machiavelli's work is exemplary. It is within this corpus of republican writing that we first encounter recognition of the idea of a governmental authority as an entity distinct from those who happen to have control of it.[16]

Although republican writers helped to formulate an understanding of the State as an impersonal apparatus which could be distinguished from those who exercise its powers, this was only a preliminary stage in the evolution of the modern idea of the State. Republican writers made no comparable distinction between the powers of the State and those of citizens; for these theorists, the State was equated with its citizens. Skinner argues, however, that the modern State has a "doubly impersonal character" and, in addition to differentiating between the apparatus and the personality of those exercising the powers, the State must also be distinguished from society. This latter aspect was most clearly highlighted by those early-modern political theorists who were critical of the idea that sovereignty in reality vests in the people. And amongst these theorists, the work of Thomas Hobbes is particularly important.

Whilst, as we have seen,[17] Hobbes treats government as having been based on an original contract of the people, he is unusual in viewing the power of the State as a form of alienation rather than delegation. Although the people covenant with one another to establish the Sovereign, the Sovereign does not make any covenant with his subjects. Rather, "that great Leviathan . . . hath the use of so much power and strength conferred on him, that by terror thereof, he is enabled to conform the wills of them all, to peace at home and mutual aid against their enemies abroad".[18] Although Hobbes's treatment seems

---

[16] See Quentin Skinner, "The State" in T. Ball, J. Farr & R.L. Hanson (eds), *Political Innovation and Conceptual Change* (Cambridge: Cambridge U.P., 1989), 90; Quentin Skinner, *The Foundations of Modern Political Thought. Vol. 1 The Renaissance* (Cambridge: Cambridge U.P., 1978), chs.1–3.

[17] Ch. 2 above, 27.

[18] Thomas Hobbes, *Leviathan* [1651] Richard Tuck ed. (Cambridge: Cambridge U.P., 1996), 122, 120–1.

absolutist in form, Skinner stresses it must not be confused with the views of divine right theorists; the latter tended to obliterate the distinction between the office and person of the king and Hobbes is unequivocal in maintaining that the sovereign's powers are never personal but belong wholly to his status as holder of "the office of sovereign".[19]

In this great work of Hobbes, a study of the "matter, form and power of a Commonwealth . . . or State",[20] we arrive at a modern conception of the State as a political authority differentiated not only from the people who originally established it but also from the personality of those office-holders for the time being. For Hobbes, the State's power to command is absolute. All notions of charisma, dignity and honour are subsumed within the idea of power; honour is simply "an argument and sign of power".[21] It is Hobbes, then, "who first speaks, systematically and unapologetically, in the abstract and unmodulated tones of the modern theorist of the state."[22] Hobbes completes the process which Machiavelli and his Italian contemporaries had started.

THE FOUNDATIONS OF POLITICAL ORDER

During the Middle Ages, sovereignty was a mark of superiority signified through some divine source. With the emergence of the modern idea of the State, however, political power becomes differentiated from heavenly authority, and sovereignty is transformed into a symbol of an earthly, depersonalized authority.[23] This transformation occurs alongside the gradual rejection of the idea that the socio-political order was

---

[19] Hobbes, above n. 18, ch. 30.

[20] Ibid. 1, 9.

[21] Ibid. 65.

[22] Skinner, "The State", above n. 16, 126.

[23] Hobbes expresses this in his statement that both swords—that of justice as well as war—belong to the sovereign: see Ch. 4 above, 60. Here Hobbes signals his rejection of the medieval doctrine of two swords, the spiritual and the temporal, which vested in the Church and the prince. The doctrine is said to derive from Luke: "And they said, Lord, behold, here are two swords. And he said unto them, It is enough." (Luke, 22:38). In *Unam Sanctum*, his famous bull of 1302, Pope Boniface VIII, claimed: "Both then are in the power of the Church, the material sword and the spiritual. But the one is exercised for the church, the other by the church, the one by the hand of the priest, the other by the hand of kings and soldiers, though at the will and sufferance of the priest. One sword ought to be under the other and the temporal authority subject to the spiritual": see Brian Tierney, *The Crisis of Church and State, 1050–1300* (Englewood Cliffs, NJ: Prentice Hall, 1964), 188, 189.

a natural organism linked to a chain of being. How then could the political order be justified? In the sixteenth century, Bodin had asserted that sovereignty is the "highest power of command" and constitutes "the absolute and perpetual power of a commonwealth".[24] In this definition, sovereignty becomes the basic principle of ordering and the foundation on which a system of states rests. Bodin, however, still maintained the old world order; without God at apex of his system, there could be no sovereignty.[25] The breakthrough—the establishment of sovereignty as the founding principle for secular political power— was decisively achieved by Hobbes.

Taking his cue from the revolution in the natural sciences, Hobbes freely made use of the modern languages of science and mathematics. Many have remarked, as indeed did Hobbes himself,[26] that he was the first to apply the methods of the natural sciences to the study of social and political phenomena. Hobbes conceives of human action, for example, in terms of physical matter in motion[27] and suggests that reason "is nothing but *reckoning* (that is, adding and subtracting) of the consequences of general names agreed upon for the *marking* and *signifying* of our thoughts".[28] Nevertheless, he is best understood as a theorist who, though adopting scientific idiom, is really devising a new form of rhetoric.[29] Hobbes certainly acknowledges the primacy of language: "The most noble and profitable invention was that of speech . . . whereby men register their thoughts . . . declare them to one another for mutual utility and conversation" and "without which there has been amongst men neither commonwealth, nor society, nor contract,

---

[24] Jean Bodin, *Six livres de la république* [1576], Bk I, ch. 8. See Bodin, *On Sovereignty*, Julian H. Franklin ed. (Cambridge: Cambridge U.P., 1992), 1.

[25] Ibid. 10: "If we say that to have absolute power is not to be subject to any law at all, no prince of this world will be sovereign, since every earthly prince is subject to the laws of God and of nature and to various human laws that are common to all peoples."

[26] In *Elements of Philosophy*, written in 1655, Hobbes suggests that the scientific study of politics is "no older . . . than my own book *De Cive*". See *The English Works of Thomas Hobbes of Malmesbury*, Sir William Molesworth ed. (London: John Bohn, 1839), vol. I, ix.

[27] Hobbes, above n. 18, 9: "For what is the *heart*, but a *spring*; and the *nerves*, but so many *strings*; and the *joints*, but so many *wheels* . . .".

[28] Ibid. 32 (emphasis in original).

[29] See Quentin Skinner, *Reason and Rhetoric in the Philosophy of Hobbes* (Cambridge: Cambridge U.P., 1996), ch. 9, which argues that in *Leviathan* Hobbes attempts to bring together the methods of science with the rhetorical techniques of Renaissance humanism. See also David Johnston, *The Rhetoric of Leviathan: Thomas Hobbes and the Politics of Cultural Transformation* (Princeton: Princeton U.P., 1986).

nor peace."[30] For Hobbes, the problem is that harmonious relations between words and things are no longer the result of divine order: "all this language gotten ... by Adam and his posterity was lost again at the tower of Babel, when by the hand of God, every man was stricken for his rebellion, with an oblivion of his former language."[31] Hobbes's conception of life in a state of nature can be read as an extension of the Babel story.[32]

Through his depiction of life in a state of nature, Hobbes deliberately rouses our fear of death and draws on our instincts for safety and self-preservation. But this device is used not only to justify vesting absolute power in a sovereign authority. The quest for security, peace and order is also closely linked to the search for certainty in language. Without a common vocabulary, there can be no social order. And without a sovereign power there can be no authoritative vocabulary, since "Covenants, without the Sword, are but Words, and of no strength to secure a man at all".[33]

For Hobbes, there can be no order without an orderer. He uses the story of the state of nature primarily as a device which will enable us rationally to consent to the establishment of a political order in which some person or body is vested with an absolute power. Consequently, "by Art is created that great *Leviathan* called a *Commonwealth* or *State*".[34] This "mortal god", however, is not dependent for the source of its authority on any conception of divine law or heavenly revelation. Instead, Hobbes finds justification for this political order in the human condition itself. Political life, he suggests, is a life of emotions and passions. No mere effort of abstract thought is able to rule these passions, or to set them definite boundaries, or to direct them to a rational end. Since "the passions of men are commonly more potent than their reason",[35] it is authority, not wisdom, which is needed. It is for this reason that Hobbes ambiguously calls the sovereign Leviathan, the name given to the monster of the deep who appears in the book of Job as "king of all the children of pride".[36]

In *Leviathan*, Hobbes gradually moves away from the metaphor of the body politic to that of the State as an artificial construct. At the

[30] Hobbes, above n. 18, 24.
[31] Ibid. 25.
[32] See Ch. 2 above, 23, 27.
[33] Hobbes, above n. 18, 117.
[34] Ibid. 9.
[35] Ibid. 131.
[36] Job 41: 34. See ibid. 221.

beginning, he uses the metaphor of the sovereign as the "artificial soul" giving "life and motion to the whole body"[37] and he develops the metaphor, with government Ministers being analogized to "the nerves and tendons that move the several limbs of a body natural", judges being compared to "the organs of Voice in a Body natural", and the commonwealth mentioned as being potentially afflicted by infirmities or diseases.[38] But Hobbes increasingly allows mechanical metaphors to take over as he tries to explain the nature of this "artificial man", likening the State to those "engines that move themselves by springs and wheels as doth a watch".[39] The main significance of this changing metaphor rests on his contention that these are human, not God-given, constructs; we construct these devices for the purpose of promoting our own sense of the good.

Hobbes provides us with the basis for a modern language in which we not only express in "scientific" terms the nature of the political order but also make empirical statements about the manner in which states carry on their business. In this idiom, power is the key concept of politics; glory, in the sense used by the ancients, is anathema in a world which conceives of politics as a struggle over interests.[40] This shift towards treating "interests" as the central concern of politics is important. The passion for glory, revenge or honour is displaced by a more calculated focus on such material objectives as self-preservation or the promotion of economic advantage. Even war is "no longer understood as the outcome of providence or blind fate, but as an object of human knowledge and as an instrument of power, susceptible to human control."[41] But above all, the pursuit of interests emerges as a driving force behind the movement for democracy, since an acknowledgement of the legitimacy of the particular interests of citizens provides some indication that, whatever their social status, citizens may have concerns which are worthy of the attention of the State.

---

[37] Hobbes, above n. 18, 9.
[38] Ibid. 167, 169, 228–30.
[39] Ibid. 9.
[40] See A.O. Hirschmann, *The Passions and the Interests: Political Arguments for Capitalism before its Triumph* (Princeton: Princeton U.P., 1977).
[41] Jens Bartleson, *A Genealogy of Sovereignty* (Cambridge: Cambridge U.P., 1995), 110. Bartleson points out that the classic example of this mode of thought is Machiavelli, *The Art of War* [1521].

SOVEREIGNTY AND LAW

During the Middle Ages, it was not obvious that there was any discrete category of human activity which might be labelled "politics". Throughout this period, the business of government was expressed primarily through the language of law, although law here referred to a relatively fluid collection of customary practices.[42] The modern idea of politics evolved at the same time as the emergence of the modern State. The critical link in this development is the identification of the concept of sovereignty. Sovereignty provides the foundation on which the nation-State emerges and thereafter a system of international relations based on the conduct of relations between such states develops. But with the establishment of this modern idea of the sovereign State, we see not only the emergence of politics as a distinctive activity but also a transformation in our understanding of law. Law, in the modern period, comes to be recognized as a human artefact promulgated by a governing authority. To the medieval mind, law took the form of crystallized custom, embodying traditional practices or even some type of natural reason. In the modern world, we think of law primarily as command.

It is Hobbes who makes the decisive break with the ancient world. Against Coke he argues that "it is not Wisdom, but Authority that makes a Law."[43] And against Fortescue he reasons that "Law . . . is not Counsel, but Command".[44] For Hobbes, law is "the Reason of this our Artificial Man the Commonwealth" and it is "his Command that maketh Law".[45] Hobbes in fact defines the sovereign as that person or body with supreme law-making authority. This sovereign cannot be bound by law, in the sense that there is no law that it cannot make or repeal; it is not "possible for any person to be bound to himself, because he that can bind can release".[46] As supreme law-maker, the sovereign is made the sole source of right and wrong.

---

[42] See Walter Ullmann, *A History of Political Thought: the Middle Ages* (Harmondsworth: Penguin, 1965), 15–17.

[43] Thomas Hobbes, *A Dialogue between a Philosopher and a Student of the Common Laws of England* [1681] Joseph Cropsey ed. (Chicago: University of Chicago Press, 1971), 55.

[44] Hobbes, above n. 18, 183.

[45] Ibid. 187.

[46] Ibid. 184.

Hobbes works through his position quite rigorously. The covenant to form a State is an act of mutual agreement in which the parties agree "to appoint one Man or Assembly of Men to bear their Person . . . and therein to submit their Wills . . . to his Judgment".[47] This "person is called Sovereign, and said to have sovereign power; and every one besides, his Subject".[48] Since this sovereign exists to enact laws for the common benefit, any attempt to judge the justice of the law is absurd: "the measure of Good and Evil actions is the Civil Law".[49] That is, a ruler cannot pass a law which infringes the basic precepts of justice, precisely because the measure of justice is supplied by the laws themselves.

It is important not to misconstrue Hobbes. Although an authoritarian, he was no absolutist. The sovereign is absolute in two respects only: first, in requiring the absolute surrender of an individual's natural right in forging the original covenant and, secondly, in the requirement that there be no appeal from the legitimacy of the sovereign's commands.[50] But although a law cannot be unjust, Hobbes did accept the idea of a good law. "By a Good Law", he suggests, "I mean not a Just Law: for no Law can be Unjust". Rather, good laws should be understood by reference to their purpose. That is, laws do not exist "to bind the people from all voluntary actions; but to direct and keep them in such a motion, as not to hurt themselves by their own impetuous desires, rashness or indiscretion; as hedges are set, not to stop travellers, but to keep them in the way." He also recognizes that "unnecessary laws are not good laws."[51] Hobbes implies that the sovereign should enact only those rules which are required for the maintenance of order and the promotion of the common benefit. Citizens remain free to pursue their "voluntary actions" in those spheres of life left unregulated by the sovereign's commands. Civil liberty thus depends "on the silence of the law". That is, "in cases where the Sovereign has prescribed no rule, there the subject hath the liberty to do, or forbear, according to his own discretion".[52] Where law ends, it might be said, there liberty begins.

[47] Hobbes, above n. 18, 120.
[48] Ibid. 121.
[49] Ibid. 223.
[50] See Michael Oakeshott, "Introduction" to Hobbes, *Leviathan* (Oxford: Blackwell, 1946), lvi–lvii.
[51] Hobbes, above n. 18, 239–40.
[52] Ibid. 152.

THE BRITISH STATE TRADITION

Although Hobbes was a relatively neglected figure in the eighteenth century, his influence was restored in the nineteenth. This rehabilitation was achieved mainly through the work of Bentham, James Mill, Austin, Dicey and Pollock,[53] writers who expressed little interest in the contractarian and egalitarian aspects of Hobbes but who devised their theories of government mainly from "habits of obedience" and the principle of utility. These writers found Hobbes of value mainly because of his attack on the idea of inalienable rights, an idea which as positivistic utilitarians they found offensive. "The formula of the greatest happiness", wrote Pollock, "is made a hook to put in the nostrils of Leviathan, that he may be tamed and harnessed to the chariot of utility."[54] Such "public moralists"[55] as Dicey and Pollock felt a particular need for the idea of an absolute sovereign authority. Their objectives, it would scarcely be going too far to say, were to place the law above criticism, and in this sense Hobbes served as a useful vehicle for bolstering Victorian conservatism. This achievement, Mark Francis comments, would be amusing were it not one of their legacies to the twentieth century. "Their absolute sovereign is still ours", he concludes, "and though the nineteenth century has long since ceased to dominate scholars of Hobbes, it still seems to affect the thought of more ordinary men, such as jurists and politicians."[56] It is, of course, the beliefs of jurists and politicians with which we are primarily concerned.

Amongst the jurists, Dicey has been pre-eminent. The entire thrust of his work had been to demonstrate that "Parliament does constitute such a supreme legislative authority or sovereign power as, according

[53] See, e.g., John Austin, above n. 2, 231n: "I know of no other writer (excepting our great contemporary Jeremy Bentham) who has uttered so many truths, at once new and important, concerning the necessary structure of supreme political government, and the larger of the necessary distinctions implied by positive law."

[54] Sir Frederick Pollock, *An Introduction to the History of the Science of Politics* (London: Macmillan, 1906), 101.

[55] See Stefan Collini, *Public Moralists: Political Thought and Intellectual Life in Britain, 1850–1930* (Oxford: Clarendon Press, 1991). Collini uses the phrase "public moralists" to refer to a distinctive group of writers who, being integrated into the governing élite of society, spoke with the confidence of those who have the ear of the important audience (ibid. 58).

[56] Mark Francis, "The Nineteenth Century Theory of Sovereignty and Thomas Hobbes" (1980) 1 *History of Political Thought* 517, 540.

to Austin and other jurists, must exist in every civilised state."⁵⁷ The sovereignty of the Queen-in-Parliament is set in place as the fundamental principle on which the British constitution rests, and this means that Parliament has "the right to make or unmake any law whatsoever; and, further, that no person or body is recognised . . . as having the right to override or set aside the legislation of Parliament."⁵⁸ It follows, as the judiciary recognized, that judges sit "as servants of the Queen and the legislature" and that "so long as [an Act of Parliament] exists as law, the courts are bound to obey it".⁵⁹ This notion of Parliamentary sovereignty has formed the bedrock of British constitutional law and practice ever since.

The achievement of the Victorian jurists, as Pollock realized, was to have "separated the actual existence and authority of the government from the foundations and reasons of government."⁶⁰ By the late nineteenth century, the British State had assumed its form through a combination of conquest, treaty, Acts of Parliament and rebellion, and it maintained an extensive Empire overseas. Given this elaborate process of state formation, it seemed highly unlikely that any political principle would provide a legitimating foundation.⁶¹ States are invariably constituted from above by the governing classes; they are not established from the bottom up. The facts of authority and obedience generally provide their own justification. Dicey sought to avoid the entanglement of lawyers in these contentious political issues by drawing a clear conceptual distinction between legal and political sovereignty. All that lawyers are required to acknowledge is the fact of legal sovereignty, the unlimited law-making power vested in the Queen-in-Parliament.

Victorian jurists did, nevertheless, accept the importance of the political question of where, within this corporate or compound sovereign authority, political power actually resides. These writers generally remained unimpressed by those, such as Montesquieu and De Lolme, who had emphasized the checks and balances within formal constitutional arrangements. Recognizing that a distinction had to be drawn

⁵⁷ Dicey, above n. 3, 59.
⁵⁸ Ibid. 37–8.
⁵⁹ *Lee v. Bude & Torrington Junction Rly Co.* (1871) LR 6 CP 582, *per* Willes J.
⁶⁰ Pollock, above n. 54, 105.
⁶¹ See Michael Oakeshott, "On the Character of a Modern European State" in his *On Human Conduct* (Oxford: Oxford U.P., 1975), 185, 191: "The claims of governments to authority have been supported, for the most part, by the most implausible and gimcrack beliefs which few can find convincing for more than five minutes together and which bear little or no relation to the governments concerned: 'the sovereignty of the people' or of 'the nation', 'democracy', 'majority rule', 'participation' etc."

between the dignified parts of the constitution, "those which excite and preserve the reverence of the population", and its efficient parts, "those by which it, in fact, works and rules", the jurists tended to follow Bagehot's line that the "efficient secret of the English constitution" is that of "the close union, the nearly complete fusion, of the executive and legislative powers."[62] As Pollock put it, the "machine works as well as it does, not because the powers are balanced, but because in the last resort there is only one power . . . the British constitution in its modern form gives the practical sovereignty to the majority of the House of Commons."[63]

Although the Victorian jurists maintained a formal distinction between legal and political conceptions of sovereignty, there seems little doubt that this fundamental legal principle remained inextricably linked to a deep-seated political belief in the need for a strong central power able to make authoritative decisions. The clearest evidence is seen in Dicey's tenacious fight against Irish Home Rule,[64] in which he excoriated federalism as being inimical to the English way, leading to weak government. "Under all the formality, the antiquarianism, the shams of the British constitution", he noted, "there lies an element of power which has been the true source of its life and growth. This secret source of strength is the absolute omnipotence, the sovereignty of Parliament."[65] Federalism, he contended, undermines parliamentary sovereignty and "deprives English institutions of their elasticity, their strength, and their life; it weakens the Executive at home, and lessens the power of the country to resist foreign attack."[66] Right and capac-

---

[62] Walter Bagehot, *The English Constitution* [1867] R.H.S. Crossman ed. (London: Collins, 1963), 61, 65.

[63] Pollock, above n. 54, 108. See also Dicey, above n. 3, 425: "if Parliament be in the eye of the law a supreme legislature, the essence of representative government is, that the legislature should represent or give effect to the will of the political sovereign, *i.e.* of the electoral body, or of the nation." Dicey's use of such phrases as "the electoral body" or "the nation"—just as others have invoked "the people"—must be treated as a rhetorical device since political power is expressed through established procedures and institutions. The views of Pollock and Dicey may thus be understood as reflections of the Ciceronian formulation of élite rule: "*Auctoritas in Senatu, Potestas in Populo.*"

[64] Dicey wrote a book against each of the three Home Rule Bills: *England's Case against Home Rule* (London: John Murray, 1886); *A Leap in the Dark: A Criticism of the Principles of Home Rule as Illustrated by the Bill of 1893* (London: John Murray, 1893); *A Fool's Paradise: Being a Constitutionalist's Criticism of the Home Rule Bill of 1912* (London: John Murray, 1913).

[65] Dicey, *England's Case against Home Rule*, 161.

[66] A.V. Dicey, "Home Rule from an English Point of View", *Contemporary Review* (July 1882), 66.

ity—the legal and political conceptions of sovereignty—remain inextricably linked.

The work of the Victorian jurists has left an indelible mark on twentieth-century thought. Operating within the frame of the sovereignty principle, law has been conceived as a set of rules laid down by the sovereign authority. Lawyers have certainly retained their respect for the common law method of working from precedent to precedent. But the more ostentatious myths surrounding the common law—particularly those which link the common law tradition to the doctrine of the ancient constitution[67]—have had no modern resonance; at best, they are treated as a rhetorical flourishes which are indulged in on ceremonial occasions. The common law method has been defended as a pragmatic device which accords with the empiricist temperament of the British people,[68] and as such is easily reconciled to the principle of sovereignty. "When long use obtaineth the authority of a law", Hobbes noted, "it is not the length of time that maketh the authority, but the will of the sovereign signified by his silence (for silence is sometimes an argument of consent)".[69]

Although the modern State founded on the sovereignty principle may present itself as an authoritarian system, it would be wrong to view it as hostile to the promotion of liberty. An absolute right to rule should not be equated with the existence of extensive government. When Macbeth orders Banquo's death with the words, "I could with barefaced power sweep him away from my sight and bid my will avouch it," Shakespeare vividly dramatizes Macbeth's dynamic

---

[67] The myth of the ancient constitution—that our history may be understood as a struggle to rid the English of the Norman yoke and return to the fair simplicity of the Anglo-Saxon constitution—is closely associated with the thought of Sir Edward Coke: see J.G.A. Pocock, *The Ancient Constitution and the Feudal Law* (Cambridge: Cambridge U.P., rev. edn, 1987). We might note that Dicey had no truck with this belief: "the illusion . . . that modern constitutional freedom has been established by an astounding method of retrospective progress ["that every step towards civilisation has been a step backwards towards the simple wisdom of our uncultured ancestors"] . . . conceals the truth both of law and of history." (above n. 3, 17).

[68] See Sir Alfred Denning, "The Spirit of the British Constitution" (1951) 29 *Canadian Bar Rev.* 1180, 1194–5: "The English distrust abstract philosophy as much as they distrust formal logic. Some suggest that this is because they do not understand philosophy or logic, but the better reason is because they know that they are apt to lead to error. The English approach is empirical. The solution to every problem depends on the question, Will it work? that is to say, Will it help to ensure justice and liberty? But they do not seek to define justice and liberty. They take those conceptions as well understood and busy themselves with the machinery to enforce them."

[69] Hobbes, above n. 18, 184.

authority.[70] And while Macbeth may have recognized no fetters, a prince "with a keen ear might have learned something about the illusion of absolute power from Macbeth's tragedy."[71] Good government requires restraint on the actions of the sovereign power.[72] Prudence in politics may often be a more effective method than entrenched laws for realizing this objective.

To be able to exercise power effectively, the sovereign authority must cultivate a reputation for trustworthiness, and this requires the sovereign to play by the rules. In the British system, these "rules" are often not rules of law, but are what have generally become known as constitutional conventions. The evolving authority of these practices may be taken as an illustration of the principle that self-binding is often an effective technique for indirectly enhancing the capacity to rule. So also with the law. The idea of law as the command of the sovereign seems to vest unlimited authority. But since a command is "the signification of desire" backed by the power "to inflict an evil or pain in case the desire be disregarded",[73] it will not generally be in the interests of good government to make extensive use of this power to make law.[74] Sovereignty and liberty are reconciled through the workings of the informal practices which ensure that power is exercised in the public interest and through a political process in which we appeal to our tradition of civil liberty to protect ourselves from the rigours of the law.

---

[70] *Macbeth*, Act III, sc.1.

[71] Kenneth Pennington, *The Prince and the Law, 1200–1600: Sovereignty and Rights in the Western Legal Tradition* (Berkeley, Calif.: Univ. of California Press, 1993), 202.

[72] See, e.g., Edmund Burke's speech on American taxation (19 April 1774) in which, urging restraint on the use of coercive action against the American colonists in the aftermath of the Boston tea party, he stressed that he was not "going into the distinctions of rights, nor attempting to mark their boundaries . . . But if intemperately, unwisely, fatally, you sophisticate and poison the very source of government, by urging subtle distinctions, and consequences odious to those you govern, from the unlimited and illimitable nature of supreme sovereignty, you will teach them by these means to call that sovereignty itself in question . . . If that sovereignty and their freedom cannot be reconciled, which will they take? They will cast sovereignty in your face." Burke, *On Government, Politics and Society*, B.W. Hill ed. (Glasgow: Fontana, 1975), 120, 150–1.

[73] Austin, above n. 2, 21.

[74] Oliver Wendell Holmes Jr., *The Common Law* (Boston: Little, Brown & Co., 1881), 96: "State interference is an evil, where it cannot be shown to be a good."

10

Fractured Sovereignty

SOVEREIGNTY CONTINUES TO be a potent force in the contemporary world. Many of the most intractable of political disputes—such as those in relation to Northern Ireland, the Falklands and between Israelis and Palestinians in the Middle East—focus on the question of sovereignty over a particular territory. Disputes of this nature also remind us that the concept of sovereignty is closely linked to the struggle for national identity and the idea of the "nation-state". Notwithstanding the importance of these conflicts, many commentators now argue that the impact of recent economic and social change is beginning to undermine the coherence of the nation-state and that, as a consequence of the resulting political realignment, sovereignty no longer provides an adequate expression of the structure of political authority. In this chapter, I propose to examine the nature and impact of these trends and to assess their implications for thinking about the relationship between law and politics. I begin by considering the relationship between sovereignty and the nation-state.

SOVEREIGNTY, THE NATION-STATE AND CONTEMPORARY TRENDS

The nation-state is a relatively modern phenomenon. Its emergence has been traced to the period after the Treaty of Westphalia of 1648, an era in which the western world was divided into more clearly delineated jurisdictions and the modern map of Europe began to take shape.[1] But the idea of the nation-state which emerged in modern European history is not one in which a close congruence between ethnicity and the structure of government has been forged.[2] Given the circumstances in which states have been formed, such congruency is almost never realized.

---

[1] See Martin van Creveld, *The Rise and Decline of the State* (Cambridge: Cambridge U.P., 1999), ch. 2.

[2] See Mark Mazower, *Dark Continent: Europe's Twentieth Century* (Harmondsworth: Penguin, 1998), ch. 2.

Rather, nation-states are best viewed as "imagined communities",[3] or "groups which *will* themselves to persist as communities".[4] They exist despite differences of race and language, and largely because they are united by "common sympathies"[5] or a history of common suffering. A nation can thus be understood as "a grand solidarity constituted by the sentiment of sacrifices"[6] and the nation-state in terms of *oblivion*: "the members of the nation, and hence of the state, have simply *forgotten* their diversity of cultural origin."[7] This is what might be called a civic conception of the nation-state. The French, for instance, constitute a nation-state, whether their ancestors were Gauls, Bretons, Normans, Franks, Romans or whatever. Similarly, the English, Irish, Scots and Welsh—notwithstanding their ethnic differences—have been forged into the nation-state of the United Kingdom. In this civic conception, the nation-state can be seen as a device through which class, ethnic and religious tensions within a defined territorial unit can be managed.

These nation-states present themselves as independent units in the international arena. From the time of Vattel's pioneering work on *The Law of Nations* in the mid-eighteenth century, it has generally been accepted that the fundamental principle of international law is that of the formal equality of states,[8] a principle which in turn yields those of independence and territorial integrity.[9] These principles of the independence, equality and territorial integrity of sovereign states form the basis for the conduct of international relations. However, since the principles of international law are general and, more importantly, because they lack an overarching sovereign authority capable of providing an effective sanction, they do not always provide clear and effective ground rules in accordance with which states may compete against one another for power, wealth and influence. The international arena

---

[3] Benedict Anderson, *Imagined Communities: Reflections on the Origin and Spread of Nationalism* (London: Verso, rev. edn. 1991).

[4] Ernest Gellner, *Nations and Nationalism* (Oxford: Blackwell, 1983), 53 (emphasis in original).

[5] John Stuart Mill, *Considerations on Representative Government* [1861] H.B. Acton ed. (London: Everyman, 1972), 359.

[6] Ernest Renan, "Qu'est-ce qu'une nation?" [1882] in John Hutchinson & Anthony D. Smith (eds), *Nationalism* (Oxford: Oxford U.P., 1994), 17.

[7] Ernest Gellner, *Nationalism* (London: Phoenix, 1998), 45 (emphasis in original).

[8] Emerich de Vattel, *The Law of Nations* [1758] Charles G. Fenwich trans. (Washington: Carnegie Institute, 1902).

[9] See United Nations Charter, art. 2.

therefore occasionally appears to be analogous to a Hobbesean state of nature in which states engage in a ceaseless struggle for survival.[10]

Nevertheless, certain structural changes are occurring in the international arena which appear to challenge the traditional role of the nation-state in political and economic affairs. These structural changes involve the twin processes of integration and fragmentation. Although these processes seem to be pulling in opposite directions, both present threats to the position of the nation-state as the predominant actor in the political affairs.

The process of integration is the result of the global impact of economic and technological change. The world which we inhabit is now genuinely global. It has been noted, for example, that today even illiterate labourers working in the deepest recesses of tropical rain forests understand that their livelihoods are not determined by forces operating at the level of their localities or even within the territorial borders of their states, but by the vagaries of world markets and the habits, tastes and capacities of consumers in distant countries.[11] But this observation now applies not only to the cocoa labourers of Ghana but also to workers in the semi-conductor plants of Scotland and north-east England. With the emergence of global markets we see the growth in scale and power of transnational corporations and also the establishment of a variety of international organizations trying to respond to the regulatory issues which are presented. This process of world-wide economic integration necessitates a reconfiguration of the international political arena.

The process of fragmentation is, to some extent, a by-product of economic and political integration. With the growth of world markets, for example, the trend has been towards the regionalization of economies, and some of these regional entities (e.g., Singapore/Indonesia or Vancouver/Seattle) have become linked primarily to the global economy rather than to their host nation-states.[12] In response to these economic trends, which have contributed to the resurgence of issues of ethnic identity, more extensive powers of government have been given to regional bodies within the nation-state. This has occurred throughout Europe,

[10] See Raino Malnes, *The Hobbesian Theory of International Conflict* (Oslo: Scandinavian U.P., 1993).

[11] John Dunn, "Social theory, social understanding and political action" in his *Rethinking Modern Political Theory: Essays 1979–1983* (Cambridge: Cambridge U.P., 1985) 119, 128.

[12] Kenichi Ohmae, *The End of the Nation State: The Rise of Regional Economies* (London: Harper Collins, 1996), ch. 7.

notably in the autonomous regions of Spain and the *Länder* of Germany and as the recent establishment of a Welsh Assembly and a Scottish Parliament indicates, this process has also affected governmental arrangements within the United Kingdom.[13] In Benedict Anderson's words, the "nation" has "proved an invention on which it was impossible to secure a patent".[14] Fragmentation undermines the traditional structures of the nation-state and has prompted the reconfiguration of the national political system. Such contemporary trends of integration and fragmentation are commonly viewed as responses to one powerful phenomenon—globalization.

THE CHALLENGE OF GLOBALIZATION

Since the end of the Second World War, there has been a spectacular growth in transnational investment, production and trade. In turn, this has led to the establishment of global financial markets as the major US, European and Japanese banks have become locked into an international circuit regulating the flow of capital. The major transnational corporations which have emerged now account for a large proportion of the world's production and these corporations, able to disperse their centres of production, are no longer bounded by the territories of any particular State.

Many of these changes have been driven by technological development. A revolution has occurred in transportation and communication systems and, in conjunction with the micro-chip revolution and the digitalization of information, this has had a profound impact on economic activity. Production is now much less tied to specific localities; enterprises increasingly possess the capacity to shift capital and labour

---

[13] Government of Wales Act 1998; Scotland Act 1998. See, e.g., *Towards Scotland's Parliament: A Report to the Scottish People by the Scottish Constitutional Convention* (Edinburgh: Scottish Constitutional Convention, 1990), 8: "The Scottish Parliament will look not only to Westminster, but also to Brussels and Strasbourg. An effective Scottish voice in the EEC is a pressing priority. This does not mean struggling to establish a nation state at the very time Europe is moving away from this narrow concept. The mood in Europe is very different with the German Länder, Spanish autonomous regions and the Italian provinces coming together to press common claims. Scotland, using the strength of the United Kingdom and her new independence of action, would be well placed to play a full part. . . . Developments within other member states towards decentralised decision-making to regional and provincial Governments are seen as parallel moves to the Convention's own proposals."

[14] Anderson, above n. 3, 67.

at low cost and high speed. Money is now able to circulate around the world through invisible networks, in vast quantities and at high velocity.[15] These developments—universalized communication, supersonic transportation, hi-tech weaponry and the like—have presented a series of serious challenges to the nation-state. The success of the modern State over the last two hundred years has been based mainly on its ability to promote economic well-being, to maintain physical security and to foster a distinctive cultural identity of its citizens. Yet it is precisely these claims which are now being undermined by such forces as "global capitalism, global proliferation of nuclear weapons and global media and culture."[16] For example, many of the social democratic theories of justice, such as that of Rawls,[17] are devised on the assumption that states are able to assume control over their economies.[18] And war becomes a much less credible instrument of policy today than it appeared in the age of Clausewitz,[19] not least because the sophistication of modern weaponry now means that states are vulnerable to attack from missiles which can be launched hundreds of miles from their borders.

Globalization has created a world of greater interdependence. Nevertheless, although the phenomenon seems to undermine the power of the nation-state, it is unlikely to lead to its demise.[20] Indeed, there seems little doubt but that the modern State will remain the primary form of political organization for the foreseeable future. The real threat which globalization poses is to traditional structures through which political authority is exercised. Globalization may not destroy the State, but it may lead to the obliteration of the principle of sovereignty as an expression of the manner in which power is wielded by rulers and conceded by the ruled.

The nature of this threat is highlighted by considering the distinction between the normative (legal) and empirical (political) conceptions of

---

[15] For analysis see: Joseph A. Camilleri and Jim Falk, *The End of Sovereignty? The Politics of a Shrinking and Fragmented World* (Aldershot: Edward Elgar, 1992); Paul Q. Hirst and Grahame Thompson, *Globalization in Question: the international economy and possibilities* (Cambridge: Polity Press, 2nd edn. 1999).

[16] Roland Axtmann, *Liberal Democracy in the Twenty-First Century: Globalization, Integration and the Nation-State* (Manchester: Manchester U.P., 1996), 134.

[17] See Ch. 7 above, 96–100.

[18] See John Gray, *False Dawn: The Delusions of Global Capitalism* (London: Granta, 1998), ch. 4.

[19] See above Ch. 1, 12.

[20] See Michael Mann, *Sources of Social Power, Vol. 2: The Rise of Classes and Nation-States, 1760–1914* (Cambridge: Cambridge U.P., 1994).

sovereignty, that is, between the formal legal authority of the State and its actual capacity to achieve policy objectives. The emergence of the global economy has reduced the ability of nation-states successfully to regulate their own economies and has made them increasingly vulnerable to the fluctuations of international financial markets.[21] This is a loss of power or capacity which cannot be recovered or reversed by edict of the sovereign body. That body might retain the legal authority to protect the domestic economy by erecting tariff barriers, levying exchange controls and regulating the flow of capital. But the retention of such formal legal powers does not demonstrate that the State is able to maintain directive control over the performance of the national economy. A vivid illustration of this point was provided by the experience of Black Wednesday—16 September 1992—when the pound was forcibly withdrawn from the exchange rate mechanism of the European Monetary System and the UK government lost billions of pounds in a futile attempt to protect sterling against the actions of international currency speculators.[22]

The State is still the principal agency for managing the economy and promoting the welfare of its citizens. The critical point for our purposes is that, as a result of structural changes, the State must acknowledge that, to be effective, it must be prepared to work with other powerful agencies. To be successful, the State must be able to harness the immense power now located in private corporations and it must also work in tandem with a range of supra-national governmental bodies. The State, in short, is obliged to share power.[23]

Contemporary trends have thus had the effect of subverting the political conception of sovereignty. The empirical tradition of sovereignty which stretches from Bodin to Dicey—based on the image of the sovereign authority as "the most high, absolute and perpetual power over the citizens and subjects"[24] and of the State as providing the locus of the "sovereign power [which] must exist in every civilised state"[25]—

---

[21] See Susan Strange, *The Retreat of the State: The Diffusion of Power in the World Economy* (Cambridge: Cambridge U.P., 1996).

[22] Philip Stephens, *Politics and the Pound: The Tories, the Economy and Europe* (London: Macmillan, 1996), esp. ch. 10.

[23] It is this basic realization which underpins the emergence of what is generally called "third way" politics: see Anthony Giddens, *The Third Way: The Renewal of Social Democracy* (Cambridge: Polity Press, 1998).

[24] Jean Bodin, *Six livres de la république* [1576], Bk I, ch. 8. See Bodin, *On Sovereignty*, Julian H. Franklin ed. (Cambridge: Cambridge U.P., 1992), 84.

[25] A.V. Dicey, *An Introduction to the Study of the Law of the Constitution* [1885] (London: Macmillan, 8th edn. 1915), 59.

is now effectively at an end. Sovereignty no longer provides an adequate expression of the nature of political power relations, a point exemplified in Bodin's contention that the right of coining money is one of the critical "marks of sovereignty". Bodin believed that, after the power of law-making, "there is nothing of greater consequence than the title, value, and measure of coin . . . and in every well-ordered state, it is the sovereign prince alone who has this power."[26] Those who agitate today in defence of the pound, however, have precious little control over its "value and measure"; to all intents and purposes, they are rallying around an entirely symbolic right of title—the right to retain the monarch's head on the coinage.

Over the last two hundred or so years it has been the all-powerful Hobbesean sovereign which has overshadowed our politics, and the main concern has been its potentially absolutist character. One consequence of change in the post-war period, however, has been that the State's traditional claims to pre-eminence have been eroded. The State remains a highly powerful institution, but it is now locked into an interdependent and globally-organized economic and political power network. On occasions—most vividly seen perhaps in the contemporary experience of Russia and other east European states—the most basic apprehension is not that of the State's omnipotence but its impotence. If the political conception of sovereignty is dead, then what of the legal doctrine? Throughout the twentieth century, the empirical and normative aspects of sovereignty have been differentiated and the normative conception has assumed an autonomous existence as a legal doctrine which defines the relationship between the legislature and the judiciary. What impact if any has the questioning of the political conception had on the legal doctrine? The position of the United Kingdom within Europe offers some answers.

THE EUROPEAN PROJECT

The map of Europe has been decisively shaped in modern times by the emergence of, and struggles between, nation-states. This process culminated in the devastating impact of two European-generated world wars, which led after 1945 to concerted efforts to overcome these traditional rivalries through a project of western European integration. This European movement evolved from the original six signatories to

---

[26] Bodin, above n. 24, 78.

the Treaty of Rome which established the European Economic Community (EEC) in 1957, to nine (including the UK) in 1973, twelve by 1986 and currently comprises fifteen member-states. The EEC has also evolved into the European Community (EC) and, after the Treaty on European Union (the Maastricht Treaty) in 1992, the European Union (EU). The European project is a classic illustration of the type of political restructuring required in response to the trend towards globalization and an analysis of the structure of the EU might reveal something about the character of contemporary political configurations. The EU is not a typical international organization. The Treaty of Rome specifically referred to the determination of signatory states "to lay the foundations of an ever closer union among the peoples of Europe",[27] a commitment which has been periodically reiterated.[28] More importantly, it established the institutional trappings of a system of government with its own law-making powers, through the formation of the Council, Commission, Court and Parliament. Designed to achieve the Union's objectives of "establishing a common market"[29] and of promoting "economic and social progress . . . through the creation of an area without internal frontiers, through the strengthening of economic and social cohesion and through the establishment of economic and monetary union"[30], this body of European law takes precedence over the laws of the member-states.[31] In the language of the European Court of Justice, "the Community constitutes a new legal order of international law for the benefit of which the states have limited their sovereign rights."[32] Since there are no provisions or procedures within the Treaties for withdrawal,[33] the project of European

---

[27] EEC Treaty of Rome (1957), Preamble.

[28] See, e.g., Treaty on European Union (1992), Preamble: "to mark a new stage in the process of European integration undertaken with the establishment of the European Communities".

[29] EEC Treaty, Art. 2.

[30] TEU, Title I, Art. B.

[31] Case 6/64, *Costa* v. *ENEL* [1964] ECR 585, 594: "the law stemming from the Treaty . . . could not . . . be overridden by domestic legal provisions, however framed, without being deprived of its character as Community law and without the legal basis of the Community itself being called into question."

[32] Case 26/62, *Van Gend en Loos* v. *Nederlandse Administratie der Belastingen* [1963] ECR 1, 12.

[33] EC Treaty, Art. 240 (as amended by TEU): "This Treaty is concluded for an unlimited period." For a discussion on formal and selective exist see J.H.H. Weiler, "The Transformation of Europe" in his *The Constitution of Europe: "Do the New Clothes have an Emperor?" and Other Essays on European Integration* (Cambridge: Cambridge U.P., 1999), ch. 2.

Union appears to be an irreversible movement in which the nation-state will be overcome and, ultimately, relegated to history.

Nevertheless, this integrationist analysis of the European project, suggesting that the economies, administrations and societies of member nation-states will gradually become merged into a supranational entity, remains highly questionable. Whether seen as a strategy dictated by the technological imperative of long-run economic development[34] or as a strategy aligned to the American cold war policy of unifying western Europe,[35] theories of integration carry a great deal of ideological baggage. Rather than assuming that the nation-state and the EU are antithetical, a better starting point for understanding the nature of the European project is to treat the EU as a new type of international framework which is designed not so much to transcend the nation-state but rather to promote the interests of the nation-state in an era of growing interdependence.[36]

This type of analysis originates in the catastrophe of the Second World War, which demonstrated that the nation-states of Europe were no longer able to discharge their most basic duty of protecting their citizens from aggression and their national boundaries from invasion. "Of the twenty-six European nation-states in 1938", notes Alan Milward, "by the close of 1940 three had been annexed, ten occupied by hostile powers, one occupied against its wishes by friendly powers, and four partially occupied and divided by hostile powers. Two others has been reduced to satellite status which would eventually result in their occupation."[37] Milward argues that the key issue concerning post-war reconstruction was not whether the nation-states could be replaced with a supra-national Europe but whether the State could find a political and economic base for survival. The nation-states of western Europe were prepared to work in the context of an international framework primarily for the purposes of supporting their own domestic policies and re-asserting the nation-state as the most fundamental unit of political life. The framework of the EEC was partly based on

[34] See Stephen George, *Politics and Policy in the European Community* (Oxford: Clarendon Press, 1991), ch. 2.

[35] See W.W. Rostow, *The Stages of Economic Growth: A Non-Communist Manifesto* (London: Cambridge U.P., 2nd edn. 1971).

[36] See Robert O. Keohane and Joseph S. Nye, *Power and Interdependence* (New York: HarperCollins, 2nd edn. 1989); Paul Taylor, *The European Union in the 1990s* (Oxford: Oxford U.P., 1996); Andrew Moravcsik, *The Choice for Europe: Social Purpose and State Power from Messina to Maastricht* (London: U.C.L. Press, 1998).

[37] Alan S. Milward, *The European Rescue of the Nation-State* (London: Routledge, rev. edn. 1994), 4.

interdependence and was also integrationist. Crucially, the "choice between interdependence and integration [in the development of the EC] was made according to the capacity of either system of international order to best advance and support domestic policy choices."[38]

There is plenty of evidence to support this interpretation of developments within the EC. The initial objective—the customs union—operated to the benefit of member-states as "an instrument both protectionist and expansionist which gave all [member-states] an increasing share of the trade within the common market until the 1970s."[39] Similarly, the common agricultural policy is a highly protectionist measure fashioned to promote the national policies of key member-states. And although other EC initiatives have been integrationist in objective, they too have been accepted essentially because they further the national interest of members. The primary advantage of integrationist measures is the relative certainty which they provide; the knowledge that once an agreement has been reached it is unlikely to be reversed gives a degree of predictability which provides a long-term guarantee of the continuity of commercial policy. Since integration requires national sovereignty to be ceded, however, states will want to maintain control over the range of such transfers. This is precisely what was achieved through the decision-making structure of the Council of Ministers; by requiring unanimity, each member-state effectively possessed a veto over any new initiatives of the Community. Indeed, this technique was reinforced through the formal establishment of the European Council in 1974. Being intergovernmental in nature, the Council provided a forum in which government representatives of member-states would become directly involved in discussions over any new policy initiatives and could therefore ensure that EC developments take full account of national policy objectives.

But what about recent integrationist developments, such as the shift to majority voting and the single currency? On the former, the Single European Act (SEA) 1986 extended majority voting only to those measures needed to bring about the completion of the internal market. Moreover, the impetus behind this programme for completing the internal market was not an integrationist one, but had been motivated by member-states' loss of economic competitiveness both inside and

[38] Milward, above n. 37, 438.
[39] Alan S. Milward, Frances M.B. Lynch, Federico Romero, Ruggero Ranieri & Vibeke Sørensen, *The Frontier of National Sovereignty: History and Theory 1945–1992* (London: Routledge, 1993), 10.

outside the common market. The single-market programme was thus designed primarily to safeguard member-states' future economic performance in the face of enhanced global competition.[40] One of the goals of the SEA was to complete the single market by December 1992; this would then be used as a lever by those who sought monetary union. But this project of monetary union, promoted by the Treaty on European Union, does seem to be integrationist. Nevertheless, it is important to remember that the single currency maintained its impetus largely because of nation-state considerations: France promoted it in order to obtain reassurance that its security would not be undermined by German reunification, Germany agreed to it only on condition that the former East Germany obtained full inclusion into the EC, and the UK and Denmark were permitted to opt-out of the arrangements.

This brief overview suggests that the evolution of the EC has been closely controlled by national policies and has had little to do with the realization of some abstract ideal of achieving a federal Europe. The development of the EC has been motivated primarily by the inability of nation-states, against a backcloth of globalization, to maintain their capacity to promote the economic and social expectations of their citizens. The special institutional arrangements of the EC have been forged to protect the interests of the nation-states of western Europe. The establishment of the EC certainly does not signal the end of the nation-state. However, the European project does indicate that to be able to act effectively within contemporary conditions of interdependence a different, more negotiative, style of politics has evolved. In certain circumstances, this requires what is sometimes termed a "pooling" or even a transfer of sovereignty. But the more general point is that these European developments may signal the destruction of sovereignty as a foundational political concept.

PARLIAMENTARY SOVEREIGNTY

It is important to stress that the European project has been managed and controlled by the states of western Europe precisely because the proto-federal vision of the EC is one which has been most vigorously promoted by lawyers.[41] This emphasis is a consequence of lawyers'

[40] Milward *et al.*, above n. 39, 27–8.
[41] See, e.g., Eric Stein, "Lawyers, Judges and the Making of a Transnational Constitution" (1981) 75 *American J. of International Law* 1; Trevor C. Hartley,

attempts to make sense of the institutional framework of the EC. The federalist project has been promoted, implicitly at least, by the European Court of Justice (ECJ), which has undertaken this work through its explication of the nature of the "new legal order". The ECJ has in effect "constitutionalized" the EC Treaty and taken the view that the Treaty, "albeit concluded in the form of an international treaty, none the less constitutes the constitutional charter of a Community based on the rule of law."[42] If, as a political project, the EU has undermined the political conception of sovereignty, the structure of the EU, especially as interpreted by the ECJ, also subverts the normative legal principle of sovereignty. The implications of these developments need to be unravelled.[43]

As we have seen, in Dicey's scheme the legal conception of sovereignty, based on a normative relationship between legislature and judiciary, was inextricably linked to the political conception, a condition of effective political action.[44] During the twentieth century, however, the legal conception of sovereignty came to be treated as a distinct and autonomous doctrine. "It is often said", Lord Reid has stated, "that it would be unconstitutional for the United Kingdom Parliament to do certain things, meaning that the moral, political and other reasons against doing them are so strong that most people would regard it as highly improper if Parliament did these things. But that does not mean that it is beyond the power of Parliament to do such things. If Parliament chose to do any of them the courts would not hold the Act of Parliament invalid."[45] Consequently, notwithstanding the growing recognition of the political limitations of the British state, sovereignty remained the foundational principle of British constitutional law. Sovereignty as a political concept may have been on its last legs, but it lived on as a legal doctrine expressing the unrestricted right of Parliament to make or unmake any law whatever.

Given the impact of the EU on both political and legal conceptions of sovereignty, however, the nature of the link between these two con-

---

"Federalism, Courts and Legal Systems: The Emerging Constitution of the European Community" (1986) *American J. of Comparative Law* 229; G. Federico Mancini, "The Making of a Constitution for Europe" (1989) 26 *Common Market Law Rev.* 595

[42] Opinion 1/91, *Re the Draft Treaty on a European Economic Area* [1991] 1 ECR 6079 para. 21; [1992] CMLR 245, 269.

[43] For an analysis of European law which is critical of neo-federalist legal view and which shares some affinities with Milward's analysis see Weiler, above n. 33.

[44] See Ch. 9 above, 138.

[45] *Madzimbamuto* v. *Lardner-Burke* [1969] 1 AC 645, 723.

ceptions needs re-evaluation. The legal doctrine is absolutist in form. The only restriction on the omnipotence of Parliament was that Parliament could not bind its successors. Since that rule exists to ensure the continuing authority of the sovereign body, this apparent qualification actually provides an illustration of the doctrine. Parliament cannot impose fetters on future legislative action by seeking to protect an Act of Parliament from subsequent repeal; any attempt to entrench legislation by requiring, for example, a referendum or a special Parliamentary majority before it can be altered would be ignored by the courts—or so it was thought. Recently, as has been seen in relation to the *Factortame* litigation,[46] the British judiciary, in order to give effect to the principle of supremacy of Community law enacted in the European Communities Act 1972, has been obliged to overturn that rule and, in effect, to invalidate Acts of the UK Parliament. The question is: should this action be understood as a reflection of the peculiar EC legal arrangements, or does it signal a more general reconceptualization of sovereignty as a legal doctrine?

Governments, it might be noted, have occasionally found it necessary to include statements of political intent—in effect, conventions—in Acts of Parliament: thus, certain "guarantees" were drafted for the benefit of the Scottish people in the Act of Union 1707,[47] for the protection of the self-governing Dominions in the Statute of Westminster 1931,[48] and for the Unionist community in the successive Northern Ireland Acts.[49] The consensus of judicial opinion has been that such protections are not enforceable at law. When Canada patriated her constitution in the Canada Act 1982, for example, the chiefs of the First Nations objected on the ground that their interests had been prejudiced without their consent. But in their legal action to challenge the validity of the 1982 Act, Sir Robert Megarry V-C held that "from first to last I

[46] See Ch. 3 above, 39–40.

[47] Act of Union 1707, art. XVIII: "no alteration be made in laws which concern private right except for the evident utility of the subjects within Scotland." For a different interpretation see Neil MacCormick, "The United Kingdom: What State? What Constitution?" in his *Questioning Sovereignty: Law, State, and Nation in the European Commonwealth* (Oxford: Oxford U.P., 1999), ch. 4.

[48] Statute of Westminster 1931, s. 4: "No Act of the Parliament of the United Kingdom passed after the commencement of this Act shall extend, or be deemed to extend, to a Dominion as part of the law of that Dominion, unless it is expressly declared in that Act that that Dominion has requested and consented to the enactment thereof."

[49] See, e.g., Northern Ireland Constitution Act 1973, s. 1; Northern Ireland Act 1998, s. 1(1): "It is hereby declared that Northern Ireland in its entirety remains part of the United Kingdom and shall not cease to be so without the consent of a majority of the people of Northern Ireland voting in a poll . . ."

have heard nothing in this case to make me doubt the simple rule that the duty of the court is to obey and apply every Act of Parliament, and that the court cannot hold any such Act to be ultra vires."[50] As an expression of the traditional relationship between the legislature and the judiciary, this ruling is non-contentious. But what would the judiciary rule if Parliament sought unilaterally to legislate for Canada? Here, the courts have already accepted that although "Parliament could, as a matter of abstract law, repeal or disregard section 4" of the Statute of Westminster, they also acknowledge that "that is theory and has no relation to realities".[51] Legal theory, in short, must march alongside political necessity.

What the judiciary appear to have accepted is the fact that capacity—a minimum of effectiveness—is a condition of validity. When colonies obtain their independence and assume the status of sovereign states in the international arena, a point is reached when the UK Parliament cannot *lawfully* legislate to re-assert their former colonial authority. This suggests that ultimately a linkage between the political and legal conceptions of sovereignty remains. Consequently, the basic issue is not whether the judiciary should take note of political conditions but rather the extent to which, and the circumstances under which, they will do so. Given the structure of the European Union, and in particular the lack of any specified procedure for withdrawal, what view will the British judiciary take if at some point in the future the UK government sought unilaterally to withdraw from the Union? Might the judiciary at some critical stage be prepared to give legal effect to the referendum pledge in the Northern Ireland Act? And although the Scotland Act 1998 takes the form of a devolution of legislative authority to a subordinate body, is it inconceivable that the courts would rule that powers conferred on the Scottish Parliament cannot lawfully be withdrawn without the consent of that institution? To apply a Hobbesean metaphor, it might be said that the (legal) skeleton of sovereignty has, for the moment, been retained but in order to retain the life of the concept, the (political) nerves, arteries and vital organs must continue to work effectively. The prognosis does not look good.

---

[50] *Manuel* v. *Attorney-General* [1983] Ch 77, 86.
[51] *British Coal Corporation* v. *The King* [1935] AC 500, 520.

SOVEREIGNTY, LAW AND GLOBALIZATION

With the emergence of the modern State, law, initially pronounced in the indistinct language of medieval custom, has come to be proclaimed in the clear and authoritative voice of command. The image of law as command, however, is often misunderstood. The command theory of law only makes sense when it is embedded within a tradition of political behaviour. It is linked, in particular, to the political belief that there must exist within all states an authoritative centre which is capable of taking decisive action and which all, including judges, must obey. Although that political theme runs through the versions of sovereignty articulated by Bodin, Hobbes, Blackstone and Dicey, it would be an error to assume that, within the scheme of these writers, sovereignty is an absolutist doctrine. Sovereignty and command are ideas rooted in a particular belief system concerning the nature of political power and of how that power might best be exercised.

This belief system recognizes that governance is a distinctive type of activity and that politics is the medium through which this activity is carried on.[52] The State is founded on sound laws and sound arms, on the power of the sword tempered by the scales of justice, and although force may be the ultimate foundation of the State, the power of the prince "cannot be measured by his capacity to command a bending of the knee."[53] If the sovereign is to govern effectively, he must be able to harness the interests of other power-brokers to his designs, and one vital method for achieving this is by cultivating a reputation for trustworthiness. By permitting power to be restricted, the sovereign enhances his authority and thereby increases the likelihood of his edicts being obeyed. In an astute analysis of the work of Bodin, Stephen Holmes shows how Bodin redefines natural law as a set of prudential maxims for avoiding revolution. Bodin, he contends, "treats restrictions on power, unconventionally, as a set of authority-reinforcing, will-empowering, and possibility-expanding rules" and suggests that through these "strategically designed limitations on supreme power ... [Bodin] explains how he can become sovereign in fact as well as in

---

[52] See Ch. 8 above, 120.
[53] Stephen Holmes, "The Constitution of Sovereignty in Jean Bodin" in his *Passions and Constraint: On the Theory of Liberal Democracy* (Chicago: University of Chicago Press, 1995), 100, 119.

law."[54] The authority of the State is strengthened when its sphere of operations is restricted and the methods by which it acts are stipulated. The messages conveyed by Machiavelli and Bodin have been absorbed within the British State tradition. The idea that the authority of the State depends on it being able to limit its actions to those which are necessary to the realization of its critical objectives goes some way towards explaining how, during the eighteenth century, the British State was able to promote a domestic philosophy of economic liberalism whilst maintaining a strong imperial presence—the invisible hand of the market at home being operated in conjunction with the all-too-visible fist of the State abroad.[55] It also provides a key to understanding how, within a centralized State founded on the sovereignty concept, a tradition of local government was able to flourish.[56] The establishment of such practices indicate how the idea of law as command is reconcilable with liberalism; since commands involve the infliction of an evil, the governing class conceded that law should be enacted only when it is demonstrably in the public interest. More generally, it was accepted that the business of government should be undertaken only in accordance with conventional understandings of how power should be exercised: political practices rather than rules of law provided the restraints on the exercise of State power and, to that extent, the idea of the rule of law was acknowledged as an important political precept. These constraints can all be seen to be techniques for reinforcing State power. But perhaps the most critical point for our purpose is that these techniques are prudential political devices which generally are not incorporated into positive law.

This State tradition has encountered certain basic problems in the twentieth century. Many of these precepts of what Bagehot called "club government",[57] having been devised for an aristocratic era, have struggled to retain their authority; with the extension of democracy, and especially given its institutional expression through a system of party politics, the force of conventions has waned and pressure has grown for law to be utilized as the primary instrument for controlling government. This is a movement which cannot easily be accommo-

---

[54] Ibid. 110.

[55] See John Brewer, *The Sinews of Power: War, Money and the English State, 1688–1783* (London: Unwin Hyman, 1989).

[56] See Martin Loughlin, *Legality and Locality: The Role of Law in Central–Local Government Relations* (Oxford: Clarendon Press, 1996), ch. 1.

[57] Walter Bagehot, *The English Constitution* [1867] R.H.S Crossman ed. (London: Collins, 1963), 156.

dated with a tradition of law as the command of the sovereign body. Secondly, with the evolution of "popular government",[58] we enter an era of big government. As the tasks of government increase, there is a need for new bodies of law—administrative law—to be created to establish a framework within which these new activities are to be conducted. While this movement can be accommodated with the idea of law as command, it is not easily reconciled with the political tradition of liberalism. Checks and controls are needed on the exercise of these new powers vested in Ministers and executive bodies and, to the extent that these checks are institutionalized through law, the system of administrative law cannot easily be squared with the image of law as command. Thirdly, with the growth of big government—in conjunction with the complexity of its tasks in an emerging interdependent world—the idea of power being located in a centralized sovereign authority no longer appears convincing.[59] Power seems in reality to be located within structures rather than being vested in a person or even an institution, and these power structures cut across both the public-private and local-global divides.

As a result of these twentieth-century developments, the precepts of sovereignty and command no longer provide adequate expressions of manner in which the State undertakes its business. Under the political conditions of the nineteenth century, when Britain was at the height of its potency as an imperial power, sovereignty may indeed have served to strengthen the power of the State and federalism could sensibly be viewed as a weak and divisive form of government, a point which would not have been hard to demonstrate in the light of the US Civil War during the 1860s. But under the changed conditions of the late twentieth century, sovereignty seems to have become a shibboleth, an expression to which we pay lip-service and which obscures, and in certain circumstances may even accentuate, the weaknesses of the contemporary State. By clinging to the concept of sovereignty, in both its political and legal conceptions, politicians and lawyers have evaded their responsibilities of trying to engage with, and respond effectively to, the challenges of a novel economic and political situation.

---

[58] Henry Sumner Maine, *Popular Government* (London: John Murray, 1885).

[59] Cf. Michel Foucault, *Power/Knowledge* (Brighton: Harvester, 1980), 121: "political theory has never ceased to be obsessed with the person of the sovereign. Such theories still continue today to busy themselves with the problem of sovereignty. What we need, however, is a political philosophy that isn't erected around the problem of sovereignty, nor therefore around the problems of law and prohibition. We need to cut off the King's head: in political theory that has still to be done."

IV

Constitutionalism

11

The Social Contract

AS THE UNITY of the medieval world disintegrated, the belief that humans occupied a fixed place within a universal order was placed in question. But if the political order was not divinely ordained, on what foundation did it rest? Some looked for answers in the mysterious workings of history, arguing that evolution had yielded a relatively stable system. In the words of Strafford, loyal servant of Charles I, "the authority of a king is the keystone which closeth up the arch of order and government, which, once shaken, all the frame falls together in a confused heap of foundation and battlement".[1] Appeals to custom, tradition or the natural processes of evolution, however, proved insufficient to solve the conflicts which were emerging in early-modern England. These conflicts came to a head during the seventeenth century, a period of dramatic political and constitutional change and one in which England's position in the world was transformed and a modern State forged.[2] Justification for the political order was no longer sought in tradition but in the autonomous powers of reason.

The shift towards reason was not unprecedented; much earlier, Plato had tried to rid the world of myth and uncover the basic principles of an ideal State. The early-modern thinkers tended to share Plato's view that the founding of the State was an analytical, rather than a historical problem: in seeking a justification of political order, they recognized the necessity of working from first principles. But unlike Plato, the pioneering early-modern thinkers accepted the need to find an explanation based on the centrality of individual moral will. By starting with the value which individuals ascribe to themselves, these thinkers based their theories mainly on the platform of natural rights, meaning a universal set of rights which all communities and creeds could embrace. At the core of this idea of natural right lies the belief that all people are free and equal by nature. Once this is recognized, the

---

[1] Cited in J.H. Grainger, *Character and Style in English Politics* (Cambridge: Cambridge U.P., 1969), 31.

[2] See, e.g., Christopher Hill, *The Century of Revolution, 1603–1714* (London: Abacus, 1978).

critical question they faced becomes obvious: if all people are free and equal, how is it that societies invariably possess a governing order in which a small group rule and the rest are ruled? Or, as Rousseau put it: "Man was born free, and he is everywhere in chains."[3]

With this idea of natural rights as the starting point, it follows that questions of authority, legitimacy and obligation in the political realm must rest on the principle of consent. Individuals, it may be assumed, will freely relinquish their natural rights to the collectivity only in return for securing certain objectives. The relationship between the individual and the State, in short, is one of contract.

In this chapter, I propose to examine how the device of the social contract came to be invoked as a foundational principle in politics, first (with Hobbes) to establish the authority of government and later (with Locke) to impose limits on that governmental authority. I shall argue that the use of this device marks an important stage in the evolution of politico-legal thought: not only is it associated with the emergence of a belief that political power vests ultimately in individuals who consensually and conditionally delegate that power to the State, but it also provides the source from which springs the notion that governance is a function of law rather than of political will. The notion of the social contract thus is central both to the evolution of a modern idea of the constitution and to the elaboration of a political theory of rights, themes which are developed in the following two chapters. In this chapter, however, my main objective will be to sketch the ways in which this contractual metaphor has been used to establish a form of political authority and, given its legal connotations, to consider the extent to which it has been used for the purpose of inscribing law into the foundations of politics.

NATURAL RIGHTS, COVENANTS AND POLITICAL ORDER

Most of the early-modern political thinkers accepted the existence of a fundamental law of self-preservation. They believed in a law of nature which recognized the basic right of all individuals both to defend themselves against attack and to acquire the necessities of life. They also accepted that mutual recognition of these natural rights would not, in itself, be sufficient to sustain a social order. For Hobbes, the lack of a

---

[3] Jean-Jacques Rousseau, *The Social Contract* [1762] Maurice Cranston trans. and intro. (Harmondsworth: Penguin, 1968), Bk. I, ch. I.

self-evident, objective moral law meant that, in a state of nature, there would be a perpetual war of all against all.[4] The rational solution was for individuals seeking their own preservation to renounce their natural rights by covenanting with one another for the purpose of establishing a sovereign authority. These individuals should "appoint one Man, or assembly of men, to bear their Person; and every one to own, and to acknowledge himself to be Author of whatsoever he that beareth their person shall Act, or cause to be acted, in those things which concern the Common Peace and Safety."[5]

Hobbes used this idea of the covenant in which individuals cede their natural rights as a device designed not to reveal the origins of the State, but to explain the validity of the political order. The function of this covenant is to legitimate coercive political order through the principle of mutual consent. The Hobbesean covenant, it must be emphasized, is an act of alienation in which natural rights are relinquished. It is therefore not strictly a contract between rulers and ruled, but is better understood as a covenant through which the authority of rulership is established.

It is Hobbes's assertion of the indissoluble nature of this covenant— a pact of submission in which individuals renounce their natural rights to forge a collective will incorporated in the sovereign authority— which is challenged, albeit indirectly, by Locke. The first of Locke's *Two Treatises of Government* is an extended critique of Sir Robert Filmer's patriarchal view of the nature of government. Filmer, a Royalist defender of absolute monarchy, had claimed biblical proof that God had ordained a social order of gradations in which fathers were placed over sons, men over women, elders over the young, and kings above everyone.[6] Locke therefore undertakes a detailed textual analysis of the Bible with the objective of refuting Filmer's interpretation. In the *Second Treatise*, Locke presents a novel conceptualization of government. Government, he contends, is not a relation of sovereign and subject but one between rulers and free citizens. Like Hobbes, Locke begins with the state of nature, but Locke's image is not one of perpetual war. There are two critical differences between the narratives.

---

[4] Thomas Hobbes, *Leviathan* [1651] Richard Tuck ed. (Cambridge: Cambridge U.P., 1996), ch. 13. See Ch. 2 above, 27.

[5] Ibid. 120.

[6] Robert Filmer, *Patriarcha and other political works of Sir Robert Filmer* [1628–52] Peter Laslett ed. (Oxford: Blackwell, 1949).

The first variation is that, whereas for Hobbes the primary threat is physical security, for Locke it is hunger. In the state of nature, the basic threat to survival comes from being unable to acquire the means of subsistence. Individuals sustain themselves by appropriating the fruits of the earth. In doing so, Locke argues, they are not dependent on the consent of others. They have a natural right to acquire those things needed for nourishment and they acquire ownership of these commodities through the expenditure of their labour: "The *labour* that was mine, removing them out of that common state they were in, hath *fixed* my *Property* in them."[7] Property therefore enters the world through labour and, because it is rooted in the natural right to the means of subsistence, it exists prior to the establishment of political order. His second basic difference concerns social order in the state of nature. "We are born free as we are born Rational",[8] he contends, and it is this rationality which guides individuals in a state of natural freedom. For Locke, absolute freedom has no meaning since "where there is no Law, there is no freedom".[9] But where is law to be found within the state of nature? Locke's answer is that it is found in the law of nature. Natural law, understood as an expression of God's will, guides individuals in their natural condition, providing the basis for social order in the state of nature.

Locke's interpretation suggests that, under these natural conditions, individuals enjoy a relatively benign form of existence. People labour to nourish and maintain themselves, and thus acquire property. They also come to recognize the benefits which the exchange of commodities brings and, as bartering increases, the medium of money is invented. Consequently, through a series of economic exchanges which people enter into both as labourers and owners, a rudimentary form of socialized existence evolves. Locke here is suggesting that civil society precedes the State. He then poses the basic question: "If Man in the State of Nature be so free, as has been said; If he be the absolute Lord of his own Person and Possessions, equal to the greatest, and subject to no Body, why will he part with his Freedom? Why will he give up this Empire, and subject himself to the Dominion and Control of any other Power?"[10]

---

[7] John Locke, *Two Treatises of Government* [1680] Peter Laslett ed. (Cambridge: Cambridge U.P., 1988), II, § 28 (emphases in original).
[8] Ibid. II, § 61.
[9] Ibid. II, § 57.
[10] Ibid. II, § 123.

His answer is that, although the law of nature guides individuals, that law is unwritten "and so [is] no where to be found but in the minds of Men." Consequently, "they who through Passion or Interest shall mis-cite, or mis-apply it, cannot so easily be convinced of their mistake where there is no established judge".[11] There are, then, three basic deficiencies which the establishment of civil government is designed to remedy: the lack of "an established, settled, known Law . . . and common measure to decide all controversies"; the need for "a known and indifferent Judge"; and the want of "power to back and support the Sentence when right, and to give it due execution".[12] It is to avoid these inconveniences that people abandon the state of nature to form a political order.

There is, however, a rather basic point which Locke's narrative is designed to highlight. It is this: since the "chief end . . . of men's uniting into Commonwealths, and putting themselves under Government, is the preservation of their property",[13] government is both defined and limited by the end for which political society is established. Absolutism is therefore inimical to the maintenance of civil society. From this point, Locke concludes that government is formed by a covenant of delegation, and not of alienation. The covenant establishing the form of government thus constitutes "the fundamental Appointment of the Society".[14] In other words, the covenant establishes a formal constitution.

THE CONSTITUTION OF SOCIETY

"The great question which in all ages has disturbed mankind", Locke contends, "has been, not whether there be power in the world, nor whence it came from, but who should have it."[15] In his *Second Treatise*, Locke makes an important innovation in asserting that political power rests in individuals and that this power is delegated through their consent to an institution (whether monarch or parliament or both) which, in some form or other, can be taken to be representative of the people. Until this moment, it had been generally accepted that

[11] Locke, above n. 7, II, § 136.
[12] Ibid. II, §§ 124, 125, 126.
[13] Ibid. II, § 124.
[14] Ibid. II, § 214.
[15] Ibid. I, § 106.

political power was vested in a collective representation of the people—the monarch as head of the body politic—and that the monarch, being sovereign, was above the law. By contrast, Locke contends that absolute monarchy is "inconsistent with civil society, and so can be no form of civil government at all."[16] Government, he asserts, is not a personal matter, a matter of *will*; it must always be an institutional matter, a matter of *law*. In short: "no man in civil society can be exempted from the laws of it."[17]

Through this reconceptualization of the foundations of political power, Locke promotes a theory of limited government. The power of government should never be arbitrary and is "limited to the public good of the society". "It is", he elaborates, "a power that has no other end but preservation, and therefore can never have a right to destroy, enslave, or designedly to impoverish the subjects."[18] Consequently, government "ought to be exercised by established and promulgated laws" so that both "the people may know their duty, and be safe and secure within the limits of the law" and that "the rulers too be kept within their due bounds".[19] Government must be subject to the rule of law, a principle which ensures the maintenance of freedom.

Unlike Hobbes, Locke does not take freedom to mean simply the absence of constraint. Locke believed in natural law as a set of objective moral principles which expresses what we ought to do and which therefore guides our actions. He also believed that with the establishment of a political order subject to the rule of law, freedom is not restricted or diminished. Within a properly regulated State, civil liberty flourishes, since "the end of Law is not to abolish or restrain, but to preserve and enlarge freedom."[20] The condition of civil liberty is maintained, Locke suggests, so long as government, established by consent, acts "according to the trust put in it."[21] And, as we have seen, a vital aspect of that trust must be that government acts as the guarantor of property.[22]

---

[16] Locke, above n. 7, II, § 90.
[17] Ibid. II, § 94.
[18] Ibid. II, § 135.
[19] Ibid. II, § 137.
[20] Ibid. II, § 57.
[21] Ibid. II, § 22.
[22] The significance of property within Locke's scheme has been a highly contentious issue within political thought. See James Tully, *An Approach to Political Philosophy: Locke in Contexts* (Cambridge: Cambridge U.P., 1993), ch. 3. The important point for legal study is that this conceptualization of civil rights as property rights has played a pivotal role in British constitutional development. See, e.g., *Ashby* v. *White* (1703) 2 Ld.

So, government is exercised by established and promulgated laws. For this purpose, there exists a legislative power which formulates the standing rules in accordance with which all must live. But because these laws have a constant force, there is also a need for an executive power to ensure that they are properly applied. Since the need for governmental action may not always be anticipated, Locke argues that this executive power, though ultimately subordinate to the legislative, must be given sufficient authority to respond to unforeseen occurrences and to adapt the laws to provide for the public good: "This power to act according to discretion, for the public good, without the prescription of the law, and sometimes even against it, is that which is called prerogative."[23] Locke also identifies a third power—the conduct of foreign relations—which he labels the federative power, and notes that it is generally left under the control of the executive.

Although it is tempting to interpret Locke's scheme as a precursor to the modern idea of the separation of powers, this would be a mistake. Locke has little to say, for example, about the judiciary. He does mention the fact that the judges must be known and authorized[24] and he believes that the judiciary should be "indifferent and upright",[25] but that is all. The judiciary, it appears, performs an important, though not particularly complex, role as an agency of the executive power to ensure the proper enforcement of the laws. But since Locke conceives State power as divided between the legislative and the executive, there is the potential for conflict between these authorities. How is this to be resolved? On this important issue, Locke has only this to say: "between an Executive Power in being and a Legislative that depends on his will for their convening, there can be no judge on earth: as there can be none between the Legislative and the People should either the Executive or the Legislative, when they have got the power in their hands, design, or go about to enslave or destroy them."[26] If Locke's system yields a modern message, it is on this point. Although the legislative power is ultimately supreme, the necessities of political life dictate that the

---

Raym. 398 (in which the right to vote was treated as a property right); *Entick* v. *Carrington* (1765) 19 St.Tr. 1029 (in which the plaintiff brought a successful action in trespass against the King's messengers for breaking and entering and seizing papers, Lord Camden CJ noting: "The great end, for which men entered into society, was to secure their property. That right is preserved sacred . . .")

[23] Locke, above n. 7, II, § 160.
[24] Ibid. II, § 136.
[25] Ibid. II, § 131.
[26] Ibid. II, § 168.

executive wields considerable power. This disjuncture between normative and the factual—the inclusion of "the extraconstitutional within the constitution"[27]—strikes at the core of the problem of the executive in modern government.[28]

For Locke, then, it is clear that the proper functioning of the powers of the State cannot be settled by separation. Instead, it is resolved by the notion of trust. The powers of government constitute "only a fiduciary power to act for certain ends."[29] Locke denied that rulers exercised absolute power but, by referring to the relationship between government and governed as one of trust, he was also rejecting the idea that it was strictly contractual. Were the relationship contractual, each party must derive some benefit and this suggests that governors obtain something from governing which the governed are obliged to provide. As Peter Laslett has noted, "this is what Locke was most anxious to avoid."[30] People enter into contract with one another to form a political order, but they are not contractually bound to government and rulers obtain benefit only to the extent that people in general profit from the establishment of government. As delegates, the governors are trustees whose powers are limited to that of achieving the ends of government—that is, the pursuit of the public good.

This stress on the fiduciary nature of political power raises certain questions. What happens if governors act in breach of the trust which has been placed in them? The answer is simple. Giving expression to the idea of popular sovereignty, Locke acknowledges that "the community perpetually retains a supreme power of saving themselves" from the foolish or wicked actions of their governors. If governors act contrary to their fiduciary responsibilities, the bond of obligation is forfeited "and the power devolve[s] into the hands of those that gave it, who may place it anew where they think it best for their safety and security."[31] But who decides whether the governors are acting in breach of trust? "The people shall be judge", Locke states, "for who shall be judge whether his trustee or deputy acts well, and according to the trust reposed in him, but he who deputes him . . . ?".[32] But will this

---

[27] Harvey C. Mansfield Jr., *Taming the Prince: The Ambivalence of Modern Executive Power* (Baltimore: Johns Hopkins U.P., 1993), 204.
[28] See Pierre Manent, *An Intellectual History of Liberalism* Rebecca Balinski trans. (Princeton: Princeton U.P., 1995), 48–9.
[29] Locke, above n. 7, II, § 149.
[30] Ibid. "Introduction", 127.
[31] Ibid. II, § 149.
[32] Ibid. II, § 240.

not, in Locke's words, "lay a ferment for frequent rebellion"[33] and, as Hobbes had suggested,[34] destabilize the political order? To this, Locke answers that people are tolerant and rebellion is likely only when oppression affects most of the people: "rebellions happen not upon every little mismanagement in public affairs."[35] It is precisely this threat of legitimate rebellion, Locke believes, which will ensure that those in power are not tempted to abuse it.[36] For Locke, it is this notion of trust, rather than contract, which is the fundamental principle in the constitution of political society.

THE SOCIAL CONTRACT TRADITION

The emergence of social contract theory is linked to the evolution of equality as a fundamental principle of politics. The basic thrust of the social contract tradition which flourished during the seventeenth and eighteenth centuries was to deny the legitimacy of any claim to the right to rule which is rooted in birth, in divine right, in charisma or, indeed, in sheer physical force. The authority to govern, social contract theorists contend, is ceded by free and equal individuals who accept the arrangements as being conducive to the pursuit of the public good. The foundation of governmental authority rests on the voluntary transfer of power and liberty by the people to their rulers. Government is based on the principle of consent.

Contractualism is also associated with the growth of individualism. This is evident in Locke's account of the state of nature, in which property enters the world through individual labour, and economy and society precede the formation of the State. Contrary to Aristotle's belief that "man is by nature a political animal",[37] Locke portrays individuals as pre-political labourers and owners who agree to unite to form a Commonwealth with the primary objective of preserving their property.[38] The individualistic thrust of contractualism, which is manifest

---

[33] Locke, above n. 7, II, § 224.

[34] Hobbes argues against leaving it to the individual to decide whether the sovereign has complied with the terms of the covenant on the ground that "it exposes any King, good or bad, to the risk of being condemned by the judgement, and murdered by the hand, of one solitary assassin." Thomas Hobbes, *On the Citizen* [1647] Richard Tuck and Michael Silverthorne ed. and trans. (Cambridge: Cambridge U.P., 1998), 134.

[35] Locke, above n. 7, II, § 225.

[36] Ibid. II, § 226.

[37] See Ch. 1 above, 7.

[38] Locke, above n. 7, II, § 123.

in the very essence of the arrangement, has an impact on the character-ization of the State. Being revealed as a human artefact constructed for particular purposes, the State is portrayed as a clear and understand-able entity. The holistic, almost mystical idea of the body politic is sup-planted by agreement amongst individuals to establish a form of political order, a process in which organic metaphors are replaced by metaphors of construction.[39]

In this way, social contract theories erode much of the mystery and symbolism surrounding the State; there is, after all, nothing less myste-rious than a contract between individuals. Nevertheless, seventeenth-century social contract theory is deeply rooted in the religious beliefs of the period. The sixteenth-century Reformation had resulted in various conflicts over claims to religious orthodoxy and Calvinist theologians had been instrumental in developing a right of popular resistance to their rulers.[40] The Reformation had renewed interest in the Bible as a source for understanding the nature of political obligation, and it is therefore not surprising that the biblical theme of the covenant provided a useful device for Protestant writers who sought to lay bare the foundations of governmental authority. Locke's *Second Treatise* can therefore be understood as "the classic text of radical Calvinist politics."[41]

The theocratic conception of natural law which lies at the heart of Locke's work was subjected to extensive criticism in the eighteenth century. One of the most acute critics was David Hume, who argued that even if the origins of government were rooted in some notion of contract, this cannot provide the foundation for legitimate political authority since, once government is established, its will can be imposed without regard to the people's consent. Hume's point is that the ques-tion of the origins of government must be differentiated from that of the source of its authority. For Hume, political obligation is not grounded in contract but rests firmly on the foundation of utility.[42] The thrust of these criticisms was recognized by Jean-Jacques Rousseau,

[39] See Giuseppa Saccaro-Battisti, "Changing Metaphors of Political Structures" (1983) 44 *J. of the History of Ideas* 31.
[40] See Quentin Skinner, *The Foundations of Modern Political Thought* (Cambridge: Cambridge U.P., 1978), vol. 2, Pt. III.
[41] Ibid. 239.
[42] David Hume, "Of the original contract" [1748] in his *Essays Moral, Political and Literary* E.F. Miller ed. (Indianapolis: Liberty Classics, 1985), 465. Hume is followed by Bentham, who attacks Sir William Blackstone's use of the idea of an original contract and contends that political society does not emerge from an original contract but is merely the result of a habit of obedience: Jeremy Bentham, *A Fragment on Government* [1776] Wilfrid Harrison ed. (Oxford: Blackwell, 1948) ch. 1, § 10. See also Ch. 9 above, pp. 125–40.

who believed that the institution of private property and political authority had destroyed natural liberty, entrenched inequality and condemned the species to labour, slavery and misery.[43] Consequently when, in *The Social Contract*, Rousseau examined the conditions under which political authority could be rendered legitimate, his solution took the form of an ideal, rather than an actual, contract.[44] This treatment of contract as a hypothesis is echoed by Immanuel Kant who, although postulating an original contract rooted in the freedom, equality and unity of its members, readily admits that the device is "merely an *idea* of reason".[45]

During the eighteenth century it became evident that the idea of the social contract could not provide an answer to the historical question: what are the origins of the State? Rather, the social contract was invoked for the purpose of resolving a vital analytical problem: how can the validity of the social and political order be explained? Once recognized to be a logical device, social contract theory lost much of its potency. John Dunn has noted that "the trenchancy of Kant's proclamation of human equality as the universal standard of public right" sits rather uneasily with "the feebleness and vagueness of his treatment of the means for achieving this standard in political practice". In conjunction, "they foreshadowed both the intellectual convenience of the hypothetical contract as a device for analysing human value and its extremely limited capacity to furnish clear and convincing direction for political actions."[46] Kant himself implicitly acknowledged this problem. If the social contract is essentially a requirement of reason—that is, if it only provides a rational criterion of the just polity—how can it bind in practice? His solution was to claim that politics must be subordinated to morality; "politics must bend the knee before right".[47]

But the practical issues of politics are not resolved by some generalized appeal to "reason".[48] This point can be illustrated by reflecting on

---

[43] Jean-Jacques Rousseau, *Discourse on the Origin and Foundation of Inequality among Mankind* [1754] Franklin Philip trans. (Oxford: Oxford U.P., 1994).

[44] Rousseau, above n. 3.

[45] Immanuel Kant, "On the common saying: 'This may be true in theory, but it does not apply in practice'" [1793] in his *Political Writings*, Hans Reiss ed. (Cambridge: Cambridge U.P., 2nd edn. 1991), 61, 79 (emphasis in original).

[46] John Dunn, "Contractualism" in his *The History of Political Theory and other essays* (Cambridge: Cambridge U.P., 1996), 39, 60.

[47] Kant, "Perpetual Peace: A Philosophical Sketch" [1795] in his *Political Writings*, above n. 45, 93, 125.

[48] Cf. Thomas Paine, *Rights of Man* [1791–2] in his *Rights of Man, Common Sense and other Political Writings* Mark Philp ed. (Oxford: Oxford U.P., 1995), 83, 321: "The

the scheme of Locke's thought. Given its grounding in equality and liberty, its universalistic pretensions, and its rejection of theological and patriarchal categories of thought, Locke's analysis is rather skewed. Mary Wollstonecraft, for example, uses Lockean arguments to insist that universal rights must include women[49] and, more recently, Carole Pateman has argued that, although Locke rejects Filmer's patriarchalism, he replaces it with a form of "fraternal patriarchy" which continues to deny full equality and status to women.[50] Locke's treatment of the European "discovery" of America is similarly revealing. Notwithstanding the existence of societies of aboriginal peoples, Locke sees seventeenth-century America as a state of nature: "in the beginning, all the world was *America*"[51] and, through the deployment of this device, he provides a justification for the imperial acquisition of land and the imposition of sovereignty. Tully argues that in Locke's narrative, the "invasion of America, usurpation of Aboriginal nations, theft of the continent, imposition of European economic and political systems, and the steadfast resistance of the Aboriginal peoples are replaced with the captivating picture of the inevitable and benign progress of modern constitutionalism."[52] Those who claim to be guided by reason alone are invariably bound up with the prejudices of their age.

Under the weight of such criticism, contractualist thinking fell from favour during the nineteenth and twentieth centuries.[53] Nevertheless, it has recently re-emerged in America, mainly through the work of Rawls

present age will hereafter merit to be called the Age of reason, and the present generation will appear to the future as the Adam of a new world."

[49] Mary Wollstonecraft, *Vindication of the Rights of Women* [1792] (London: Everyman, 1929).

[50] Carole Pateman, *The Sexual Contract* (Cambridge: Polity Press, 1988).

[51] Locke, above n. 7, II, § 49.

[52] James Tully, *Strange Multiplicity: Constitutionalism in an Age of Diversity* (Cambridge: Cambridge U.P., 1995), 78.

[53] Note might be made, in particular, of Hegel's rejection of contract as providing the basis of political obligation. Hegel rejected contractualism primarily because it assumes the autonomy of the individual and gives priority of the private over the public. For Hegel, contract is a casual bond which arises from a subjective need, whereas the political relationship is qualitatively different, being objective, necessary, and not a matter of choice: see G.W.F. Hegel, *Philosophy of Right* [1821] T.M. Knox trans. (Oxford: Oxford U.P., 1967), 215. In criticizing contractualism as bourgeois ideology, Marx builds on Hegel's foundation: see Karl Marx "On the Jewish Question" [1843] in Jeremy Waldron (ed.), *Nonsense on Stilts: Bentham, Burke and Marx on the Rights of Man* (London: Methuen, 1987), 147. This line of criticism lies at the core of modern communitarian thought: see Michael Sandel, *Liberalism and the Limits of Justice* (Cambridge: Cambridge U.P., 1982).

and Nozick. Rawls's work on justice, which has already been considered,[54] is a reformulation of Kantian contract theory which aims to show how political institutions should be designed, and what practices they should follow, if they are to meet the criteria of justice. What is most surprising about Rawls's theory, however, is the gap between its social democratic ideals and the actual social and economic differences in those societies which today claim to be social democracies. Nozick, by contrast, provides a modern variant of the Lockean argument; he starts with the idea of the individual as a holder of rights to life, liberty and property in some pre-political state in order to justify the claim of the minimal State as the only just State.[55] Unlike Locke's natural rights, Nozick's individual rights are not derived from God's natural law, but are taken to inhere in the idea of the person as a free and equal subject. The source of these rights, however, is never adequately explained. But what is most intriguing about the work of Rawls and Nozick is that, having asserted different starting premises (needs for Rawls, entitlements for Nozick) they use a contractual metaphor as a device to justify very different political regimes.[56]

The social contract, then, is a device which is often used to show how political obligation rests on individual consent. The technique is to relate a story about life without political order, both to indicate why we might bind ourselves in allegiance to a governing authority and what functions the State should be expected to undertake. The more brutal the story about the pre-political state, the more authoritarian the form of the political order to which we bind ourselves. If life in a state of nature is presented in a less grotesque light, the more likely it is that a system of limited government will be articulated. Similarly, the more we focus on individuals as bearers of property the more we are likely to devise a limited role for the State, and the more we focus on individuals as possessors of needs the more likely it is that the device will be used to justify redistribution. Social contract theory has been unable to avoid the politics of identity, of inclusion and exclusion, which lies at the heart of political issues.[57]

[54] John Rawls, *A Theory of Justice* (Oxford: Oxford U.P., 1972). See Ch. 7 above, 96–100.

[55] Robert Nozick, *Anarchy, State, and Utopia* (Oxford: Blackwell, 1974).

[56] See Alasdair MacIntyre, *After Virtue: A Study in Moral Theory* (London: Duckworth, 2nd edn. 1985), ch. 17.

[57] See, e.g., William E. Connolly, *Identity/Difference: Democratic Negotiations of Political Paradox* (Ithaca, NY: Cornell U.P., 1991).

CONTRACTUALISM AND LAW

Contractualism has been an important device in modern political thought.[58] The deployment of contractual metaphors has been particularly useful for the purpose of conveying a belief that political order is rooted in the agreement of free and equal individuals; contractualism is therefore associated with the values of liberty and equality. The idea of the social contract strips away much of the mysticism which surrounds foundational issues, revealing the State to be a human construction designed for particular purposes. Although the earliest thinkers who used contractual metaphors drew their inspiration from the Old Testament, with its images of the covenant between God and people, contractualism has been a vital part of a secularizing movement in modern political thought.

But contract is also a legal concept. The question thus arises: what, if any, has been the impact of the deployment of these metaphors on our understanding of the relationship between politics and law? Hobbes was clear on this point. The covenant was not a contract between rulers and ruled but one through which the authority of rulership is established. Sovereignty expresses the nature of the relationship between governors and governed and this is fundamentally a political relationship. It follows that Hobbes is opposed to any division of the sovereign power: "for what is it to divide the power of a commonwealth", he suggests, "but to dissolve it?"[59] One concern was that, if power were divided formally, then law might be assumed to provide the foundation of politics. This, for Hobbes, was heresy: "And for these doctrines, men are chiefly beholding to some of those, that making profession of the Laws, endeavour to make them depend upon their own learning, and not upon the Legislative Power".[60] The affairs of the State are quintessentially political, and if practices are to evolve as to how the power of the State should best be exercised, then these must be understood to be prudential practices of politics and not formal rules of law.

Whereas Hobbes uses the contract metaphor to establish authority, Locke employs it to limit the authority of the ruler. But if the basis of

---

[58] See Harro Höpfl and Martyn P. Thompson, "The History of Contract as a Motif in Political Thought" (1979) 84 *American Hist. Rev.* 919.

[59] Hobbes, above n. 4, 225.

[60] Ibid.

all political power is a contract of rulership which has certain limits, then surely law will provide the foundation of political order? Locke, however, avoids this conclusion, using the term "contract" only occasionally and more commonly invoking such expressions as "compact" or "agreement". This usage, Laslett argues, is deliberate: these terms "are further removed from the language of the law" and "[v]ague as Locke is, we seem to have here a deliberate attempt to avoid being specific and to leave legal models on one side".[61] Locke was careful to avoid the suggestion that the establishment of political order was essentially a legal, rather than political, event. For Locke, the relationship between the ruler and the people is not essentially a legal relationship of contract, but a political relationship of trust. The idea of trust secures the principle of the sovereignty of the people, instils the principle of limited government and generates a sense of accountability of governors to governed. But these all express fundamentally political—not legal—relationships. Consequently, even though Locke acknowledges the need for a division of State power, this is not a formal legal separation; it is a division which flourishes through the evolution of trust.

Early-modern political thinkers therefore did not believe that social contract theory implied that the practices of politics are either rooted in, or defined by, positive law. This was to come later, as modern thinkers unpacked the implications of Kant's belief that "[t]he rights of man must be held sacred" and "all politics must bend the knee before right".[62] This later development may explain Maine's rather jaundiced view that "the only real connection between political and legal science has consisted in the last giving to the first the benefit of its peculiarly plastic terminology".[63]

[61] Above n. 7, "Introduction", 126.
[62] Kant, above, n. 47, 125.
[63] Sir Henry Sumner Maine, *Ancient Law: Its Connection with the Early History of Society and its Relation to Modern Ideas* [1861] (London: John Murray, 10th edn., 1884), 307.

12

Modern Constitutions

EARLY-MODERN SOCIAL contract thinkers form the bridge between the ancient and modern worlds. According to Locke and his associates, the political relationship is not one between sovereigns and subjects, but between rulers and free citizens. Political order is established through an act of delegation by free and equal individuals to a governing body, and the activities of rulers are limited to the pursuit of the collective good. These beliefs had a powerful impact on eighteenth-century radicals. When in 1776 Thomas Jefferson drafted the American Declaration of Independence, the language he used reflected this shift in thought. Indeed, Lockean ideas seemed so obvious as to be in need of no further demonstration. "We hold these truths to be self-evident", Jefferson asserted: "that all men are created equal; that they are endowed by their Creator with certain inalienable rights; that among these are life, liberty and the pursuit of happiness. That, to secure these rights, governments are instituted among men, deriving their just powers from the consent of the governed."[1]

The American revolution marked the beginning of the end of the Aristotelian idea that "man is by nature a political animal". Following its success, certain political beliefs were built into the foundation of the governing order: that civil society and the State are separate; that the State exists to realize particular and limited social objectives; and that a division between the public and private spheres must be recognized. More generally, it was assumed that people are not political animals, but are creatures of labour. They come together and forge an agreement to establish a collective power primarily for the purposes of self-preservation, the maintenance of freedom and the protection of their acquired property rights. And if the collective power acts unjustly, then the people have the right of rebellion. It was, after all, precisely this right to resist an unjust power which the American colonial pamphleteers had asserted in order to justify their struggle for independence.

[1] Cited in Max Beloff, *Thomas Jefferson and American Democracy* (Harmondsworth: Penguin, 1972), 49.

From these ideas emerged a belief in the constitution as a construction. In *The Philosophy of Mind*, Hegel gave expression to the old understanding when he stated that "what is . . . called 'making' a 'constitution' is . . . a thing that has never happened in history" since a constitution "only develops from the national spirit."[2] With the benefit of hindsight, however, the founders of the modern American republic did indeed make a constitution. "It has been . . . reserved to the people of this country," Alexander Hamilton noted, "to decide an important question, whether societies of men are really capable or not of establishing good government from reflection and choice, or whether they are forever destined to depend for their political constitutions on accident and force."[3] The American constitution takes its place as the first modern constitution. Constitutions, in this modern sense, are of human design; the constitution is conceived as a formal mechanism devised to hold rulers to their bargains.

This chapter examines the modern idea of a constitution. It is an idea apparently at odds with the principle of sovereignty. Being a concept expressing the conviction that political power could be freed from subjection to religious authority, sovereignty had been a liberating idea. But some were concerned that, through sovereignty, a power had been created which might be used to oppress. Although Hobbes and Locke recognized this problem, both believed that a solution could be found in political behaviour. For Hobbes, the sovereign was enjoined to act only when it was necessary to maintain order and promote the common good.[4] Locke went further: he rejected the idea of absolute governmental power and asserted the principle of popular sovereignty. By making the legislature responsive to the wishes of the people, Locke anticipated that governors would not use their powers oppressively. But his solution—the sovereignty of the people instead of the sovereignty of the king—did not ensure the protection of individual liberties and it is for this reason that he provided a longstop of the right of rebellion. Nevertheless, the argument remained to be made that, once the principle of limited government is established, there was no place for such absolutist ideas. This is the argument that lies at the foundation of a modern constitution.

[2] G.W.F. Hegel, *The Philosophy of Mind* [1830] William Wallace trans. (Oxford: Clarendon Press, 1971), § 540.

[3] Alexander Hamilton, James Madison and John Jay, *The Federalist* [1787–8] Benjamin Fletcher Wright ed. (Cambridge, Mass: Belknap Press, 1961), 89 (no. 1, Hamilton).

[4] See Ch. 9 above, 135.

By advocating a division of State power between the legislature and executive, Locke had taken us some way along this road. He had suggested, however, that a conflict between these two powers could not be resolved by any "judge on earth".[5] After the Glorious Revolution of 1688, an accommodation was reached between legislature and executive, which meant that the British had no need to determine the precise source of the sovereign authority of the State. It was therefore left to a French scholar, Charles Louis de Secondat, Baron de Montesquieu, to identify the basis of the English system.[6] It is generally accepted that *The Spirit of the Laws* provides "an enthusiastic but mistaken tribute to the system that he had so falsely imagined to prevail in England."[7] Nevertheless, despite this rather basic flaw, Montesquieu's book rapidly gained acceptance, in part because it explained the unwritten British constitution in such clear terms. By copying from it for his *Commentaries*, Blackstone "gave that version semi-official standing, especially in the American colonies"; and, by making the British constitution intelligible, Montesquieu and Blackstone together "made the equivalent of a first draft available to constitution-makers on a distant continent."[8]

In this chapter, I propose to examine the nature of this activity of constitution-making, to identify the ideas and values which underpin such an exercise, and to highlight the way in which constitution-makers tend to conceive of the relationship between politics and law. I shall argue that the modern idea of the constitution is closely associated with the emergence of the principle of the separation of powers and that this in turn leads to recognition of a modern idea of the rule of law. And as a consequence of these developments, law presents itself not as an assortment of customary practices nor as the commands of a sovereign power but as a set of foundational principles which exist to constrain and channel the conduct of politics.

[5] John Locke, *Two Treatises of Government* [1680] Peter Laslett ed. (Cambridge: Cambridge U.P., 1988), II, § 168.
[6] Montesquieu, *The Spirit of the Laws* [1748] Anne M. Cohler, Basia Carolyn Miller and Harold Samuel Stone trans and ed. (Cambridge: Cambridge U.P., 1989)
[7] Isaiah Berlin, "Montesquieu" in his *Against the Current: Essays in the History of Ideas* Henry Hardy ed. (Oxford: Clarendon Press, 1989), 130, 131.
[8] Judith N. Shklar, *Montesquieu* (Oxford: Oxford U.P., 1987), 112.

THE SEPARATION OF POWERS

Montesquieu's objective in *The Spirit of the Laws* went far beyond that of revealing the basis of the English constitution. He set out to explain the development of the entire institutional framework of government and thereby to expound the social laws of political development. Montesquieu, in short, sought to establish a rational science of government. This venture was scarcely an unqualified success. Berlin's overall assessment is that Montesquieu's science was merely a collection of epigrams and maxims: "his errors of fact were too numerous, his social history a string of anecdotes, his generalisations too unreliable, his concepts too metaphysical, and the whole of his work, suggestive though it might be in parts, and an acknowledged masterpiece of literature, was unsystematic, inconsistent, and in places regrettably frivolous."[9] Though it fails as science, it is nonetheless a major work of political and legal theory. And the one foundational idea he has bequeathed is that of the doctrine of the separation of powers.

Montesquieu's primary concern was with the power of monarchy, the predominant mode of government throughout mid-eighteenth century Europe. The power of the monarch, he contends, is necessarily bounded: "in a monarchy, the prince is the source of all political and civil power . . . [but] if in the state there is only the momentary and capricious will of one alone, nothing can be fixed and consequently there is no fundamental law."[10] Monarchy is rooted in the principle of honour and this mode of governance is sustained only if monarchical power is encircled by laws, institutions and practices which prevent the prince's personal will from being directly imposed on his subjects. Unless power is dispersed, monarchs are unable to maintain their constitution, which is likely to be transformed either into a republican or a despotic order. Montesquieu believed that republican constitutions are able to work only in traditional, highly politicized, societies. Looking to the future, his main concern was to counsel against the degeneration of monarchy into despotism: just as "rivers run together into the sea," he notes, so also "monarchies are lost in despotism."[11]

---

[9] Berlin, above n. 7, 131–2.
[10] Montesquieu, above n. 6, Bk. 2, ch. 4. This is, of course, a traditional theme: see, e.g., Fortescue, above 112.
[11] Ibid. Bk. 8, ch. 17.

For Montesquieu, despotism is the prevalence of fear and "its end is tranquillity". But this does not signal peace; "it is the silence of the towns" brought about by the destruction of social life. Despotism brings in its train a stifling uniformity.[12] Within free societies, by contrast, citizens pursue a variety of ends. The challenge for government is to be able to permit freedom of choice, since without liberty society will degenerate. The best constitution for society, therefore, is one in which power is dispersed. There must exist a system of interlocking and mutually checking interests.

It has been suggested that Montesquieu's genius is to have identified the essence of the political problem in the conflict between *power* and *liberty*.[13] Rather than following Locke in asserting a natural right that provides the foundation for a claim to liberty, Montesquieu focuses on the power that threatens it. And rather than speculating on the origins of power, he simply examines its effects. For Montesquieu, liberty and power are both to be understood as concepts which acquire meaning within social frameworks. Since, in making this move, he is generally acknowledged to have provided us with the definitive language of liberalism, it is worth examining further this conflict between power and liberty.

Liberty should not be conceived as a state of total independence, of being able to do whatever one wishes. This, Montesquieu believes, will lead only to anarchy, and thence to the despotism required in order to control the situation. He argues, rather, that "liberty can consist only in having the power to do what one should want to do and in no way being constrained to do what one should not want to do."[14] But how do we know this? The answer, he contends, is to turn to the law: "Liberty is the right to do everything the laws permit."[15] Montesquieu concedes that there can be oppressive laws. But in a society rooted in justice, which he defines as "the necessary relations deriving from the nature of things,"[16] the law will always aim at the protection of liberty. Liberty he describes elsewhere as a good net in which the fish do not feel constrained.[17] Freedom is achieved through the operation of

---

[12] Montesquieu, above n. 6, Bk. 5, ch. 14.
[13] Pierre Manent, *An Intellectual History of Liberalism* Rebecca Balinski trans. (Princeton: Princeton U.P., 1995), 55.
[14] Montesquieu, above n. 6, Bk. 11, ch. 3.
[15] Ibid.
[16] Ibid. Bk. 1, ch. 1.
[17] *Pensées*, 943; cited in Shklar, above n. 8, 86.

political and legal arrangements which protect citizens against the oppressive instincts of their rulers. Political power is also the consequence of social arrangements. "It has been eternally observed", Montesquieu notes, "that any man who has power is led to abuse it; he continues until he finds limits." In order to prevent this happening, "power must check power by the arrangement of things."[18] Within this scheme, there is no need to vest absolute power in a Hobbesean sovereign for the purpose of keeping the ambitious or rebellious under control. The temptation amongst people to exploit their power is neutralized through the allocation of powers to a variety of institutions so that a system of countervailing powers is established. It is just such a division of powers—needed to permit liberty to flourish—which Montesquieu contends prevailed in republican Rome and was present in eighteenth-century England.

Like Locke, Montesquieu accepts the need to divide power between the legislature and the executive. But he makes two innovations. First, he views the danger for liberty as emanating primarily from the legislative power. Rooted in the principle of representation, the legislature might be tempted to increase the range of its powers and act abusively. One function of the executive, then, is to provide a check on the legislature: "If the executive power does not have the right to check the enterprises of the legislative body, the latter will be despotic, for it will wipe out all the other powers, since it will be able to give to itself all the power it can imagine."[19] Secondly, he draws a distinction between two aspects of executive power: the "executive power of the state" to make peace or war, to establish security and prevent invasions; and the "power of judging" through which crimes are punished and disputes between individuals adjudicated. Consequently, he contends not only that "when the legislative power is united with executive power in a single person or single body of magistracy, there is no liberty" but "nor is there liberty if the power of judging is not separate from legislative power and from executive power".[20]

Montesquieu here clearly expresses the principle of the separation of powers. Although distinguishing between legislative and executive power, Locke treated judges as forming part of the executive. By elevating the judiciary to a third, independent branch of government, Montesquieu opened up the possibility of law acting as an autonomous

---

[18] Montesquieu, above n. 6, Bk. 11, ch. 4.
[19] Ibid. Bk. 11, ch. 6.
[20] Ibid. Bk. 11, ch. 6.

force in government. But surely this would lead to a direct clash between law and politics? Hobbes certainly would have contended that the divided powers of the State are likely to work against one another and prevent the State from acting effectively.[21] Montesquieu, however, believed that, "as they are constrained to move by the necessary motion of things, they will be forced to move in concert,"[22] and that the legislative, executive and judiciary will act collectively to maintain and promote liberty. But if law and politics are not held in conflict, surely Montesquieu establishes a system in which, as Manent provocatively suggests, liberty "is produced through the neutralization of the political"?[23] In order to take further this line of inquiry, we must explore how the principle of separation of powers generates a distinctively modern understanding of the rule of law.

THE MODERN IDEA OF THE RULE OF LAW

Constitutional liberty, says Montesquieu, is achieved when the exercise of governmental power is constrained through institutional checks and balances. This system of formal constraints is what we now recognize as a modern liberal constitution and it provides us with a contemporary understanding of the idea of constitutionalism. It is only once these understandings have been set in place that we can appreciate what is meant by the modern idea of the rule of law.

The ancient (Aristotelian) idea of the rule of law, as we have seen, is best understood as the rule of "aristocratic" reason.[24] Its potency rests on the virtue, character and dispositional habits of the governing élite. In the modern version, these traits of virtue and character are of secondary importance. According to modern sensibilities, the exercise of State power, even when placed in the hands of the wisest, contains an arbitrary element which must be checked and controlled. This system of checks—the separation of powers—ensures that the power vested in governors cannot be turned to personal advantage and that the personalized rule by men is replaced by the impersonal rule of rules. In its modern formulation, the rule of law is closely associated with the

---

[21] Thomas Hobbes, *Leviathan* [1651] Richard Tuck ed. (Cambridge: Cambridge U.P., 1996), ch. 17. See also Robert Filmer, "The Anarchy of a Limited or Mixed Monarchy" [1648] in his *Patriarcha and Other Political Works* Peter Laslett ed. (Oxford: Blackwell, 1949), 275.

[22] Montesquieu, above n. 6, Bk. 11, ch. 6.

[23] Manent, above n. 13, 61, 60.

[24] See Ch. 5 above.

separation of powers—the political theory of constitutionalism—and presents itself as a fence which can protect the citizen's liberties from the potentially oppressive power exercised by rulers. One of the main facets of this modern conception is that of an independent judiciary in acting as a bulwark against executive power. It is this aspect of the rule of law which is critical in distinguishing between liberal and despotic regimes. Montesquieu makes it clear that a dispute is referred to the judiciary not because of their innate wisdom (*phronēsis*) but because they are strict and impartial rule-appliers: "the judges of the nation are . . . only the mouth that pronounces the words of the law, inanimate beings who can moderate neither its force nor its rigour."[25] Whereas in Locke's scheme the judiciary hardly figured at all, in Montesquieu's they perform a pivotal role as guardians of the liberties of the citizen.

In contrast to the ancient conception of the rule of law, which had great ethical weight but was applied only to the governing élite, Montesquieu's modern version places formal restrictions on the conduct of governors, restrictions intended to operate for the benefit of every member of society. Whereas the Aristotelian conception is compatible with a slave society or with a modern "dual state" (one in which a proportion of the population might be declared to be sub-human and excluded from the legal order), this is anathema to the modern conception which is devised to preserve the liberty and equality of the individual. Both operate through a public–private distinction, but the manner in which the lines are drawn varies. In the ancient conception, women, children and slaves form part of a private, domestic economy which is ordered on patriarchal lines and is not governed by norms of justice or law. In the modern version, all individuals possess—in theory at least—a formal legal and political equality. However, it is precisely because the norms of justice and law apply equally to all, that certain types of human conduct—issues of personal morality such as the expression of religious belief, sexual identity or political views—must be removed from the control of the State. Montesquieu emphasizes the point that if the State attempts to regulate this private sphere, governors will be drawn into taking repressive action, leading to despotism.

This modern version of the rule of law creates a zone of freedom within which citizens are able to pursue their own vision of the good life. This zone of civil liberty is defined by the general framework of

---

[25] Montesquieu, above n. 6, Bk. 11, ch. 6.

rules under which all—including rulers—are obliged to live. This is what is meant by freedom under the law: the rules provide a framework or set of boundaries within which individuals may act as they please, protected from the arbitrary will or aggression of the rulers. The celebrated case of *Entick* v. *Carrington* in 1765—in which the plaintiff successfully brought an action for trespass against officers of the Secretary of State who searched the plaintiffs house and seized his papers—provides a good illustration of the principle in operation. Having taken action to protect the security of the State against seditious pamphleteering, the officers had relied on past practice, claiming "reason of State". To this argument, the Chief Justice replied that: "If it is law, it will be found in our books. If it is not to be found there, it is not law." Lord Camden here asserts that judges are rigorous rule-appliers, applying the rules in order to protect the liberties of citizens: "it is too much for us without such authority to pronounce a practice legal, which would be subversive of all the comforts of society." If the judiciary were "to mould an unlawful power into a convenient authority" then "[t]hat would be, not judgment, but legislation."[26]

For this idea of the rule of law to flourish, what is needed is a division of governmental functions such that power is checked by power in order that neither the exigencies of the executive, nor the enthusiasms of the legislature could function in such a manner as would oppress the individual. Within the structure of governance, the judiciary—the "least dangerous" branch, possessing neither the power of the purse nor the sword[27]—do not need exceptional virtue. What they require is, first, a set of relatively clear and general rules which can establish an impartial system and, secondly, independence in order to apply the law without fear or favour. While much of this thinking derives from Montesquieu, it was taken up in the nineteenth century by Dicey, who expressed the belief that "the rule of law is contrasted with every system of government based on the exercise by persons in authority of wide, arbitrary, or discretionary powers of constraint."[28] This modern version has been highly influential in twentieth-century debates.[29]

[26] (1765) 19 St.Tr. 1030.
[27] Hamilton *et al.*, above n. 3, 490 (no.78, Hamilton). See further Alexander Bickel, *The Least Dangerous Branch: The Supreme Court at the Bar of Politics* (New Haven: Yale U.P., 1962).
[28] A.V. Dicey, *An Introduction to the Study of the Law of the Constitution* (London: Macmillan, 8th edn. 1915), 188.
[29] See, e.g., F.A. Hayek, *The Constitution of Liberty* (London: Routledge, 1960), Pt. II; L.L. Fuller, *The Morality of Law* (New Haven, Yale U.P., rev. edn. 1969); Joseph Raz,

LAW, LIBERTY AND DEMOCRACY

Montesquieu believed that, being necessary for the maintenance of liberty, law is of the utmost importance in shaping human conduct in modern societies. Although in ancient Rome, mores were determinative and laws were enacted only when mores failed, in modern England, he argued, it was the other way round: there, the laws shaped mores.[30] Montesquieu also links the foundational importance of law to the growth of commerce. Commerce, he notes, "cures destructive prejudices" and leads to peace amongst nations: "it is an almost general rule that everywhere there are gentle mores, there is commerce and that everywhere there is commerce, there are gentle mores."[31] Whilst commerce eradicates banditry on the one hand and altruism on the other, "it produces in men a certain feeling for exact justice."[32] Commerce promotes self-interest and the collective pursuit of self-interest requires the establishment of a clear framework of laws under which all must live.

The linkage between the development of commerce, the promotion of self-interest, the maintenance of political stability, the retention of liberty, the establishment of a clear framework of laws and the achievement of progress provided what was probably the most vital theme in the political discourse of the eighteenth and nineteenth centuries.[33] What is most interesting for our purposes is the connection between these various themes and the emergence of democracy. If, as Montesquieu suggests, commerce promotes self-interest, then we might also note that this is essentially an egalitarian movement, in the sense that this development also advances the idea that no individual's interest should be treated as being intrinsically more valuable than another's. Progress, it would appear, is linked to the evolution of democracy in government. But will not democracy both undermine the stability of the social order and generate mediocrity, as government by the wise is replaced by government by the many? Further, since the

"The Rule of Law and its Virtue" in his *The Authority of Law: Essays on Law and Morality* (Oxford: Clarendon Press, 1979), ch. 11. Cf. E.P. Thompson, Ch. 1 above, 15.

[30] Montesquieu, above n. 6, Bk. 19, chs. 23, 27.

[31] Ibid. Bk. 20, chs.1, 2.

[32] Ibid. Bk. 20, ch. 2.

[33] See Istvan Hont and Michael Ignatieff (eds), *Wealth and Virtue: The Shaping of Political Economy in the Scottish Enlightenment* (Cambridge: Cambridge U.P., 1983); J.G.A. Pocock, *Virtue, Commerce and History* (Cambridge: Cambridge U.P., 1985).

involvement of the many in government might have the tendency to extend the legitimacy of governmental activity, might not the legislative power of the majority be deployed to subvert the liberties of minorities? Debate on the impact of democracy on government was highly polarized during this period. Some, such as Thomas Paine, extolled the virtues of democracy, arguing that "government on the old system is an assumption of power for the aggrandizement of itself; on the new, a delegation of power, for the common benefit of society."[34] Many remained sceptical, however, and extolled the virtues of maintaining an evolutionary constitution. Edmund Burke, for example, claimed that "we are resolved to keep an established church, an established monarchy, an established aristocracy and an established democracy, each in the degree it exists, and in no greater."[35] Within this charged debate, Tocqueville's classic analysis is particularly instructive.

In his preface to the twelfth edition, Tocqueville highlighted one of his key objectives in writing *Democracy in America*. Writing in 1848, he noted that, while "almost all Europe was convulsed by revolutions, America has not had even a revolt."[36] His point was that democracy is not to be feared, but is a tendency which had to be managed. Tocqueville was not starry-eyed about the coming of democracy: "Nothing conceivable is so petty, so insipid, so crowded with paltry interests—in one word, so anti-poetic—as the life of a man in the United States."[37] He did not believe that democracy should be embraced because it was intrinsically just, or that it would promote civic virtue, or that it would lead to more enlightened government. On the contrary, he recognized that "it is incontestable that the people frequently conduct public business very badly."[38] Instead, he promotes a thesis which, typically, he presents in a paradoxical form: "that extreme democracy obviates the dangers of democracy."[39]

What is it, he asks, that enables us to maintain order during a period of great social change? The nature of the changes which were taking

---

[34] Thomas Paine, *Rights of Man* [1791–2] in his *Rights of Man, Common Sense and other Political Writings* Mark Philp ed. (Oxford: Oxford U.P., 1995), 223.

[35] Edmund Burke, *Reflections on the Revolution in France* [1790] Conor Cruise O'Brien ed. (Harmondsworth: Penguin, 1968), 188.

[36] Alexis de Tocqueville, *Democracy in America* [1835] Henry Reeve trans., Daniel J. Boorstin intro. (New York: Vintage Books, 1990), vol. 1, xxi.

[37] Ibid. vol. 2, 74.

[38] Ibid. vol. 1, 251.

[39] Ibid. vol. 1, 198.

place meant that class deference was on the wane. Further, given the secularizing tendencies of the age, the power of religion to maintain order, and especially to reconcile the poor to their poverty, was likely to be eroded. In these circumstances, Tocqueville contended, the extension of democracy can ensure that the citizens will obey the law. Social egalitarianism stabilizes society; once everyone owns some property it is unlikely that the institution of private property will be subject to a sustained assault, since "only those who have nothing to lose ever revolt."[40] Similarly, egalitarianism in politics will bind all to the political order. If everyone has an equal voice in government, people will voluntarily submit to the authority of collective decisions, and not solely because they believe this to be right: the losers respect majority decisions on the ground they expect on another occasion to be able to benefit from the system. The people do not obey the law because it expresses reason, truth or justice. Nor do they obey out of fear, since this motivation may ultimately have the effect of leading to revolution. The law is obeyed not because it is *necessary* but because it is *contingent*: "the people . . . obey the law, not only because it is their own work, but because it may be changed if it is harmful; a law is observed because, first, it is a self-imposed evil, and, secondly, it is an evil of transient duration."[41]

Within a democracy, then, the laws "are frequently defective or incomplete; they sometimes attack vested rights, or sanction others which are dangerous to the community."[42] Tocqueville also maintains that aristocracies "are infinitely more expert in the science of legislation than democracies ever can be," since they are "possessed of a self-control that protects them from the errors of far-reaching designs" and that aristocratic government "proceeds with the dexterity of art."[43] Democracy certainly is not to be valued because it is more enlightened. Popular government should be promoted mainly because it generates loyalty amongst citizens and thus makes society easier to control. In short, the more democratic the system, the less revolutionary it is likely to be.[44]

[40] Tocqueville, above n. 36, vol. 1, 248.
[41] Ibid.
[42] Ibid. vol. 1, 237.
[43] Ibid. vol. 1, 238.
[44] See Stephen Holmes, "Tocqueville and democracy" in David Copp, Jean Hampton and John E. Roemer (eds), *The Idea of Democracy* (Cambridge: Cambridge U.P., 1993), ch. 1.

Following Montesquieu, Tocqueville believes that commerce and democratic politics go hand-in-hand. Under democracy, citizens become more active and energetic and although democratic government "does fewer things well, it does a greater number of things." The "grandeur" of the system thus lies "not in what the public administration does, but in what is done without it or outside of it."[45] This is not to say that democracy is without its dangers. Tocqueville recognizes that, given the release of energy which democracy unleashes, there is a likelihood that for many economic activity—the private sphere—will become all-absorbing and this will result in citizens ceasing to involve themselves in public affairs. Democracy is likely to engender a type of individualism which will cause people no longer to participate actively in public affairs.[46] And this gives rise to a danger of a new form of despotism.[47] Tocqueville believed that the only defence against this threat is the maintenance of a vibrant political culture which would ensure that political power was widely dispersed. What role might law have to play in ensuring that power remains dispersed so that both liberty and pluralism in politics might be maintained? For many, the answer to that question lies in the use of law as an instrument of institutional design.

CONSTITUTIONAL DEMOCRACY

Can liberalism be reconciled with democracy? For most contemporary writers working in the tradition of Montesquieu and Tocqueville, the answer is found in the political theory of constitutionalism. Based on the idea that no individual is intrinsically more worthy than any other, constitutionalism expresses an egalitarian ethos. But constitutionalism, being also underpinned by a belief that people are motivated by self-interest, does not assume that individuals possess some innate sense of civic virtue. Working from these assumptions, constitutionalism asserts that the basic danger posed by democracy is that of majoritarianism, the threat that majorities motivated by self-interest might use their power to tyrannize minorities. Since action motivated by

---

[45] Tocqueville, above n. 36, vol. 1, 252.

[46] Tocqueville suggests that within democracy, the passions of the individual are quelled, his horizons are narrowed and he becomes confined "entirely within the solitude of his own heart" (ibid. vol. 2, 99).

[47] See Ch. 2 above, 29–30.

self-interest might infringe the principle of the equal moral worth of individuals, constitutionalism prescribes a set of constraints on those wielding political power. These constraints—the rules of political engagement—are incorporated in basic principles of the constitution. In this modern understanding, "a constitution is a thing *antecedent* to a government, and a government is only the creature of a constitution."[48] Since a constitution, in this modern sense, establishes and controls the government, it is generally accepted that the constitution must be a body of written and fundamental law, the meaning of which is determined ultimately by a supreme court. Constitutional law constrains political behaviour.

If democracy means the rule of the majority, then the restrictions imposed by this body of fundamental law—restrictions which might not be capable of being overturned by a simple majority—seem not to be justified on democratic grounds. Why, it might be asked, should citizens and their representatives be constrained in the legitimacy of their political actions by the terms of a constitutional document which was drafted and adopted many years previously? Surely this is simply a new form of ancestor-worship? How can the actions of the judiciary in striking down democratically-enacted legislation on the ground that it infringes the constitution be justified? Is this not to trump the rule of the living by the rule of the dead? How, if modern constitutions are framework documents which the people give themselves,[49] can constitutions frustrate the expressed will of the people? Is it not the case, in short, that constitutional democracy is an oxymoron?

Liberal democrats contend that these tensions are not contradictions and that it is a paradox of democracy that majoritarianism must presuppose certain restrictions on the exercise of the will of the majority. Constitutional constraints, they argue, must not be seen simply to be limitations on power. Following Montesquieu's point that power and liberty are products of social arrangements, they argue that constitutional rules also create and apportion powers in a manner which enables democracy to function.[50] Like rules of grammar which facili-

---

[48] Thomas Paine, *Rights of Man*, above n. 34, 122.

[49] See, e.g., the Preamble to the Constitution of the United States of America: "We the People of the United States, in order to form a more perfect Union . . . do ordain and establish this Constitution for the United States of America."

[50] See, e.g., John Hart Ely, *Democracy and Distrust: A Theory of Judicial Review* (Cambridge, Mass: Harvard U.P., 1980), who argues that constitutional constraints can be democracy-reinforcing insofar as their function is that of ensuring that the channels of political competition work properly.

tate the speaker's ability to communicate, constitutional rules should be treated as being enabling not disabling: the limits fixed by such rules, they argue, do not weaken government but, by organizing the exercise of political power and channelling its direction, the rules enhance and strengthen government.

If we are properly to appreciate the idea that constitutional rules express rather than restrict democracy, further consideration must be given to the meaning of democracy. If we believe that democracy reflects the aspiration of self-government by a people, then it cannot be reduced simply to an expression of the will of a transient majority. Understood as self-government, democracy requires decision-making after public discussion amongst free and equal citizens. Consequently, rules which ensure the freedom and equality of citizens to participate in public debate, and which thereby protect the right to express unpopular views, can be understood as democracy-reinforcing rules.[51] And this means that it is impossible to make sense of the idea of democratic government without having regard to a system of rules which establish the institutional framework through which expression can be given to the popular will.

Understood in this light, constitutions might not be presented as restrictions on the power of rulers, but as instruments of collective self-rule. This is what Stephen Holmes refers to as "positive constitutionalism".[52] Constitutions, he argues, not only limit power and prevent tyranny, but also construct power and guide it towards socially desirable ends; they establish the rules which put democracy to work. Thus, the articulation of a majority will is dependent on the existence of rules which encourage wide-ranging debate, and which therefore dictate restrictions on the exercise of censorship and on the ability of economically powerful interest groups to dictate the agenda or intimidate others. Furthermore, those majorities will need the co-operation or acquiescence of outvoted minorities, and this can be attained only if the basic rights of minorities are respected. One particularly important function of constitutional rules is to quell the passions and promote reflective deliberation on the central issues of collective life. Self-government involves more than the free play of the appetites; it also

[51] For an argument that the checks and balances in the US Constitution are designed not only to promote limited government but also to institutionalize deliberative democracy, see Cass R. Sunstein, *The Partial Constitution* (Cambridge, Mass: Harvard U.P., 1993).

[52] Stephen Holmes, *Passions and Constraint: On the Theory of Liberal Democracy* (Chicago: University of Chicago Press, 1995).

requires the self to assume control of the desires. It is precisely because we start from the assumption that individuals are motivated by self-interest that there is a need to establish institutions which are able to curb the destructive passions and encourage people to deliberate and to act rationally.

CONSTITUTIONAL LAW AND POLITICS

The political theory of constitutionalism brings the metaphor of the scales from the sphere of justice into the heart of the governmental process. The objective of the theory is to establish a balance between the different branches of government, primarily for the purpose of ensuring that the passions of rulers are tempered and that government acts reflectively and proportionately in furtherance of the collective good. If politics is to be viewed as a competitive struggle for power and aggrandizement, the aim of establishing a binding constitution which devises the basic rules of the game is to provide some stability into what might otherwise be a rather volatile contest.

The modern constitution seeks the realization of this stabilizing objective not only through the imposition of formal procedures with respect to the processes of public decision-making, but also by removing certain issues of social contention from the agenda of government. Consensus can be achieved over the rules of the game, it is suggested, only if some of life's basic issues—most notably those concerning the nature of religious belief—are removed from the field of play. Through this type of exercise, referred to variously as "gag rules,"[53] the "precept of avoidance",[54] and "constitutional abeyances",[55] a private sphere protected from political controversy is created. By having these unre-solvable issues removed from the public agenda—by, for example, drawing a clear line between Church and State[56] or, in a gesture of rec-onciliation during the transition of a State to democracy, by offering amnesties to power-wielders in the old regime[57]—the political process

[53] Holmes, *Passions and Constraints*, ch. 7.

[54] John Rawls, *Political Liberalism* (New York: Columbia U.P., 1993), 29, 151–2.

[55] Michael Foley, *The Silence of Constitutions: Gaps, "Abeyances" and Political Temperament in the Maintenance of Government* (London: Routledge, 1989).

[56] See, e.g., the First Amendment to the US Constitution: "Congress shall make no law respecting an establishment of religion, or prohibiting the free exercise thereof . . ."

[57] See, e.g., Ruti Teitel, "Transitional jurisprudence: the role of law in political trans-formation" (1997) 106 *Yale Law Journal* 2009 (on post-communist states); David

is able to do its work more effectively. Constitutionalism not only formalizes the rules of political decision-making, but also circumscribes the range of issues to be addressed by government. Constitutional rules thus are both constraining and enabling. Stephen Holmes argues further that, since the restrictions imposed on the powers of government can function to enhance the State's capacity to mobilize public power for common purposes, limited government is more powerful than unlimited government. Viewed in this light, constitutionalism emerges as "one of the most effective philosophies of state building ever contrived".[58] Constitutionalism, it should be noted, also generates a particular conception of the relationship between politics and law. It suggests that law must be conceived as a structure of rules and principles which provides the foundation of political order. To some, this will appear to be an elementary proposition. Nevertheless, it is one which the British tradition has not embraced. Notwithstanding the fact that Montesquieu identified the English system as the cradle of constitutionalism, the evolutionary British constitution has never accepted the need for the institutional differentiation of the State to be regulated by positive law.[59] Although the efficacy of this tradition has been questioned on a number of fronts in recent years,[60] the system still operates within the framework of a command-based conception of law. The system has not yet developed a structural conception of law—law as a set of foundational principles—which the institutionalization of positive constitutionalism would seem to require.[61]

Although this structural image of law shaping and limiting the conduct of politics conveys a reassuring message, it is one which may be deceptively seductive. For one thing, it is often the case today that modern constitutions perform a function similar to that of public relations departments of large corporations: they portray the system as those in authority would wish to see it presented. There is an ambiguity—some would argue a deliberate ambivalence—between the formal

Dyzenhaus, *Judging Judges, Judging Ourselves: Truth, Reconciliation and the Apartheid Legal Order* (Oxford: Hart, 1998) (on post-Apartheid South Africa).

[58] Holmes, above n. 52, xi.
[59] See Ch. 9 above, 136–40.
[60] See Ch. 10 above, 155–7.
[61] See David Marquand, *The Unprincipled Society: New Demands and Old Politics* (London: Fontana, 1988), which presents the thesis that Britain's constitutional heritage and legal tradition has become a major obstacle to our ability successfully to adjust to the realities of late twentieth-century life.

constitution and the manner in which government actually conducts its business, and these ambiguities are, arguably, an indispensable aspect of the system.[62] Constitutional abeyances not only insulate certain issues from political controversy, but also amount to "condoned obscurities"[63] through which certain unresolvable conflicts can be dissipated and defused and in accordance with which the exercise of executive power can escape the categories of law. Consequently, to the extent that the establishment of a framework of fundamental law conveys the belief that answers to all political disputes can ultimately be found in law, this achievement may well lead to an intense politicization of legal processes.

One final point might be raised about the relationship between law and politics within a constitutionalist framework. Drawing on Weber's view that the three major justifications for domination are the claims of tradition, charisma and legality,[64] it might be noted that the trajectory of change in political systems seems generally to be away from traditional sources of authority and towards the legitimacy of legality. For some, this increased rationalization and bureaucratization of political order is leading to a loss of meaning, or sense of disenchantment with the world. Political systems today exhibit an impersonal power which is insufficiently connected to the "lifeworld" to be able to command people's allegiance.[65] From this perspective, constitutionalism is simply an exercise in bootstrapping, of trying to lift ourselves by our own boots.[66] Such feelings contribute to the growing gulf which appears to be opening up between citizens and the political system, and this may cause people to retreat to a simple primordialism in order to make sense of their lives.[67] This occasionally manifests itself when, as over the public debates throughout Europe over the Maastricht Treaty, it becomes evident that politicians are failing fully to carry the citizens

[62] See Harvey C. Mansfield Jr., *Taming the Prince: The Ambivalence of Modern Executive Power* (Baltimore: Johns Hopkins U.P., 1989).

[63] Foley, above n. 55, 114.

[64] Max Weber, "Politics as a Vocation" [1921] in H.H. Gerth and C. Wright Mills (eds), *From Max Weber: Essays in Sociology* (London: Routledge & Kegan Paul, 1948), 77, 78–9.

[65] See Jürgen Habermas, *Between Facts and Norms: Contributions to a Discourse Theory of Law and Democracy* William Rehg trans. (Cambridge: Polity Press, 1996).

[66] We might, e.g., compare the present situation with Jefferson's declaration, above n. 1, which was able to establish an authoritative value framework only by appealing to the work of "a Creator".

[67] See Clifford Geertz, "The Integrative Revolution: Primordial Sentiments and Civil Politics in the New States" in his *The Interpretation of Cultures* (London: Fontana, 1993), ch. 10.

with them. But we see that it also carries specific messages about the contemporary meaning of such abstractions as the rule of law, a point that was thrown into stark relief when Colonel Oliver North was transformed into a national hero during the Iran–Contra investigation in the United States, notwithstanding clear evidence that he had been party to the flouting of some of the most basic constitutional requirements.[68] Constitutionalism may place politics within a framework of law, but this does not resolve the issue of the relationship between law and politics. What remains is a set of contentious issues concerning the politics of constitutionalism.

---

[68] See Harold Hongju Koh, *The National Security Constitution: Sharing Power after the Iran–Contra Affair* (New Haven: Yale U.P., 1990).

13

The Age of Rights

MONTESQUIEU'S GENIUS was to have located the essence of politics in the struggle between power and liberty.[1] He argued that since the extension of power entails the restriction of liberty, the objective of constitutionalism must be to provide checks on the exercise of power for the purpose of ensuring the preservation of liberties. But throughout his extensive discussions on politics and law, the concept of rights is scarcely mentioned. This, in retrospect, seems significant, if only because today it is often assumed that constitutionalism is bound up with the protection of rights. In this chapter, I examine the way in which the ideal of constitutionalism seems to have shifted away from a concern with limited government and towards the protection of individual rights. Before outlining the evolution of rights discourse in modern times, however, we should first reconsider the influence of thinkers like Locke on the political activists of the late eighteenth century.

As against Aristotle, Locke had argued that the true state of mankind is not political society but a state of nature. And as against Hobbes, he claimed that this state of nature, rather than being a war of all against all, is one in which people exist as free and equal beings. Applying these ideas of natural law, Locke contended that political society is an artificial construct devised for the purpose of maintaining and extending natural freedom and equality. It follows, he believed, that individuals possess certain natural rights which they cannot renounce or alienate and which cannot be expunged by anyone, even the State. Locke's views on natural rights had a major influence on late eighteenth-century debates.

The first indication of the translation of natural rights rhetoric from philosophical debate to political action is found in the Declaration of Rights of Virginia in 1776. It maintained that "all men are by nature equally free and independent, and have certain inherent rights, of which, when they enter into a state of society, they cannot by any

---

[1] See Ch. 12, above 181.

compact deprive or divest their posterity."[2] The American colonists
here were asserting a right of resistance against the Crown on the
grounds that their natural rights were being violated. Of even greater
political significance, however, was the *Declaration of the Rights of
Man and the Citizen* approved by the French National Assembly on
26 August 1789. The Declaration not only signalled the outcome of an
act of rebellion but what was to become a full-scale revolution, the
overthrow of the *ancien régime* and a total reconstruction of the political order. Here, too, Locke's influence can be detected. In proclaiming
the liberty, equality and sovereignty of the people, the Declaration
recognized that the "end of all political associations" is the "preservation of the natural and imprescriptable rights of man."[3]

The American and French Revolutions opened a new era in political
history, one of the defining features of which has been the role accorded
to rights within the political structure. Before these revolutions, rights
and liberties were invariably treated as concessions to be extracted
from the sovereign. This is precisely the form in which rights are
expressed in the celebrated English charters of Magna Carta (1215), the
Petition of Right (1628) and the Bill of Rights (1689).[4] But within this
new revolutionary discourse, rights are recognized as existing prior to
the power of the sovereign. Rights do not derive from the political constitution, but are antecedent to constitutional order and provide the
foundation on which all constitutions are constructed. This innovation
leads to the establishment of a new form of political rule, one which
contains at its core the necessity of maintaining and protecting the
"natural rights" of individuals.

In this chapter, I propose to examine the growing influence of this
political movement to promote natural rights and to chart its success in
having rights institutionalized and thereby transformed from political
claims into legal entitlements. I hope to show that the range of interests
subject to rights claims has considerably grown and that, at the same
time, so too has the nature of the claim, as rights rhetoric extends
beyond the arena of the State and into the category of a universal
requirement. As a result of these developments, I shall argue that rights

---

[2] *Virginia Declaration of Rights*, 12 June, 1776, art. 1 in A.I. Melden (ed.), *Human
Rights* (Belmont, California: Wadsworth Publishing Co., 1970), App.1, 135. See also the
American Declaration of Independence, 4 July 1776: Ch. 12, above 177.

[3] *Declaration of the Rights of Man and the Citizen* (1789), art. 2 in Melden, ibid. App.
3, 140.

[4] See R.C. van Caenegem, *An Historical Introduction to Western Constitutional Law*
(Cambridge: Cambridge U.P., 1995), ch. 7.

discourse has today become one of the major forces shaping the development of legal orders throughout the world and an especially powerful form of political expression.

NATURAL RIGHTS DOCTRINE

The political values underpinning the American and French revolutionary movements were given popular expression in Thomas Paine's *Rights of Man*. Paine argued that a new system of government was now materializing, driven by the principle of popular sovereignty and the rapid development of commerce, and directing us towards "universal civilization."[5] The old system of government, he suggests, "is an assumption of power, for the aggrandisement of itself; on the new system, a delegation of power, for the common benefit of society."[6] The old "keep[s] up a system of war" whereas the new "promotes a system of peace"; the old "encourages national prejudices" and the new "promotes universal society."[7]

At the core of this new system lies the idea of natural rights, most clearly expressed in Article 1 of the French Declaration: "Men are born, and always continue, free, and equal in respect of their rights." For Paine, natural rights means those rights "which appertain to man in right of his existence" and which provide "the foundation of all his civil rights."[8] Whilst these natural rights, being "founded on the original inherent Rights of Man," are ancient, the system of government emerging on the platform of these principles is genuinely innovative, precisely because "tyranny and the sword have suspended the exercise of those rights for many centuries past."[9] Government founded on these indefeasible rights, having received its spark from America, had ignited in Europe and "is now revolving from west to east, by a stronger impulse than the government of the sword revolved from east to west."[10] The present age merits being called "the Age of Reason,"[11] Paine concludes, since government is now being reconstructed in accordance with the principle of natural rights.

[5] Thomas Paine, *Rights of Man* [1791–2] in his *Rights of Man, Common Sense and other Political Writings* Mark Philp ed. (Oxford: Oxford U.P., 1995), 83, 266.
[6] Ibid. 223.
[7] Ibid.
[8] Ibid. 119.
[9] Ibid. 223.
[10] Ibid. 213.
[11] Ibid. 321.

Although natural rights doctrine flourished in the late eighteenth century, it was also subjected to sustained attack. Jeremy Bentham ridiculed the idea as "rhetorical nonsense—nonsense on stilts",[12] though it might be noted that rhetorical nonsense can often make ideological sense.[13] Reflecting a Hobbesean view, Bentham argued that such claims are destructive of political order. The idea of a right "is a child of law" and it is only "from *real* laws" that we might derive "*real* rights." Elaborating on this theme, Bentham contended that "from *imaginary* laws, from the laws of nature, fancied and invented by poets, rhetoricians, and dealers in moral and intellectual poisons, come *imaginary* rights, a bastard brood of monsters."[14]

The most celebrated attack on the French Declaration, however, was that of Edmund Burke.[15] Burke's argument was that the idea of natural rights was much too abstract and metaphysical and that, when deployed by individuals, it was an invitation to insurrection and a persistent cause of anarchy. He believed it to be a dangerous notion precisely because power is necessary to sustain order and, since it cannot be eradicated, "Kings will be tyrants from policy when subjects are rebels by principle."[16] Burke viewed English liberties as "an entailed inheritance, derived to us from our forefathers, and to be transmitted to our posterity."[17] These are real, historically-grounded rights and they vest in the people "without any reference whatever to any other more general or prior right."[18] This idea of what he calls "a liberal descent" is needed to fortify and bolster "the fallible and feeble contrivances of our reason".[19] "We fear God; we look with awe to kings; with affection to parliaments; with duty to magistrates; with reverence to priests; and with respect to nobility."[20] These are the roots of our natural sentiments and the source of our ability to reconcile order with freedom.

---

[12] Jeremy Bentham, *Anarchical Fallacies; being an examination of the Declaration of Rights issued during the French Revolution* [c.1795] in Jeremy Waldron (ed.), *Nonsense on Stilts: Bentham, Burke and Marx on the Rights of Man* (London: Methuen, 1987), 46, 53.

[13] See Michael Freeden, *Rights* (Milton Keynes: Open U.P., 1991), 18.

[14] Bentham, *Anarchical Fallacies*, above n. 12, 69 (emphasis in original).

[15] Edmund Burke, *Reflections on the Revolution in France* [1790] Conor Cruise O'Brien ed. (London: Penguin, 1986).

[16] Ibid. 172.

[17] Ibid. 119.

[18] Ibid.

[19] Ibid. 121.

[20] Ibid. 182.

Burke's essay was prescient. He foresaw the violence which came with the degeneration of the Revolution into the Terror and the eruption of the Napoleonic wars. Nonetheless, natural rights doctrine has lived on, becoming the powerful rallying cry of all who are fighting for emancipation. No greater acknowledgement of its potency is to be found than the fact that Article 1 of the Universal Declaration of Rights in 1948—declaring that "All human beings are born free and equal in dignity and rights"—reproduces Article 1 of the French Declaration almost verbatim.

The main difficulty with natural rights doctrine flows from its inherent idealism. Since the claim that humans are born equal in dignity and rights is patently untrue, adherents are required to find some way of placing this rhetorical claim on an objective foundation. One obvious method of doing so is by appealing to religious authority and invoking the intentions of a divine creator, which is precisely what Jefferson did when drafting the American Declaration.[21] In a secular age, however, this is an unreliable method of establishing the truth of these claims. An alternative would be to establish the authority of these rights by demonstrating the existence of a constant and unchanging human nature, but given the vagaries of human history, this also seems doomed from the outset. Perhaps the most challenging method—one associated with Kant—has been to discover the structure of ethical order embedded within human reason itself.[22] Nevertheless, even if fundamental rights are built on a single value—the principle of freedom—we still face the difficulty that freedom remains an essentially contested concept. The real problem is that, since fundamental rights are invoked for the purpose of achieving final values, they serve mainly as an appeal to those values and, of necessity, as Norberto Bobbio points out, "final values themselves cannot be justified but only premised; that which is final is, by its very nature, without foundation."[23] Alisdair MacIntyre is more scathing: "there are no [natural or human] rights, and belief in them is one with belief in witches and unicorns."[24] Claims to "natural," "inalienable" or "fundamental" rights, it appears, are either tautological or fictional.

---

[21] See Ch. 12 above, 177.

[22] See, e.g., Alan Gewirth, *Human Rights: Essays in Justification and Application* (Chicago: University of Chicago Press, 1982), who attempts to derive human rights from claims to necessary human goods.

[23] Norberto Bobbio, *The Age of Rights* Allan Cameron trans. (Cambridge: Polity Press, 1996), 5.

[24] Alisdair MacIntyre, *After Virtue: A Study in Moral Theory* (London: Duckworth, 2nd edn. 1985), 69.

This is not to suggest that an appeal to fundamental rights without value. What it does means is that, rather than seeking to demonstrate their truth, the strength of the claim is vitally dependent on particular rights acquiring general acceptance. Fundamental rights have force through consensus. The claim to the existence of certain fundamental human rights which all states must respect is ultimately an exercise in bootstrapping. And this means that the force of rights discourse depends not on demonstrating the requirements of some Kantian "moral law", but on our growing acceptance of certain core human values, of what Annette Baier, following David Hume, calls "a progress of sentiments."[25] The force of rights discourse is derived from the intricate and uncertain processes through which political consensus is established.

THE GROWTH OF RIGHTS DISCOURSE

Throughout the modern period, there has been a growing acceptance of the importance of rights in the conduct of politics. Why is this so? The answer, at its most basic, is that rights discourse emerges from a fundamental shift in our perception of the nature of political order. The Aristotelian idea of political society as an organic whole has been displaced by an individualistic conception in which free, equal and rights-bearing individuals combine to promote their collective purposes. The State exists not only to promote relatively limited objectives, but also to preserve and protect the citizen's fundamental rights. Humans are not by nature political animals, nor is the political relationship one of sovereigns and subjects. With the emergence of rights discourse, the traditional relationship between State and citizen is inverted and the basic or "natural" rights of the citizen are regarded as primary.

The authoritative source of these so-called natural rights need not detain us. Rights are asserted as being natural or fundamental primarily because their existence is not felt to be dependent on the consent of the sovereign power. Although the roots of these political claims lie in the struggle for religious liberty in the early-modern era, their force

---

[25] Annette Baier, "Hume, the Women's Moral Theorist?" in Eva Kittay and Diana Meyers (eds), *Women and Moral Theory* (Totowa, NJ: Rowman and Littlefield, 1987), 40. See also Richard Rorty, "Human Rights, Rationality and Sentimentality" in Stephen Shute and Susan Hurley (eds), *On Human Rights* (New York: Basic Books, 1993), 111.

need not rest on the truth of a religious belief. In the modern, secular age many of these rights-claims have been transformed into what Tocqueville called a "civil religion."[26] This transformation in the nature of the political relationship can most clearly be seen through the growing importance of rights discourse, especially during the latter half of the twentieth century. I want to focus on five aspects of this movement: first, the intrinsically political nature of rights claims; secondly, the type of language in which these political claims are expressed; thirdly, the dramatic growth in complexity of rights-claims as the range of their protection is extended; fourthly, the institutionalization of rights claims, so that both their identification and protection becomes an issue of law; and, finally, the transformation of rights claims beyond the arena of State law and into the sphere of universal right. By briefly considering each in turn, I hope to be able to highlight the political significance of these developments.

The first feature, that rights discourse remains intrinsically a form of political discourse, is self-evident. Rights are local, historically-rooted claims, not fixed universals. Consider the varied treatment accorded to property rights over time. During the late-eighteenth century the right to property was regarded as being "inviolable and sacred"[27] and perhaps the most basic of human rights, whereas today property rights are subject to extensive restriction and regulation. Property rights are never treated as inviolable and they no longer prominently feature in more recent charters and declarations.[28] Furthermore, while certain rights have waned in importance, others, such as the right to work or to enjoy a healthy, sustainable environment, have recently begun to figure in charters of rights.

That the recognition and status accorded to particular rights is a political matter is also highlighted by the fact that today many of the most intractable political issues concern the question of how disputes between conflicting rights claims are to be resolved. How is the right to artistic or political self-expression to be reconciled with the citizen's right not to be subjected to offensive speech or behaviour? How can a woman's right to control her reproductive behaviour be squared with

[26] For a modern rendering see Sanford Levinson, *Constitutional Faith* (Princeton, NJ,: Princeton U.P., 1988).

[27] *Declaration of the Rights of Man and the Citizen*, art. 17.

[28] It might be noted that political movements to make the protections of charters apply only to humans, and thus to prevent corporations from taking advantages of charters of rights, derive primarily from the objective of ensuring that such charters cannot be used for the purpose of protecting extensive claims to property rights.

the right to life of an incipient person? On these and many other clashes between rights, the State is obliged to reach a determination. And that decision is intrinsically political. But although rights recognition remains the subject of political debate—and here we come to the second feature of the rights movement—the language of politics uses a different register. No longer is the issue addressed in the textured dialect of citizenship claims; instead, it is articulated in the strident, universalistic, egalitarian and individualistic jargon of rights. When rights clash, the political issues at stake are presented in a polarized form.

With this in mind, Marshall's account of the evolution of conceptions of citizenship[29] can be re-interpreted through the language of rights. Marshall, we may recall, charts the trajectory of modern political history from the claim of civil citizenship (rooted in the wars over religious liberty), through the political idea of citizenship (based on parliamentary struggles), and on to social and economic claims of citizenship (founded in the protections accorded by the Welfare State). Within rights discourse, this basic scheme is retained, but the language is transformed: liberties are converted into rights, concessions into entitlements, and governmental powers into duties. The full impact of this changing language becomes apparent, only when we turn to the third feature of the rights movement: the gradual extension in the scope of protections accorded by rights.

It is beyond question that the rhetoric of rights has evolved very rapidly over the last two hundred or so years and now colonizes broad swathes of political discourse. What began life as the abstract claims of certain natural rights theorists, comes to provides the foundation of established political systems. Since the American and French revolutions, increasing numbers of states which, at critical moments in their development, have devised modern constitutional frameworks, have also inscribed a charter of rights within these documents.[30] The range of demands within the scope of rights claims has also mushroomed. We have quickly moved from the traditional claims of "natural rights" (such as the right to life), through the sphere of political rights (such as the right to vote), and now face an extensive range of claims to such social rights as education, health, welfare and work.

The challenge here not only flows from the proliferation of rights claims, though it seems inevitable that this must lead to an escalation

---

[29] Ch. 7 above, 100.
[30] See, e.g., David Beatty (ed.), *Human Rights and Judicial Review: A Comparative Perspective* (Dordrecht: Martinus Nijhoff, 1994).

of rights conflicts. It is much more fundamental. Although civil and political rights generally inhere in the abstract entity of the person or citizen, social rights vest in particular groups of human beings—such as the old, the sick or the exploited. While civil and political rights generally impose restrictions and limitations on the State's power of action, the realization of social rights invariably requires positive action from the State. One consequence of the extension of rights to the social sphere has therefore been to fuel an intense political debate on the idea of freedom.[31] Such debate often only exposes the depth of disagreement about the nature and status of the right and highlights the gap between the generalized claim and its actual implementation.

Reference to the question of implementation brings us to the fourth feature of the movement, the institutionalization of rights in legal systems. Here, it is important to recognize that rights discourse has traditionally belonged primarily within the political sphere, with a distinction being maintained between natural rights and positive law. The English tradition of liberties illustrates this point: we have generally appealed to our (political) tradition of liberties in order to protect ourselves from the rigour of the law.[32] In earlier formulations, natural rights theories positioned rights claims in the same place as civil liberties.[33] This format is evident in the French Declaration, in which it is recognized that: "The exercise of the natural rights of every man, has no other limits than those which are necessary to secure to every other man the free exercise of the same rights; and these limits are determinable only by the law."[34] So, rights are political and the limits to a rights claim, or the resolution of a conflict of rights, will be determined

[31] The formulation of this concern varies with the preferred animal analogy: see R.H. Tawney, *Equality* (London: Unwin, 4th edn. 1964), 164 ("freedom for the pike is death for the minnows"); Isaiah Berlin, *The Crooked Timber of Humanity* (London: Fontana, 1991), 12–13 ("total liberty for wolves is death to the lambs"); cf. William Blake, *The Marriage of Heaven and Hell* Sir Geoffrey Keynes intro. (London: Oxford U.P., 1975), 24 ("One Law for the Lion & Ox is Oppression"). For the general philosophical debate see: Isaiah Berlin, "Two Concepts of Liberty" in his *Four Essays on Liberty* (Oxford: Oxford U.P., 1969), ch. 3; Charles Taylor, "What's wrong with negative liberty" in his *Philosophical Papers, vol. 2* (Cambridge: Cambridge U.P., 1985), ch. 8.

[32] See, e.g., Christopher Hill, *Liberty against the Law: Some Seventeenth Century Controversies* (London: Allen Lane, 1996).

[33] These theorists generally distinguished between two senses of right, a broad formulation (that which is right) and a narrower notion of a right in a juridical sense, a division which has affinities with Aristotle's distinction between distributive and corrective justice. See Richard Tuck, *Natural Rights Theories. Their Origin and Development* (Cambridge: Cambridge U.P., 1981), 66–7.

[34] *Declaration of the Rights of Man and the Citizen*, art. 4.

ENY 9SL

by the law. But once rights become inscribed in law on any significant scale, the nature of the system is radically altered: the legal code shifts from one based on duties to one rooted in rights. And with the establishment of codified charters of rights in the form of general principles, citizens look to the law as the source of their liberties. The institutionalization of a platform of basic citizen's rights in the legal order thus has a profound effect on the character of law.

Clearly, this development is of major importance in seeking to understand the relationship between law and politics. But before we examine it further, the final feature of the rights movement must be considered. Until the middle of the twentieth century, the struggle for rights was a domestic movement through which citizens sought rights recognition within State structures. The movement was therefore one which, although requiring a reconceptualization of the political relationship from sovereign and subject to that of citizen and State, did not impinge on the basic principle of State sovereignty as it operated in the sphere of international relations. In 1948, as a consequence of approval by the General Assembly of the United Nations of the Universal Declaration of Human Rights, all this changed. With the acceptance of the Universal Declaration, natural rights theorists—who traditionally had expressed scepticism about the attempt to find a basis for natural law in the claim to general acceptance—were presented with "the greatest historical test of the *consensus omnium gentium* in relation to a given value system."[35] For the first time in history, a set of human rights acquired universal authority, drawing its validity from general consensus.

It scarcely needs mention that, since 1948, ensuring the effective protection of these human rights has remained a matter of major controversy. There are still "deep tensions between the traditional autonomy of states (sovereignty) and international concern for individual welfare, tensions that pervade both the law and the politics of international human rights and embarrass the international effort to improve the condition of individual human beings everywhere."[36] These tensions— between the UN Charter which bans the use of force violating the basic principle of State sovereignty and Universal Declaration of Human Rights which expresses basic rights to be protected against the actions of oppressive States—have most recently been articulated over the

---

[35] Bobbio, above n. 23, 14.
[36] Louis Henkin, "The Internationalization of Human Rights" in his *The Age of Rights* (New York: Columbia U.P., 1990), 14.

action taken by NATO in 1999 against Serbia over Kosovo.[37] Notwithstanding the controversies, the establishment of international human rights norms which can be invoked by the international community against those states which violate them, marks a new stage in the evolution of a rights movement.[38] The rights-bearing individual now has a presence in the arena of international law which previously had been the exclusive preserve of states. Citizens are no longer confined to those rights recognized by their government, but are also empowered to make rights claims against their own states.[39]

During the post-war period, then, the evolutionary features of the rights movement within states has been replicated in the international sphere. Since the Universal Declaration in 1948, which condemns discrimination based on sex and race as well as over religion and language,[40] action has been taken not only to unpack these general principles and place them in a legislative form,[41] but also to extend the scope of international human rights protection. The movement to extend the range of rights protection has evolved in two main directions: first, the scope of international conventions has developed from a framework of according rights to the abstract individual towards providing special protections both for particular groups[42] and for entire peoples;[43] and secondly from providing protection for individual

[37] See Bruno Simma, "NATO, the UN and the Use of Force: Legal Aspects" (1999) 10 *European J. of International Law* 1; Antonio Cassese, "*Ex Injuria ius Oritur?* Are we moving towards international legitimation of forcible humanitarian countermeasures in the world community?" (1999) 10 *European J. of International Law* 23.

[38] Henkin, above n. 36, 14–15: "The internationalization of human rights, the transformation of the idea of constitutional rights in a few countries to a universal conception and a staple of international politics and law, is a phenomenon of the middle of our century." This constitutes a further challenge to the sovereignty principle: see above, Ch. 10, 144–7.

[39] See Fernando R. Tesón, *A Philosophy of International Law* (Boulder, Colo.: Westview Press, 1998), presenting a Kantian thesis which challenges the traditional view that states, not individuals, are the basic subjects of international law and international relations.

[40] Universal Declaration of Human Rights 1948, art. 2.

[41] The Universal Declaration is a general declaration and not an international treaty. However, the International Covenant on Civil and Political Rights and the International Covenant on Economic, Social and Cultural Rights—both completed in 1966 and in force since 1976—have given legislative effect to the principles of the Declaration.

[42] See, e.g., the Convention on the Political Rights of Women, 1953 (providing for non-discrimination in relation to electoral suffrage, candidature and access to public office); Convention on the Elimination of all forms of Discrimination against Women 1979.

[43] See, e.g., UN Declaration on the Granting of Independence of Colonial Territories and Peoples, 1960 (declaring that the "subjection of peoples to an alien subjugation, domination and exploitation constitutes a denial of fundamental human rights").

rights towards endowing certain rights of collective autonomy.[44] The principle of sovereignty may remain the core principle of the international system but, as cases such as the Pinochet extradition action indicate,[45] it is now challenged in the name of human rights. What cannot be denied, however, is the fact that such rights claims are inextricably bound up with the major political issues of our times. If we raise our eyes from the text of the Universal Declaration and look around, we see the gulf between those lofty aspirations and the stark reality of a world of instability and conflict, power and impotence, wealth and poverty.

RIGHTS AND THE RULE OF LAW

The rights movement can be understood as an evolutionary process of *generalization* (as greater numbers of political claims are expressed in the language of rights), *institutionalization* (as such claims increasingly acquire recognition in positive law), *collectivization* (as claims extend beyond the abstract individual to embrace social groups), and *internationalization* (as rights discourse enters the domain of international relations). Each of these trends contributes to the growing *politicization* of rights, fuelled by the need for the State to ensure the realization of certain rights claims. This development highlights the question of the relationship between law and politics. In part, this is because the rights movement has affected our understanding of the nature of the legal order and, in particular, of the idea of the rule of law.

Natural rights doctrine made its initial impact as part of a political movement to formulate basic standards of treatment of citizens against which the laws and practices of the State could be measured. Once these basic rights become inscribed in positive law, however, citizens need no longer appeal to a set of political values and argue for their truth; they can now demonstrate their authority by referring to the normative framework of the law. This process of institutionalizing rights has had a powerful effect on the conduct of politics. As a result, the political relationship of sovereign and subject, based on notions of duty

---

[44] See, e.g., UN Covenant of Economic, Social and Cultural Rights, 1966, art 1: "All peoples have the right of self-determination. By virtue of that right they freely determine their political status and freely pursue their economic, social and cultural development."

[45] R. v. *Bow Street Metropolitan Stipendiary Magistrate, ex parte Pinochet (No. 2)* [1999] 2 WLR 272.

and trust, has been transformed into a relationship of citizen and State, founded on rights and contract. In certain respects, this process strengthens the State: after all, Locke's claim that the people retain the ultimate natural right of rebellion in case of a breach of trust[46] can now be replaced by the argument that citizens should seek the vindication of rights through judicial, rather than political, action. But it also means that, increasingly, the pursuit of politics focuses on the recognition of these rights by legislatures and their enforcement by courts. To this extent, the evolving rights movement is leading to the legalization of politics.

Such trends effect a change in our understanding of law. If citizens are to enforce rights against the State, it is vitally important that the judiciary be independent of the executive; this, as we have seen, is a critical dimension to the modern idea of the rule of law.[47] But once the State possesses a modern constitution incorporating a charter of rights, there is a tendency to claim that the legal enterprise is mainly concerned with the articulation and elaboration of rights. Once this claim is accepted, the idea of the rule of law undergoes a further subtle shift: it is converted from its status as a political ideal[48] to that of a juridical principle. This is a controversial development, since charters of rights are drafted as general statements of principle and the process of explicating the principle to yield specific decisions and remedies can appear to be a political exercise. But this task, vested in the judiciary, is one for which the legislature no longer bears the prime responsibility. The evolutionary dynamic of the rights movement therefore leads not only to the legalization of politics but also to the politicization of law.

This process has reached its zenith (or nadir?) in the United States where, during the twentieth century, a "rights revolution" has take place. This revolution has been prompted by the willingness of Supreme Court justices to activate the provisions of the Bill of Rights to provide a new platform of civil, political and social rights, including freedom of speech, due process in criminal procedure, and rights against discrimination on the basis of race or sex. This in turn has caused judges to assume the roles of political actors by, for example, taking discretionary control over their own dockets and deciding on

---

[46] See Ch. 11 above, 168–9.

[47] See Ch. 12 above, 183–5.

[48] See, e.g., F.A. Hayek, *The Constitution of Liberty* (London: Routledge, 1960), 206: "The rule of law is . . . not a rule of the law, but a rule concerning what the law ought to be, a meta-legal doctrine or political ideal. It will be effective only in so far as the legislator feels bound by it."

which cases they will hear[49] or by fashioning remedies which require their continued involvement in the management of the process.[50] It also results in the mobilization of major political resources to advance the cause of social reform through the courts[51] and in the Supreme Court becoming a major player in the politically contentious issues of the day.[52]

For some, this amounts to no less than "a new version of an old corruption: power without (financial or democratic) responsibility."[53] This is the view of Robert Bork, the Court of Appeals judge whose nomination to the Supreme Court in 1987 provoked a national debate, leading to his candidature being rejected by the Senate. Bork argues that, as a consequence of the rights movement, the US Constitution has been turned into a source of arbitrary power. The "liberals", he maintains, have successfully claimed that "the Constitution cannot be [positive] law" with the result that interpretation of the constitution is determined by "the morality and politics of the intellectual or knowledge class".[54] Consequently, the Constitution has become "a weapon in a class struggle about social and political values" which has resulted in "the transportation into the Constitution of the principles of a liberal culture that cannot achieve those results democratically". Judges, in short, have been seduced into substituting politics for law.[55] Others, however, are less jaundiced, arguing that judicial review can be justified on democratic grounds provided judges recognize that their pri-

[49] H.W. Perry Jr., *Deciding to Decide: Agenda Setting in the United States Supreme Court* (Cambridge, Mass: Harvard U.P., 1991).

[50] J. Harvie Wilkinson, *From* Brown *to* Bakke: *The Supreme Court and School Integration, 1954–1978* (New York: Oxford U.P., 1979); Jesse H. Choper, *Judicial Review and the National Political Process* (Chicago: Chicago U.P., 1980).

[51] See, e.g., Frances Kahn Zemans, "Legal Mobilization: The Neglected Role of the Law in the Political System" (1983) 77 *American Political Science Rev.* 690; Mark Tushnet, *The NAACP's Legal Strategy against Segregated Education, 1925–1950* (Chapel Hill, NC: University of North Carolina Press, 1987); Susan E. Lawrence, *The Poor in Court: The Legal Services Program and Supreme Court Decision-Making* (Princeton: Princeton U.P., 1990).

[52] The most intractable have probably been the life and death questions of euthanasia and abortion: see *Washington* v. *Glucksberg* 117 S.Ct 2258 (1997); *Vacco* v. *Quill* 117 S.Ct 2293 (1997); *Roe* v. *Wade* 410 US 113 (1973). See, e.g., Laurence H. Tribe, *Abortion: the Clash of Absolutes* (New York: Norton, 1990); Ronald Dworkin, "Darwin's New Bulldog" (1998) 111 *Harvard Law Rev.* 1718.

[53] Kenneth Minogue, "What is Wrong with Rights" in Carol Harlow (ed.), *Public Law and Politics* (London: Sweet & Maxwell, 1986), 209, 225.

[54] Robert H. Bork, *The Tempting of America: The Political Seduction of the Law* (London: Sinclair-Stevenson, 1990), 8.

[55] Ibid. 8, 9.

mary role in enforcing constitutional rights is to safeguard the political process by ensuring that the channels of political competition work properly.[56] At the other end of the spectrum are those who argue that the courts have not been sufficiently active, having failed to recognize that the constitution establishes a form of "deliberative democracy" rooted in civic republicanism.[57] The general point is that a great deal of political energy now focuses on the constitutional role of courts, creating a peculiar form of armchair politics in which the pen may well be mightier than the sword.

Although the United States is an extreme case, the trajectory of change is following a similar path across the western world.[58] Given the peculiar nature of Britain's unwritten, evolutionary constitution, this movement has had a less profound impact on our system. But there are accumulating pressures on the court system. The increased volume of judicial business,[59] the rise of interest-group litigation,[60] the dramatic growth in judicial review,[61] the impact of European law,[62] the evolution of a rights-based public law,[63] and the introduction of a charter of rights[64] are resulting in comparable debates emerging about the role of law in the political process. Courts are undoubtedly becoming more important. In Locke's seventeenth-century scheme, the judiciary

[56] See, e.g., John Hart Ely, *Democracy and Distrust: A Theory of Judicial Review* (Cambridge, Mass: Harvard U.P., 1980).

[57] Mark Tushnet, *Red, White and Blue: A Critical Analysis of Constitutional Law* (Cambridge, Mass: Harvard U.P., 1988); Cass R. Sunstein, *The Partial Constitution* (Cambridge, Mass: Harvard U.P., 1993).

[58] See Charles R. Epp, *The Rights Revolution: Lawyers, Activists, and Supreme Courts in Comparative Perspective* (Chicago: University of Chicago Press, 1998).

[59] Consider, e.g., the fact that although the House of Lords was able to hear virtually all cases filed before it in 1960, by 1990 it was granting leave in only about 25 per cent of cases: see Epp, ibid. 130. See further Kate Malleson, *The New Judiciary: The effects of expansion and activism* (Aldershot: Ashgate, 1999).

[60] See Carol Harlow and Richard Rawlings, *Pressure Through Law* (London: Routledge, 1992).

[61] See Law Comm. No. 226, *Administrative Law: Judicial Review and Statutory Appeals* (H.C. 669, 1994), App. C.

[62] See, e.g., Derrick Wyatt, "European Community Law and Public Law in the United Kingdom" in B.S. Markesinis (ed.), *The Gradual Convergence: Foreign Ideas, Foreign Influence and English Law on the Eve of the Twenty-First Century* (Oxford: Clarendon Press, 1994), 188; Robert Thomas, *Legitimate Expectation and Proportionality in Administrative Law* (Oxford: Hart, 2000).

[63] See Sir John Laws, " Law and Democracy" [1995] *Public Law* 72; Martin Loughlin, "Rights Discourse and Public Law Thought in the United Kingdom" in G.W. Anderson (ed.), *Rights and Democracy: Essays in UK-Canadian Constitutionalism* (London: Blackstone Press, 1999), ch. 9.

[64] Human Rights Act 1998.

212 Sword and Scales

hardly figured; in Montesquieu's eighteenth-century analysis they performed a significant role as guardians of the citizen's basic liberties. But due to the rights revolution of the twentieth century, their power has increased dramatically and concern has been expressed about the emergence of a system of government by judiciary. The vital institutional question is whether courts are equipped to perform these political tasks. From an ideological perspective, however, the issue is not so much that of the place of courts in government but the position of law within politics: does the judiciary have the legitimacy to engage in this type of decision-making?

The answer depends, first, on whether these political demands can successfully be converted into rational claims and, secondly, on whether such claims are accepted as being inscribed in law. The most ambitious attempt to answer these questions is found in Ronald Dworkin's "rights thesis". Dworkin develops a theory of liberalism based on the citizen's entitlement to "equal concern and respect": citizens have moral rights and duties with respect to one another, and political rights against the State. This argument is elaborated into two bold claims. First, "[i]f someone has a right to something, then it is wrong for the government to deny it to him even though it would be in the general interest to do so".[65] This is the idea of "rights as trumps" which defeat public policy claims rooted in the collective good. Secondly, he insists "that these moral and political rights be recognized in positive law, so that they may be enforced *upon the demand of individual citizens* through courts or other judicial institutions of the familiar type, so far as this is practicable."[66] This latter claim transforms our understanding of the rule of law.

In classical doctrine, the political claim to natural rights contrasts with the demands of positive law. The struggle was conceived as one of ensuring that respect for natural rights was incorporated, through legislation, in positive law. With the articulation of general and fundamental rights in positive law, however, our conception of law undergoes a basic shift. Rights which previously received their recognition through legislation, now find their source in a rational claim to the inherent dignity and worth of the human person. And when these assume the status of "fundamental human rights", they become the

65 Ronald Dworkin, "What Rights Do We Have?" in his *Taking Rights Seriously* (Cambridge, Mass: Harvard U.P., 1977), 266, 269.
66 Ronald Dworkin, "Political Judges and the Rule of Law" in his *A Matter of Principle* (Cambridge, Mass: Harvard U.P., 1985), 9, 11 (emphasis in original).

criterion against which the legality of legislation may be measured. The rule of law is no longer treated as a set of techniques through which an independent judiciary can keep government within the bounds of the rules of law. The rights conception insists that the judiciary ensure that the moral and political rights which citizens possess—and which might be "other than and prior to those given by positive enactment"[67]—are accurately identified and fully and fairly enforced. The rights conception blurs the distinction between moral/political and legal discourse and converts the rule of law from a political ideal into a foundational juridical principle.

The most contentious ideological question is whether judicial review which evaluates governmental action (legislative and executive) against the yardstick of constitutional rights can be reconciled with the principle of democracy. This controversy does not dissipate even if it is accepted that charters of rights chosen by the people or adopted by their representatives can be justified on democratic grounds. The main difficulty is that the level of abstraction of these principles means that they yield a variety of interpretations; that is, judges who hold different theories of the nature of order and liberty—power and rights—are likely to reach different conclusions about the applications of rights to particular areas of political dispute. And if judges have discretion arising from the different political theories they hold, then judicial review can scarcely be treated as an exercise of collective self-binding designed to promote democracy. Judicial review must actually be seen as the retention of a form of aristocratic rule.[68] There may be special reasons for this limited form of aristocratic rule, but it must be recognized as such and not somehow justified as an aspect of democratic self-government.

RIGHTS AND COMMUNITY

"Liberty, equality, fraternity" may have been the clarion call of the French revolutionaries, but these aspirations do not make comfortable bedfellows. Since 1789, political debate has focused mainly on the tension between liberty and equality, and is encapsulated in the distinction between the concepts of positive and negative freedom.[69] In recent years, the tension between liberty and fraternity has come to the forefront and revolves around the question of whether a political system

---

[67] Dworkin, above n. 66, 13.
[68] Cf. Ch. 5 above 69–70, 74.
[69] See above n. 31.

erected on the foundation of individual rights is able to sustain a social order. The debate has a long lineage; in the 1840s Karl Marx was criticizing the concept of "natural rights" as resting on the idea of "an individual withdrawn behind his private interest and whims and separated from the community."[70] The contemporary debate, polarized around the camps of liberalism and communitarianism,[71] has been kindled mainly because rights rhetoric is rapidly becoming the basic coinage of political discourse.[72]

From a British perspective, the basic question is whether the dominance of rights discourse in the United States is a product of the peculiarities of that system,[73] or of Americans having lived in the future longer than anyone else. Once rights are legally entrenched, it seems evident that political organizations have less need to engage in the deliberative task of coalition-building to advance their goals through legislative and executive processes.[74] Rights rhetoric also tends rapidly to permeate popular political culture, fuelled by the perception that the gap between governors and the people is growing too wide. Individuals thus latch on to rights rhetoric as a way of gaining greater control—an illustration, perhaps, of the lure of simple ideas in a highly complex world. But not all would accept that an evolving rights discourse must lead inexorably to the atomization of society;[75] for some, the belief that the institutionalization of rights heightens the tension between individual and community simply provides an instance of the way in which political thought lives in the thrall of false polarities.[76] The subject of rights thus remains a vital and contentious political issue.

---

[70] Karl Marx, "On the Jewish Question" [1846] in Waldron (ed.), above n. 12, 147.

[71] For an analysis of the theoretical foundations see Stephen Mulhall and Adam Swift, *Liberals and Communitarians* (Oxford: Blackwell, 1992).

[72] See Mary Ann Glendon, *Rights Talk: The Impoverishment of Political Discourse* (New York: Free Press, 1991). Similar concerns have figured prominently in recent feminist political theory: see Elizabeth Frazer and Nicola Lacey, *The Politics of Community: A Feminist Critique of the Liberalism-Communitarianism Debate* (London: Harvester Wheatsheaf, 1993).

[73] Louis Hartz, *The Liberal Tradition in America* (New York: Harcourt, Brace, 1955); Byron E. Shaffer (ed.), *Is America Different?* (Oxford: Clarendon Press, 1991).

[74] See, e.g., F.L. Morton, "The political impact of the Canadian Charter of Rights and Freedoms" (1987) 20 *Canadian J. of Political Science* 31.

[75] See Jürgen Habermas, "On the Internal Relation between the Rule of Law and Democracy" in his *The Inclusion of the Other: Studies in Political Theory* Ciaran Cronin and Pablo De Grieff eds. (Cambridge, Mass: MIT Press, 1998), ch. 10.

[76] See Stephen Holmes, *Passions and Constraint: On the Theory of Liberal Democracy* (Chicago: University of Chicago Press, 1995), 28.

V
Conclusions

.

14

The Relationship between Law and Politics

IF THIS INQUIRY yields a message, it is that the relationship between law and politics has no fixed or settled form. Law and politics are related, but also competing practices through which people aspire to settle their differences. Although drawing on a common fund of ideas, the practices are distinct; law, for example, maintains a formal structure which ensures its differentiation from, and opposition to, other forms of political engagement. But the precise form which law takes changes over time and the shifts which have been effected provide a key to understanding the nature of the relationship.

It is for this reason that we should be attentive to history, and when reflecting on the history of the relationship we are, I believe, drawn to the centrality of certain basic ideas which underpin legal and political discourse. These ideas provide the tools through which order is devised, institutionalized and maintained. Political visions generate contrasting images of order. The world of Hobbes, for example, differs markedly from that of Locke and, notwithstanding their differences, each narrative draws on a common pool of ideas (notably those of justice, liberty, sovereignty and rights) and makes use of such similar devices as covenant or contract so as to present them as distinctive and rival arrangements. It is only once these ideas have been assembled into a particular configuration that they take on specific meaning, and only once this happens does law take on a precise form.

In Chapter 1, I sketched three basic conceptions of law which seem to have been influential. The first presents law as a set of customary rules which are articulated by the judiciary, acting as the guardians of the immanent values of the common law. The second defines law as an expression of the will of the community, enunciated through the highest law-making authority. And the third conceives law as an expression of rights vested in individuals, thereby determining the character of the relationship between citizen and State. The contrasts are evident. Law as custom marks out a certain sphere of public activity as being subject to control by the judiciary, suggesting a relationship of accommodation with politics. Law as command reflects the idea of law as the outcome of an institutionalized political process, thus presenting law as an instrument of politics. Law as right reveals an image of law as structuring the entire political process, thereby laying down the foundation for politics.

Although the three conceptions of law are simplifications, they do reveal something of the complexity of the law/politics relationship. In this chapter, I will therefore try to unpack the meaning of these conceptions—elements of which have been identified in those sections of the book dealing with Justice, the State, and Constitutionalism—and indicate how particular conceptions of law have carried authority at different moments in history.

LAW AS CUSTOM

The idea of law as custom reflects an understanding of law as a practical discourse rooted in "artificial reason". Since law is the product of decisions and practices which have been built up over many generations, we have no need of high theory to make sense of the practice. Knowledge of law is acquired not through theory or analysis, but by education in a tradition of behaviour. "We acquire [such] habits of conduct", Oakeshott suggests, "not by constructing a way of living upon rules or precepts learned by heart and subsequently practised, but by living with people who habitually behave in a certain manner."[1] Although law involves rule-handling, the rules are not the wellspring of knowledge but are cribs, properly used only by someone educated in the traditions of the law. To be involved in the law is to participate in the continuing development of a concrete historical tradition. So although it is evidently the product of human action, law cannot be reduced to a matter of will. We no more make law than we make language or religion; like language and religion, law evolves through time to form an important part of the cultural matrix of society.

Law, in this conception, is a set of conventional practices which frame, but do not establish, political order. Judges have a special role in acting as custodians of these practices; legislators, after all, are rela-

---

[1] Michael Oakeshott, "The Tower of Babel" in his *Rationalism in Politics* (London: Methuen, 1962), 59, 62.

tive novices in the business of law-making. But since there is no grand theory to be unpacked, nor rationalist design to be discerned, judges are neither logicians nor technicians. Their engagement is best understood as an esoteric form of political discourse. Certainly, there exist important constraints on their power of action; they wait to be petitioned by other parties and in the context of a particular dispute before pronouncing on any matter and they are expected to refrain from involvement in partisan political controversy. Judges also have special obligations when rendering decision, especially in being required to craft a judgment which is defensible in the light of the extant legal materials. But although they "proceed from case to case, like the ancient Mediterranean mariners, hugging the coast from point to point and avoiding the dangers of the open sea of system and science,"[2] they remain important actors who actively participate in an on-going political venture. As guardians of the common law, judges act implicitly as interpreters of the political constitution. At times, they may even present themselves as the nearest we have to Platonic guardians of the ship of State.

However, although judges are active participants in a political engagement, they do not attempt, in interpreting and applying positive law, to colonize the political sphere. The methods of the common law are extended to the unwritten constitution; being an assemblage of statutes, rulings and practices, the British constitution makes little sense without reference to political understandings. But the judiciary also recognizes the limitations on its role. Although judges may on occasion be obliged to pronounce on the boundaries of the respective spheres of the State in contentious circumstances,[3] they readily accept that the king, or in a modern world the executive, must maintain authority to govern. Such deference has traditionally been accorded by drawing a distinction between *jurisdictio*, a sphere of private right supervised by courts, and *gubernaculum*, an area of discretionary executive power which enabled government to be conducted effectively and into which the courts would not trespass. Devised in the Middle Ages, the distinction has continued to be influential.[4] Thus, although Locke's *Second Treatise* is celebrated as a key text advocating a separation of

---

[2] Lord Wright, "The Study of Law" (1938) 54 *Law Quarterly Review* 185, 186.

[3] The most celebrated instance of this being Coke's claim against James I that judges and not the sovereign were the fountains of the law: see above, Ch. 5, 72–3.

[4] See Charles Howard McIlwain, *Constitutionalism: Ancient and Modern* (Ithaca, NY: Cornell U.P., 1947), ch. 4.

powers and the rule of law, it also explicitly accepts the necessity of retaining an extensive prerogative power.[5] Fixed legal rules do not—indeed, cannot—eliminate the need for executive action, and this irreducible responsibility must be accepted as a sphere of extra-legal political power.[6] This division of governmental power between the executive and judicial is acknowledged by the judiciary through silences, accommodation and the explicit acceptance of the jurisdictional limits of courts.

Here, politics and law are viewed as crafts, practices through which we aspire to manage those conflicts and differences which pervade all forms of order. Politics emerges from the distinction between rulers and ruled, between State and citizen. Further, the State is not conceived as some technical, neutral mechanism, but as an institution whose purpose is to ensure that political conflicts can be effectively handled. The well-being of the State is thus essential to the maintenance of a well-ordered society. As part of that venture, the art of politics consists in the acquisition and application of certain practical skills which have been devised to manage conflict. These political skills have variously been called *technē* (Plato), *prudentia* (Cicero), and *virtù* (Machiavelli). Critical to the exercise of these skills, which involve know-how, tact, judgment and an instinct for taking decisive action at the right moment, is the cultivation of the art of rhetoric. And the acquisition of such skills is an essential requirement for judicial appointment.

Although law is often presented as transcending politics, this is an essentially rhetorical claim. Law is a form of political discourse which because of its particular functions, and because of the special roles and responsibilities accorded the judiciary, is required to draw on all the props—the rituals, myths and tropes—that can be assembled. Despite the jurisdictional division between the spheres of the legal and the political, law and politics are in fact related modes of discourse, united in the common venture of keeping the show on the road.

LAW AS COMMAND

Law as custom treats law as a sphere of social life which is the special preserve of the judiciary. By enforcing the laws and resolving disputes

---

[5] See above, Ch. 11, 167–8.

[6] See Pasquale Pasquino, "Locke on King's Prerogative" (1998) 26 *Political Theory* 198; Harvey C. Mansfield, Jr., *Taming the Prince: The Ambivalence of Modern Executive Power* (Baltimore: Johns Hopkins U.P., 1993), ch. 8.

in an even-handed manner, the judiciary bolsters the authority structure of the State. Law is "the collected reason of the ages"[7] and the constitution similarly entails a partnership between past and present. If
attempts are made radically to alter the structure of the State, this edi-
fice would be destroyed: "the whole chain and continuity of the commonwealth would be broken", Burke argues, and people loosened
from these bonds would suffer from disorientation, becoming "little
better than the flies of a summer."[8] However, the great difficulty with
this image of political order held together by custom and tradition is
that it maintains its power only in a stable and relatively stationary
world. It is an image which could not easily survive "the great transformation" brought about by the Industrial Revolution.[9]

The radical changes effected by the Industrial Revolution, Arendt
notes, "took place within a political framework whose foundations
were no longer secure", with the consequence that, "although it was
still able to understand and to judge, [society] could no longer give an
account of its categories of understanding and standards of judgment
when they were seriously challenged".[10] These social changes had a
profound effect on our understanding of law. As Woodrow Wilson
expressed it, custom was mostly superseded by acts of legislation, religion retreated mainly to a private sphere "giving law only to the con-
science", adjudication was being constrained by a process of
codification, and "all means of formulating Law tend to be swallowed
up in the one great, deep, and broadening source, Legislation."[11]
Elaborating, Wilson noted that, "spoken first in the slow and general
voice of custom, law speaks at last in the clear, the multifarious, the
active tongues of legislation."[12] Law, he concluded, "is the will of the
State concerning the civic conduct of those under its authority."[13]

The modern idea of law as command had first been voiced by
Hobbes. *Auctoritas non veritas facit legem* (authority not wisdom
makes law) was his refrain: "a law is the command of him, or them that

---

[7] Edmund Burke, *Reflections on the Revolution in France* [1790] Conor Cruise
O'Brien ed. (Harmondsworth: Penguin, 1968), 193.

[8] Ibid.

[9] Karl Polanyi, *The Great Transformation: The Political and Economic Origins of
Our Time* [1944] (Boston: Beacon Press, 1957).

[10] Hannah Arendt, "Understanding and Politics" (1953) 20 *Partisan Review* 377, 385.

[11] Woodrow Wilson, *The State: Elements of Historical and Practical Politics*
(London: Heath & Co., rev. edn. 1899), 591.

[12] Ibid. 610.

[13] Ibid. 587.

have the sovereign power."[14] This idea of law as a regulatory force is linked to the emergence of the modern State on the foundation of sovereignty. Law is perceived to be the product of human will as expressed through the sovereign body, and the primary duty of the judiciary is faithfully to give effect to that legislative will. Law now takes on a tangible form in texts. In contrast with law as custom, "the propositions in the statute books tell us which norms are valid. These propositions provide the basis of adjudication, and they provide the perspective from which legal doctrine strives to interpret law."[15] This imperative theory of law thus effects a shift in the relationship: no longer the medium of the relationship between ruler and ruled, law becomes an instrument of rule. Rather than assuming a role as the guardians of the law and the constitution, judges become functionaries whose task it is to give precise effect to the edicts of an authoritative law-giver. Law is distinguished from politics insofar as it forms a structure of rules, a code for ordering of society. But the code, being a product of will, is itself the outcome of a political process.

The institutionalization of the idea of law as command is closely linked to the emergence of representative democracy as the key legitimating principle of modern government. The people engage in self-government by electing representatives to a sovereign body which has responsibility for enacting the laws which govern us all. Though vesting unbridled power in legislative majorities, the command theory of law does not necessarily lead to a system of extensive government; since command involves "the infliction of an evil", there are powerful political arguments for suggesting that the fewer the commands, the better the regime. But a presumption does emerge that any restraint on the exercise of the will of the majority is anti-democratic. Democracy also results in the emergence of disciplined party politics which in turn has the tendency of undermining the settled (customary) understandings of the constitution. When this occurs, however, the judiciary educated in the ancient traditions of the common law occasionally manifest their disdain for the practices and outcomes of mass politics.[16] Consequently, tensions between law and politics within this frame of understanding often arise from the lawyer's objective of continuing to

---

[14] Thomas Hobbes, *A Dialogue between a Philosopher and a Student of the Common Laws of England* [1681] Joseph Cropsey ed. (Chicago: University of Chicago Press, 1971), 55, 71.

[15] Jürgen Habermas, *Between Facts and Norms: Contributions to a Discourse Theory of Law and Democracy* William Rehg trans. (Cambridge: Polity Press, 1996), 388.

[16] See above, Ch. 7, 101–5.

promote the precepts of aristocratic rule to temper the ambiguous, naïve or over-ambitious products of democratic political processes.[17] In the modern world, this ancient judicial tradition of prudence often smacks of reactionary élitism.

LAW AS RIGHT

Many who have no desire to shore up an old and crumbling order nevertheless express discomfort at the bid to reduce law to a matter of will. Laws, they argue, are not essentially imperatives; they are normative statements, rules with good reasons for being obeyed. The edict, the expression of will, is determined not simply by desires but by what can be shown to be good. In making this type of appeal, thinkers such as Locke explicitly invoke the idea of natural law as a set of objective moral principles which can be discovered through the exercise of reason. But there are others who claim that, whilst there is no need to invoke the authority of a deity, law must still be recognized as normative, concerned with what ought to be done. If democracy is the modern legitimating principle for the idea of law as command, it is liberty or autonomy which provides the normative criterion of law as right. Law in this conception is an enterprise inextricably linked to the maintenance of freedom. Law elaborates the principles of right conduct.

The politics/law relationship is now cast in a particular light. Once viewed as a noble craft, politics is now conceived as an activity in which the passions hold sway. The political sphere, being one of power conflicts, is dangerous and potentially destructive. Constraints are therefore required to ensure that passions are channelled towards right conduct. Law thus presents itself as a set of foundational principles providing the framework within which politics is to be conducted. Politics must be tamed and placed within bounds so that its energies can be harnessed positively, that is, in accordance with the dictates of reason and justice. No longer is law a conventional medium of the relationship between ruler and ruled or the pliant instrument of the ruling authority. Instead, law expresses the rational foundation of the governing relationship; it establishes the preconditions for the conduct of politics.

It has generally been accepted that since politics is not concerned with power in the sense of might or force, then it must be undertaken

---

[17] See esp. the views of Tocqueville: above, Ch. 5, 74.

within some bounds of constraint. To be effective, even a sovereign king is obliged to cultivate a reputation for trustworthiness, and this means that he must generally rule in accordance with the customary ways of doing business. This precept lies at the core of the idea of law as custom, and it persists even when the command theory assumes prominence. The sovereign authority generally accepts that, even though there may not be any legal restrictions on law-making power, the precepts of prudence severely circumscribe the imposition of will. Power, of political necessity, must be shared with others. Acquiring trust, playing the game according to conventional understandings, are techniques by which rulers indirectly enhance their power. Even the most rigorous of sovereignty theorists have recognized that State power can be enhanced by attaching limitations to its exercise.[18] The critical innovation effected by the shift from either law as custom or command to the conception of law as right is that these conventional precepts—matters of political prudence in the first two conceptions—are converted into principles of positive law. Norms which previously were treated as being either traditional maxims (rooted in precedents) or simply as empirical phenomena (that is, as conditions of effectiveness) become truly normative (criteria of rationality).

This shift in our understanding of the legal in relation to the political stems from the modern natural rights movement which reached its culmination in the work of Kant. With Kant, the Hobbesean idea of the nature of the political relationship was inverted. Hobbes contended that the aim of civil science was to undertake an investigation into "the right of a commonwealth and the duties of citizens."[19] Kant, by contrast, started with the primacy of individual rights. The rights of man "must be held sacred, however great a sacrifice the ruling power may have to make." There can be no half-measures, no fudge, and "no use [in] devising hybrid solutions such as a pragmatically conditioned right halfway between right and utility". For the fact of the matter is that "politics must bend the knee before right".[20] Law as right aims at no less than the elimination of the idea of the (political) sovereign and its replacement with the sovereignty of law. It requires a transformation

[18] See, e.g., Stephen Holmes, "The Constitution of Sovereignty in Jean Bodin" in his *Passions and Constraint: On the Theory of Liberal Democracy* (Chicago: University of Chicago Press, 1995), 100.

[19] Thomas Hobbes, *On the Citizen* [1647] Richard Tuck and Michael Silverthorne ed. and trans. (Cambridge: Cambridge U.P., 1998), 10.

[20] Immanuel Kant, "Perpetual Peace: A Philosophical Sketch" [1795] in his *Political Writings*, Hans Reiss ed. (Cambridge: Cambridge U.P., 2nd edn. 1991), 93, 125.

in understanding of the legal code from one based on duties to one founded on rights.

The historical aspects of this study help us to situate, and in the process partially to resolve, some of the confusion that has permeated discussion of the relationship between law and politics. It is common to encounter statements on this issue which appear to contradict one another. For example, reference has already been made to the expression, "where law ends, there tyranny begins",[21] as an elaboration of the idea of law as right. But if law is treated as an expression of command, we could just as easily state that "where law ends, there liberty begins".[22] And once the idea of law as customary practice rooted in a tradition of politics is unpacked, the thrust of that maxim might even be reversed to suggest that "where tyranny ends, there politics begins".[23] Statements of this nature take on meaning only within a particular historical and ideological context. Once we become conscious of this, the clarity and simplicity of the message becomes blurred. The historical texts remind us of the very different contexts in which these debates have arisen; whenever we are presented with a statement purporting to answer the question about law's relationship to politics, therefore, we should be conscious both of its context and of the particular conception of law which is being invoked.

However, although history evidently has great value, its importance should not be misunderstood. The main danger in presenting a sketch of this nature is that of implying that history is concerned with the unfolding of an idea, that is, that it involves a progressive movement from a lower to a higher state. Whilst the evolution of the conceptions of law as custom, through command, to law as right can be seen to follow a path of historical development, this should not be treated teleologically. Although a particular conception might capture the spirit of the times at a particular moment, other conceptions are never entirely subdued. Indeed, it is precisely because of the existence of these basic tensions between varying conceptions of law that law itself is able continuously to evolve.

[21] See above, Ch. 1, 13.
[22] See above, Ch. 9, 135.
[23] See above, Ch. 8, 112.

The main importance of the historical dimension, then, is much
more modest. We might say that it is only by examining the evolution
of these ideas that we become conscious both of the fluidity of these
politico-legal languages and of the way in which their usage is capable
of change.[24] This is important precisely because these languages are of
influence in shaping and limiting the lines of political action which can
successfully be followed.[25] The language of the law is anything but
tidy. It can be compared to an ancient city: "a maze of little streets and
squares, of old and new houses, and of houses with additions from various periods; and this surrounded by a multitude of new boroughs with
straight regular streets and uniform houses."[26] Old concepts thus
become extended, constrained or transformed over time;[27] terminology devised at one moment to resolve a particular difficulty is able,
because of its plasticity, to take on new life for different purposes.[28]
Occasionally the need is felt to systematize an area of the law. It is
almost impossible, however, for these new codes to remove entirely the
old jumble; they will generally provide an overlay or even, like new
boroughs, simply an extension.[29] Just as "the grammar of words is too
multiform to be represented in a theory or comprehensive rule that
stipulates the essential conditions for the correct application of words
in every instance",[30] so too it is impossible to devise a comprehensive
theory of law to accommodate its labyrinthine ways. It is this unwieldiness which promotes continuous legal evolution. But this unwieldiness

[24] See J.G.A. Pocock, "The Concept of a Language and the *Métier d'Historien*: Some
Considerations on Practice" in Anthony Pagden (ed.), *The Languages of Political Theory
in Early-Modern Europe* (Cambridge: Cambridge U.P., 1987), 19.

[25] Quentin Skinner, *Liberty before Liberalism* (Cambridge: Cambridge U.P., 1998),
105.

[26] Ludwig Wittgenstein, *Philosophical Investigations* [1945] G.E.M. Anscombe trans.
(Oxford: Blackwell, 1967), §.18. Cf. Walter Bagehot, *The English Constitution* [1867]
R.H.S. Crossman intro. (London: Collins, 1963), 265: "Our law very often reminds one
of those outskirts of cities where you cannot for a long time tell how the streets come to
wind about in so capricious and serpent-like a manner. At last it strikes you that they
grew up, house by house, on the devious tracks of the old green lanes; and if you follow
on to the existing fields, you may find the change half complete."

[27] Consider, e.g., the development of the concept of the rule of law: see Chs. 5 and 12
above.

[28] Consider, e.g., the evolution of the concept of negligence as a head of tortious lia-
bility: see Edward H. Levi, *An Introduction to Legal Reasoning* (Chicago: University of
Chicago Press, 1949), 8–27.

[29] Consider, e.g., the reforms of the 1925 property legislation: see Stuart Anderson,
"The 1925 Legislation: Setting Contexts" in Susan Bright and John Dewar (eds), *Land
Law: Themes and Perspectives* (Oxford: Oxford U.P., 1998), ch. 4, esp. 125–8.

[30] James Tully, *Strange Multiplicity: Constitutionalism in an Age of Diversity*
(Cambridge: Cambridge U.P., 1995), 104.

also highlights the distinctively pragmatic—or, it might be said, political—dimension to the deployment of particular conceptions of law. This point can be observed in a range of contexts. Consider, for example, the issue of adjudication. When rendering legal judgment, a judge is generally able to draw on various conceptions of law so as to manoeuvre between being bound by an existing precedent (law as custom), strictly adhering to an Act of Parliament (law as command), or following the path of principle (law as right).[31] While disputes over the correctness of these various approaches provide the meat-and-drink of jurisprudence,[32] the fact is that each of these conceptions forms an essential part of legal practice and the triumph of one over another, far from being an issue of "truth", is invariably a function of politics. In this particular sense, legal discourse must be rooted in political practice. There is nothing new in this observation. In the seventeenth century, Hobbes criticized lawyers on the ground that "they appeal from custom to reason; and from reason to custom, as it serves their turn; receding from custom when their interest requires it, and setting themselves against reason, as oft as reason is against them". It is, he concluded, precisely the "cause that the doctrine of Right and Wrong is perpetually disputed, both by the Pen and the Sword."[33] Whether or not one accepts Hobbes's solution—the establishment of the sovereign as the final arbiter—we must surely acknowledge the force of his sentiment that the struggle over the meaning of law is itself a political issue.

---

[31] See above, Ch. 6, 85–90.
[32] Cf. Lord Denning, "Misuse of Power" in his *What Next in the Law?* (London: Butterworth, 1982) 307, 330 ("May not the judges themselves sometimes abuse and misuse their power? . . . The judges of England have always in the past—and always will—be vigilant in guarding our freedoms. Someone must be trusted. Let it be the judges"); J.A.G. Griffith, "The Political Constitution" (1979) 42 *Modern Law Review* 1, 6 (promoting "a solid, positivist, unmetaphysical, non-natural foundation for analytical jurisprudence" founded on sovereignty); Ronald Dworkin, *Law's Empire* (London: Fontana, 1986), 404 ("we accept the adjudicative principle of integrity as sovereign over law, because we want to treat ourselves as an association of principle, as a community governed by a single and coherent vision of justice and fairness and procedural due process in the right relation.").
[33] Thomas Hobbes, *Leviathan* [1651] Richard Tuck ed. (Cambridge: Cambridge U.P., 1996), 73–4.

15

The End of Politics and the
Triumph of Law?

THE STRUGGLE OVER the meaning of law may indeed be
a political issue, but in recent years the idea of law as right
seems to have carried many in its sway. Should this be taken as
a sign that law has now evolved to some higher state of reason and
principle, from which pinnacle it triumphs over politics? It certainly is
possible to conceive of a differentiated world of norms and, as an intellectual exercise, to devise a juristic order in which the State is not the
source of these norms. But this is not the issue. The question is not
whether a conceptual framework can be constructed,[1] but whether this
conception of law as right provides an adequate representation of contemporary arrangements, one which is able to make a decisive impression on the current structure of government. By way of conclusion, I
shall try to identify the trends which have been influential in shaping
our thinking about contemporary politics and the claims of law and
also to sketch some criticisms concerning the cogency of this contention about the triumph of law.

THE DISPLACEMENT OF POLITICS

In classical thought, politics was treated as the "master-science".
Politics was studied for the purpose of gaining an insight into the
nature of the good life and acquiring an understanding of those
institutions and laws through which conflicts within society could be
managed and overall social well-being promoted. This classical conception of politics was anchored by a belief that society is a unitary

---

[1] Cf. Ronald Dworkin, *Law's Empire* (London: Fontana, 1986), 413: "Law is not
exhausted by any catalogue of rules or principles . . . Law's empire is defined by attitude
. . . Law's attitude [aims] to lay principle over practice to show the best route to a better
future, keeping the right faith with the past. . . . That is, anyway, what law is for us: for
the people we want to be and the community we aim to have."

phenomenon, one which receives its most authentic form of representation through the institution of the State. These ancient beliefs lingered on during the medieval era and were not seriously challenged until early-modern times. As portrayed in the medieval construct of the "body politic", the commonwealth was taken to *constitute* society, and politics was the language through which the voice of society was given authoritative expression. Even in the work of Hobbes, the first great theorist of modern politics, this organic representation persists: the State is represented as a magnified body, an artificial man whose soul is the sovereign, whose joints are the magistrates, whose business is the *salus populi* (the welfare of the people) and who is able to wield an absolute power (represented by the sword).[2]

In modern times, this integrative conception of politics has been severely eroded. This is seen first in the way that organic metaphors in political language are replaced by mechanical ones (especially with the growth of the idea of the State as a machine or instrument) and then, more recently, by the emergence of systems approaches to politics, in which the political system is treated merely as one sub-system amongst many operating in society.[3] Politics has certainly not come to an end, but it appears to have been displaced from its traditional role of giving expression to the character of social existence. Modern politics has thus been transformed into an activity through which certain, though not necessarily the most important, conflicts of interests amongst individuals and groups are handled. Once politics is treated as an activity which is located within a distinct and limited sphere, law and politics become more clearly differentiated, and positive law gradually comes to play an increasingly important role in the regulation of social life.

Montesquieu was probably the first to have clearly signalled this development. He believed that the displacement of politics from its exalted status was primarily attributable to the growth of commerce. Commerce, he suggested, weakened the grip of xenophobia and bigotry, the most base of the friend-enemy passions, and, since "[t]wo nations that trade with each other become reciprocally dependent . . . [t]he natural effect of commerce is to lead to peace."[4] The growth of

---

[2] Thomas Hobbes, *Leviathan* [1651] Richard Tuck ed. (Cambridge: Cambridge U.P., 1996), 9. See above, Ch. 9, 132–3.

[3] See Niklas Luhmann, *The Differentiation of Society* Stephen Holmes and Charles Larmore trans. (New York: Columbia U.P., 1982).

[4] Montesquieu, *The Spirit of the Laws* [1748] Anne M. Cohler, Basia Carolyn Miller and Harold Samuel Stone trans. and ed. (Cambridge: Cambridge U.P., 1989), Bk. 20, ch. 2.

commerce is also associated with the extension of constitutional politics. Modern politics, Montesquieu indicates, might not propagate a sense of grandeur or a nobility of spirit but, by focusing directly on conflicts of interests, it is often able effectively to manage existing social problems. Montesquieu thus goes on to note positively that "England has always made its political interests give way to the interests of its commerce" and to draw a link between the promotion of commerce and the extension of liberty.[5] These developments, as we have seen, dictate that politics is conducted within a formal framework of laws, laws which are certain, prospective and proportionate.[6] The sword of power, it might be said, should be wielded only in accordance with the scales of justice.

This connection between the establishment of a modern, more limited, conception of politics and the rise in the importance of law within government has been drawn by a number of commentators. Weber, for example, notes that since the French Revolution "the modern lawyer and modern democracy absolutely belong together."[7] This growing influence of lawyers in government emerges alongside the institutionalization of democratic party politics. "The management of politics through parties", Weber contends, "simply means management through interest groups" and this is significant because the "craft of the trained lawyer is to plead effectively the cause of interested clients."[8] Politics today is "conducted in public by means of the spoken or written word" and "[t]o weigh the effect of the word properly falls within the range of the lawyer's tasks."[9] Weber is undoubtedly correct: law and lawyers have in modern times come to play an increasingly influential role in the conduct of politics. This does not mean that law is replacing politics, but it is indicative of a change in the role and function of politics in the modern era.

These modern trends—commerce, liberty, individualism, democracy, interest competition—have cumulatively brought about a revolution in

---

[5] Montesquieu, above n. 4, Bk. 20, ch. 7.

[6] See above, Ch. 12, 186. See also ibid. Bk. 20, ch. 14: "The Magna Carta of England forbids in the event of war the seizure and confiscation of the commodities of foreign traders, except as a reprisal. . . . In the war Spain waged against the English in 1740, a law was made that punished with death those who introduced English commodities into the Spanish states . . . Such an ordinance runs counter to our mores, to the spirit of commerce, and to the harmony that should prevail in proportioning penalties."

[7] Max Weber, "Politics as a Vocation" [1921] in H.H. Gerth & C. Wright Mills (eds), *From Max Weber: Essays in Sociology* (London: Routledge & Kegan Paul, 1948), 77, 94.

[8] Ibid.

[9] Ibid. 95.

our understanding of politics. In effect, an individualist conception of society has replaced the traditional image of society as an organic whole and as a consequence our understanding of politics has been transformed. The quintessential political relationship is generally taken to be that between rulers and ruled, between those who wield power and those who are subject to its exercise. Whilst this relationship can be examined from either perspective, political thinkers have traditionally viewed it from the ruler's point of view. The questions which typically are asked include: how is power acquired and handled? what are the powers of government and how are they best assigned? what devices should rulers use to ensure that subjects acknowledge their authority? In modern times, however, politics has undergone a radical shift in perspective. Rather than being concerned with the rights of sovereigns and duties of subjects, it is scarcely an exaggeration to suggest that modern politics is primarily concerned with the rights of citizens and the obligations of government. Alongside this shift in perspective, we also see a transformation in our understanding of law. Both the conceptions of law as a set of customary practices of governance and of law as the command of the sovereign are able to be accommodated within the traditional approach to politics. With the inversion of political perspective, however, we see a revolution in our understanding of law. Once treated as a code based on duties, law now presents itself as being founded on rights.

The basic thrust behind the claim that the end of the twentieth century marks the death of politics can now be appreciated: it is best understood as a claim that the century's end marks the intellectual defeat of those totalitarian ideologies—fascism and communism—which during the twentieth century have persisted in promoting an organic and integrative notion of politics as the "master-science". Whether this global victory has actually been achieved is debateable. But even if it has, this scarcely justifies the general claim.

In modern times, politics and law have become more formally differentiated and, most recently, law has come to be viewed as establishing a cordon within which politics is conducted. But this development remains politically contentious. The project of establishing law as an objective framework of rational principles, whether treated as an exercise in philosophy[10] or in jurisprudence,[11] has not been successful. With the ascendancy of law as right we do not therefore reach the end

---

[10] See above, Ch. 7, 96–100.
[11] See above, Ch. 13, 212–13.

of history, or an escape from politics. Instead, this legalization of politics has led primarily to a politicization of law.

The age-old controversies over the meaning of liberty, equality, democracy and the like are now taking place within a more explicit legal-constitutionalist framework. This means that the institution of courts will now play a more important role in giving precise meaning to the core values of society. Whether the judiciary is adequately equipped to undertake this task and whether the formal and adversarial procedures of courts are appropriate for determining these issues must remain matters of debate. But no one should be in any doubt about the political character of the exercise. In the United States, where the jurisprudence of rights is most highly developed, powerful arguments have recently been presented for claims of fundamental rights rooted in a variety of irreconcilable positions, including the maintenance of property,[12] the promotion of the right to equal concern and respect,[13] the protection of rights of access to the political process,[14] the defence of the rights of disadvantaged groups,[15] and the realization of the conditions of "deliberative democracy".[16] Each of these claims can be justified by reference to some notion of equality, and each finds evidential support in constitutional texts. But since none can be shown to provide an objective rendering of constitutional requirements, this type of engagement must be acknowledged to be simply a more explicitly rationalized form of political discourse.

SWORD AND SCALES

Although the contemporary period does not mark the end of politics and the triumph of law, it does signal the emergence of a new phase in the interpenetration of law and politics. In this new era, whose dominant characteristics are the consolidation of extensive networks of big government and the institutionalization of the rights-bearing

---

[12] Richard A. Epstein, *Takings: Private Property and the Power of Eminent Domain* (Cambridge, Mass: Harvard U.P., 1985).

[13] Ronald Dworkin, *Taking Rights Seriously* (Cambridge, Mass; Harvard U.P., 1977), ch. 5.

[14] John Hart Ely, *Democracy and Distrust: A Theory of Judicial Review* (Cambridge, Mass: Harvard U.P., 1980).

[15] Owen Fiss, "Groups and the Equal Protection Clause" (1976) 5 *Philosophy & Public Affairs* 107.

[16] Cass R. Sunstein, *The Partial Constitution* (Cambridge, Mass: Harvard U.P., 1993).

subject, the metaphors of sword and scales no longer appear to serve as adequate images of political power and legal justice.

The symbol of the sword is a product of the early stages of the development of the State, when the State was conceived mainly as an instrument for maintaining law and order. By harnessing the forces of nationalism, however, the modern State has now built up an extensive administrative apparatus and has acquired responsibility both for disciplining the people and enhancing their welfare.[17] With this transformation in scale and function, the modern State has become a highly complex institution, operating under conditions of interdependence.[18] In such circumstances, sovereignty is no longer able to provide an adequate expression of the governing relationship and "a command, the direct translation of authority into communication, is far too simple a structural category to do justice to the complex conditions for maintaining and rationalizing [this political] system."[19] The sword, in short, no longer provides a fitting symbol of political power.

At the same time, though for different reasons, the image of the scales of justice also appears to be losing its potency. Equality has ceased to carry the religious connotation of having equal dignity before God, or to be a formal, distinctly limited, criterion of corrective justice. Instead, it now functions as the basic political and legal principle against which all social issues are to be judged, and the principle of "right proportion" is apparently to be used as the measure of all governmental action. Given our inability to identify the Archimedean point—"a point from which the basic structure [of social order] itself can be appraised"[20]—the metaphor of the scales of justice can no longer bear the weight. The claims of "justice" today have become so politicized that the figure of an authoritative, dispassionate and venerable law-giver has effectively disappeared from the scene.

If, as has been argued, we need symbol and myth to forge identity, to orientate ourselves within the world and to determine connections between things, then the loss of potency of these images—a product of the gap between fiction and reality—is serious. In the late-modern period of "disenchantment", we might be forgiven for thinking that the only remaining criterion of value is that of the achievement of material

---

[17]   See Martin van Creveld, *The Rise and Decline of the State* (Cambridge: Cambridge U.P., 1999), ch. 4.

[18]   See above, Ch. 10, 157.

[19]   Luhmann, above n. 3, 36.

[20]   John Rawls, *A Theory of Justice* (Oxford: Oxford U.P., 1972), 260.

success. For some, however, this is not a condition of freedom so much as a state of anxiety. Equality has become the watchword of contemporary society. But because it is an abstraction no longer anchored by custom and convention, a society motivated by material success and founded on the principle of individual rights fuels a passion which simply cannot be satisfied. This is a dangerous state of affairs, because it is likely to generate cynicism about politics. For those who believe that politics, understood as a clash of principles rooted in conflicting views over the good, is an existential condition, this would amount to a moral loss. This seems a pessimistic note on which to end. But if the study of the history of these ideas makes us question the trajectory of contemporary trends, then this books objective will have been realized.

Index